# Philosophical Musings for a Meaningful Life

## An Analysis of K.V. Dominic's Poems

# Edited by S. Kumaran

From the World Voices Series

Modern History Press

Philosophical Musings for a Meaningful Life: An Analysis of K.V. Dominic's Poems
Copyright © 2016 by S. Kumaran. All Rights Reserved.

2nd Printing: February 2016

Portrait of KV Dominic by Ankita Sharma.

---

Library of Congress Cataloging-in-Publication Data

Philosophical musings for a meaningful life: : an analysis of K.V. Dominic's poems / edited by S. Kumaran.
pages cm. -- (World voices)
Includes bibliographical references and index.
ISBN 978-1-61599-266-9 (pbk. : alk. paper) -- ISBN 978-1-61599-267-6 (hardcover : alk. paper) -- ISBN 978-1-61599-268-3 (ebook)
1. Dominic, K. V. (Kannappillil Varghese), 1956---Criticism and interpretation. I. Kumara_n, Es, editor.
PR9499.4.D66Z83 2015
823'.92--dc23

2015000080

---

Distributed by Ingram Book Group (USA/CAN), Bertram's Books (EU/UK)

Modern History Press, an imprint of
Loving Healing Press
5145 Pontiac Trail
Ann Arbor, MI 48105

www.ModernHistoryPress.com
info@ModernHistoryPress.com
Toll free 888-761-6268 (USA/Canada)
FAX 734-663-6861

# Contents

Foreword by Dr. Stephen Gill ............................................................................................. iii

Introduction from the Poet ................................................................................................. v

Preface ............................................................................................................................... vii

About the Editor ................................................................................................................ xi

About the Poet ................................................................................................................... xiii

Chapter 1 - Introduction: Poetic Mind of K. V. Dominic by P. C. K. Prem ..................... 1

Chapter 2 – Humanism in K. V. Dominic's *Winged Reason* by Dr. S. Kumaran) ......... 15

Chapter 3 - An Angel in Flight: A Critique of K. V. Dominic's *Winged Reason* by Dr. Sudhir K. Arora ............................................................................................................... 23

Chapter 4 - K. V. Dominic's *Multicultural Symphony*: A Critique by Dr. Sudhir K. Arora ...... 29

Chapter 5 - K. V. Dominic—A Humanitarian in Conception and Socio-Consciousness: An Analytical Study of *Write Son, Write* by Dr. D. C. Chambial ......................................... 39

Chapter 6 - K. V. Dominic's *Winged Reason*: Poems of Man's Earthly Life and Painful Realities by P. C. K. Prem ................................................................................................. 45

Chapter 7 - Social Criticism in the Poetry of K. V. Dominic by Prof. T. V. Reddy ......... 53

Chapter 8 - Concurrent Predicaments and Urge for Philanthropy in the Poetry of K.V. Dominic by Dr. Sugandha Agarwal .................................................................................. 61

Chapter 9 - Poetry for a Better World: A Critical Look at the Poetry of K. V. Dominic by Rob Harle ......................................................................................................................... 77

Chapter 10 - A Requiem for the Disconsolate: K. V. Dominic's Poetry as a Social-Criticism by Dr. J. Pamela ............................................................................................... 85

Chapter 11 - Poetry for a Meaningful Life: A Critical Analysis of K. V. Dominic's Poetry by Bhaskar Roy Barman .................................................................................................... 97

Chapter 12 - K. V. Dominic as a Social Critic: A Study of His Poems by Dr. S. Ayyappa Raja 107

Chapter 13 - Philosophical Voyage of K. V. Dominic by Arbind Kumar Choudhary ..... 117

Chapter 14 - The Poet of the Marginalized: An Analysis of Dr. K. V. Dominic's Poetry by Anisha Ghosh Paul ...................................................................................................... 123

Chapter 15 - K. V. Dominic's Poetry: Rebellion and Reticence on Winged Reason by Joe Palathunkal ....................................................................................................................... 131

Chapter 16 - Critical Analysis of K. V. Dominic as a Philosophical Poet by Patricia Prime ...... 139

Chapter 17 - The Relation between God, Man and Nature in K. V. Dominic's Poems by Mahboobeh Khaleghi .................................................................................. 145

Chapter 18 - K. V. Dominic, the Messenger of Humanity, Peace and Harmony in the Universe by Sangeeta Mahesh .................................................................................. 155

Chapter 19 - Philosophical Musings for a Meaningful Life: An Analysis of K. V. Dominic's Poetry by Dr. Radhamany Sarma ................................................................ 167

Chapter 20 - The Landscape of Kerala in K. V. Dominic's Poetry by Anisha Ghosh Paul ....... 181

Chapter 21 - Eco-Critical Perspectives in the Poetry of K. V. Dominic by Dr. S. Barathi ........ 187

Chapter 22 - Ecological Issues Reflected in the Selected Poems of K. V. Dominic by Rincy Mol Sebastian ................................................................................................ 191

Chapter 23 - Ecological and Social Issues in K. V. Dominic's Multicultural Symphony by Dr. Arbind Kumar Choudhary ................................................................................ 197

Chapter 24 - Holistic Musings: K. V. Dominic as a Poet with Purpose by Kavitha Gopalakrishnan .................................................................................................. 201

Chapter 25 - Interview with Prof. K. V. Dominic by Prof. Elisabetta Marino ..................... 209

List of Contributors .................................................................................. 213

Index .................................................................................. 217

# Foreword

*Philosophical Musings for a Meaningful Life* is a study of the poetry of Dr. K.V. Dominic, a prominent poet and literary critic of India, who draws inspiration from the well of humanity. When Dr. Dominic talks about injustices, his pen becomes as tender as the breeze of a delightful summer morning, and at the same time, it becomes as biting as that of a snake. This defines the essence of the *Philosophical Musings for a Meaningful Life*.

Dr. K.V. Dominic has edited a full-length critical study, titled *Stephen Gill's Poetry: A Panorama of World Peace*. The merits of this and other scholarly works by Dr. Dominic are commendable. His pen is not confined to India only. He has edited critical studies on Canadian and Afro-American Literatures and has written papers on the writers of other nations. He has edited literary journals that have had editors, readers, and contributors from abroad. He has taken care of writers through literary organizations. He is a retired professor of English Literature, and has authored three volumes of poems, which have been reviewed favorably in the media.

Among the salient features in Dr. Dominic's poetry, I have observed his belief that the earth is the home for all. He condemns hollow dogmas, traditions, inequity, inhumanity, and exploitation, and he approves of peace-related activities. His poetry is saturated with the pathos of the sufferers. He is absolutely appalled at the conditions under which women are treated.

I am happy to note that contributors to *Philosophical Musings for a Meaningful Life* have covered all these observations in their own individual ways. Among contributors, I see Dr. Sudhir Arora, who has released two books on my modern epic *The Flame,* my ambitious project. One is titled *The Poetic Corpus of Stephen Gill,* and the second is *The Flame Unmasked*. Dr. Arora does a good job in evaluating the poetry of Dr. Dominic as he does in these two volumes on my poetry.

Among other contributors, Dr. Arbind Kumar Choudhary has published papers on my works and co-edited a critical study *War and Peace in the Works of Stephen Gill*. Patricia Prime from New Zealand is a well-known poet and critic, and Dr. P.C.K. Prem, Dr. D.C. Chambial, Dr. Bhaskar Roy Barman, and Dr. S. Kumaran, who is the editor of *Philosophical Musings for a Meaningful Life,* have also written about me elsewhere. Because of these bonds, *Philosophical Musings for a Meaningful Life* carries profound and wider significance for me.

I have discussed in the introduction to *The Flame* and elsewhere about the difficulties a poet confronts when he or she brings out the god who is within in the shape of dreams, experiences, feelings, thoughts, and other such airy substances. The poet brings this god out in a concrete shape with the help of imagery. It is a fight that needs dedication. I am happy to confirm that Dr. Dominic is one of these fighters. Since the message is crucial, the style of Dr. Dominic is straightforward. The portrayals of his inner self makes his poetry powerful and more meaningful.

This critical study on the poetry of Dr. K.V. Dominic deserves to be read closely for evaluation and to be on the shelf of every notable library. The English Literature of India started maturing even before Rabindranath Tagore received the Nobel Prize in Literature in 1913. It has attained its own status now. I am convinced that *Philosophical Musings for a Meaningful Life* will inspire scholars from the West to find rubies and diamonds in the Indian poetry of today.

Dr. Stephen Gill<br>
Poet Laureate of Ansted University,<br>
Adjunct Professor of European-American University

# Introduction from the Poet

When more than two dozen critical articles and book reviews were written by eminent critics on my maiden collection of poems, *Winged Reason* (2010), within a year of its publication, it gave me the boost and impetus for further writing. The feedback from the critics through their papers was highly positive and motivating. It seemed that the readers liked my simple, direct way of presenting stark, burning realities in free verse. Hence, I was ignited more, and thus, I could bring out the second collection *Write Son, Write* (2011). As a poet, I was growing and becoming more philosophic, and the outcome was my longest poem "Write My Son, Write" in twenty-one sections, which proclaimed to the world my philosophic views—the interrelation among Man, Nature, and God. I am more a Realist than a Romantic, and my tendency is to stay in this world, portraying the aching issues and problems of the people around me as well as of the non-human beings, plants, and the planet itself. Thus, when I composed my third poetic collection, *Multicultural Symphony* (2014), the themes, topics, and incidents chosen for the poems were mainly those reported in the newspapers.

As a poet, I am responsible to my own conscience, and I want to convey an emotion or a message often through social criticism. I have a commitment to my students as a professor; to the reader, scholars, and writers as an editor; and to all human and non-human beings as a poet. Hence, I give priority to the content of a poem rather than to the style of language. I am of opinion that poetry should be digestible, just as short stories and novels are appealing to the ordinary layman. I adopt conversational style in poetry, which again attracts ordinary readers.

Being a social critic, I use my weapon, poetry, to attack the three mafias—Religious, Political, and Intellectual—that exploit people and Nature. The major theme of my poetry is the eternal relationship between Man, Nature, and God. Though baptized a Christian, I am primarily an Indian, and it is my duty as a teacher and poet to instill Indian values in my students and countrymen, and also to propagate these noble values to the rest of the world. I believe in the concept of *jeevatma* and *paramatma* (individual soul and universal soul) and that all living beings are part of *paramatma* (God). Again I believe in the Indian concept of *Aham Brahmasmi* (I am the God). *Advaita* seems to me more reasonable and acceptable than *Dvaita*. Thus, I find the eternal affinity between Man, Nature, and God. Man is not given liberty to kill other beings, nor is he allowed to uproot plants and trees for his luxuries. The Creator has given man permission to use plants just for his survival. That is the law of Nature.

The other important themes of my poetry are: disparities in society; gender issues; problems of the poor, the down-trodden, the marginalized, and the old; terrorism; communalism; corruption and exploitation by political parties and religions; descriptions of Nature; the multicultural beauty of the universe; developed and developing nations' irrational craze for war and defense; the sacrifice of soldiers for the nation; the need for peace relations between nations; superstitions created by religions and the exploitation of the laity by clergymen; global warming; the need for the conservation of nature; animal torture; child labor; casteism; unemployment; exploitation of the labor sector; the dignity of labor; the need of value-based education; and the celebration of man's intelligence, skills, and selfless service for society.

I believe that the best literary genre for addressing these innumerable diverse issues is poetry because with minimum use of words, I am able to impart these messages and values into the minds of the masses. Besides, since I use very simple vocabulary and diction, even an adult or child with minimum knowledge of the English language can digest what I have written. And who on this earth can spend more time reading in this busy, fast-paced world of survival? Our visual and fast-developing multi-media society dissuades the younger generation from reading serious philosophic books.

Since fiction rules the literary world now, poetry can only compete with it and survive by adapting itself to be more attractive and digestive while at the same time be enlightening and entertaining to the readers' minds. That's what I have done through my poetry, and the feedback I have received through comments, reviews, and articles ascertain the fact that the burning issues around us can be best conveyed through poetry. Hence, there should be more and more poems on these themes, as well as their reviews and studies, and thus, a revolution can take place in the minds of the readers, so gradually, we will regain our lost values.

Dr. K.V. Dominic

# Preface

This book is the culmination of the impact of Dr. K. V. Dominic's poetry on me and I believe my experience would become the collective experience of the readers. Each of the twenty-five chapters involves a paper. The papers have been arranged based on their themes, and they include: analysis of a collection, study of multiple volumes, scrutiny of rebellious attitude, and focus on ecocritical principles.

P. C. K. Prem's "Poetic Mind of K. V. Dominic" forms the first chapter of this book and also serves the purpose of an introduction. In his paper, Prem has examined all the three collections of Dominic and revealed the poet's zeal to use poetry as a means to enhance the quality of life on earth. He finds Dominic as a people's poet who "attempts to recognize pains, sufferings, and anguish of men who work hard, live a miserly life, but contribute to the building of vast empires, nations, and rulers" and informs the readers what they can expect from the poetry of Dominic.

In Chapter 2, "Humanism in K. V. Dominic's *Winged Reason*", Dr. S. Kumaran has explored K. V. Dominic's *Winged Reason* to bring out the humanistic values expressed in it. He has recognized the poems found in the collection as an ardent expression of the poetic soul to witness peace and harmony in the universe. The poems proclaim the poet's faith in the humanistic values and his belief in the inherent worth and intrinsic value of non-human others. Further, the poems reveal the poet's anguish at the evils and the inhuman attitudes prevalent in the society and necessitate harmony of existence.

Dr. Sudhir K. Arora in the third chapter "An Angel in Flight: A Critique of K. V. Dominic's *Winged Reason*", has scrutinized Dominic's *Winged Reason* and found him as "a poet with feelings and nothing else" as his poetry is an outlet of his conscience that urges him to articulate "an emotion or a message often through social criticism." Dr. Arora has also studied Dominic's *Multicultural Symphony* in the fourth chapter "K. V. Dominic's *Multicultural Symphony*: A Critique" and recognized Dominic's portrayal of the plight of his countrymen and his projection of the shortcomings of the materialistic attitude.

The fifth chapter "K. V. Dominic—A Humanitarian in Conception and Socio-Consciousness: An Analytical Study of *Write Son, Write*", by Dr. D. C. Chambial elucidates Dominic's brilliant understanding of life around him and "his humanitarian philosophy steeped in contemporaneous societal consciousness, making him an advocate of the down-trodden and human values." Further, P. C. K. Prem has identified Dominic's *Winged Reason* as a rare collection of poems in Indian English poetry as it is written in simple and plain language, showing "genuine anxiety for socially neglected segments of society" and the philosophy of life in totality in the sixth chapter "K. V. Dominic's *Winged Reason*: Poems of Man's Earthly Life and Painful Realities."

In Chapter 7, "Social Criticism in the Poetry of K. V. Dominic", Prof. T. V. Reddy has identified Dominic's profound concern for the marginalized sections of the society in almost all the lines of the three collections and revealed the poets persistent efforts 'to dissect' corruption at all levels—religious, political, social, and academic. Dr. Sugandha Agarwal has examined all the three collections of Dominic and found him a didactic poet who writes poetry for the benefit of the world and not to fulfill any sort of aesthetic appeal or sensuous gratification, as he writes in the eighth chapter—"Concurrent Predicaments and Urge for Philanthropy in the Poetry of K. V. Dominic."

In Chapter nine, "Poetry for a Better World: A Critical Look at the Poetry of K. V. Dominic," Dr. Rob Harle acknowledges Dominic's poems as indispensable collections "to bring about positive change and equality for all individuals" and "to raise awareness in others with the hope of making the world a better place for all." Dr. J. Pamela in Chapter 10, "A Requiem for the Disconsolate: K. V. Dominic's Poetry as a Social Criticism", has declared Dominic as a multifaceted personality whose poems are social criticisms and are devoid of absurdity or obscurity. She has noted that it is the poet's sensitivity to the world that has urged him to pen down some of the mournful poems to impart his message to the reader.

In Chapter 11, "Poetry for a Meaningful Life: A Critical Analysis of K. V. Dominic's Poetry", Dr. Bhaskar Roy Barman has unveiled Dominic's philosophical musings in the three poetry collections. He asserts that every poem of Dominic is "infused with the poet's philosophical thought and his personal ideas, because the life of human beings is itself a philosophy." Dr. S. Ayyappa Raja has closely observed the three collections of Dominic in Chapter 12, "K. V. Dominic as a Social Critic: A Study of His Poems", and has brought out Dominic's wish toward universal brotherhood and his treatment of the social issues, such as child labour, exploitation of nature, corruption, religious intolerance, poverty, casteism, the sad plight of women, superstitious beliefs, and abandonment of aged people in the society.

In Chapter 13, "Philosophical Voyage of K. V. Dominic", Dr. Arbind Kumar Choudhary has emphasized the fact that the appeal of Dominic's poetry lies in "his candid expression, simple language, mind-blowing thought, and innovative ideas that provoke the imagination of the muse lovers to its utmost degrees" and declares that the highly detailed observation and skilled presentation of the poet would prove to be a "milestone in the poetic world of Indian-English poetry." Anisha Ghosh (Paul) in Chapter 14, "The Poet of the Marginalised: An Analysis of K. V. Dominic's Poetry", has identified the doctrines of Advaita Vedanta philosophy in the poems of Dominic and has shown the influence of humanitarians and thinkers like Swami Vivekananda, Marx, Darwin, Said, Fanon, Mother Teresa, Adi Sankara, Salim Ali, Steve Irwin, Gandhi, and Nehru, as well as from the tenets of Hinduism, Christianity, and Buddhism in the collections of Dominic. Further, she has stated that the imagination of Dominic is triggered by the major English, American, and Indian poets like Wordsworth, Blake, Shelley, Keats, Frost, Emily Dickinson, Kamala Das, Nissim Ezekiel, and Jayanta Mahapatra. She has also claimed that "In all three collections of his poems, Dominic voices his proletarian sentiments in poems about the working classes, the daily wagers and the teeming millions suffering the pangs of poverty."

In Chapter 15, "K. V. Dominic's Poetry: Rebellion and Reticence on Winged Reason", Joe Palathunkal has brought out the "streaks and streams of rebellion, a shriek of revolt" in the *Winged Reason* as Dominic "has heard the call of the situational imperatives and has responded with his mind and heart, which reflect the strands of emotions and thoughts one comes across in his poetry." Patricia Prime in Chapter 16, "A Critical Analysis of K. V. Dominic as a Philosophical Poet", has scrutinised the poetic elements, such as style and content, vocabulary, and subject matter in the poetry of Dominic, and has found the technique and subject matter match each other and are mutually supportive. Further, she avers that his collections need a critical insight to comprehend their sublime philosophy. Ecocritical principles necessitate the interconnectedness of all lives and the poems of Dominic propose the interdependence of all beings as a means to achieve a harmonious world.

In Chapter 17 "The Relation between God, Man and Nature in K. V. Dominic's Poems", Dr. Mahboobeh Khaleghi has divulged Dominic's insistence of interdependence of all lives in his

*Philosophical Musings for a Meaningful Life*

collections of poems and his desire to establish peace on earth. Sangeeta Mahesh in Chapter 18, "K. V. Dominic, the Messenger of Humanity, Peace, and Harmony in the Universe", has apprehended the theme of humanism, peace, and harmony in the poems of Dominic and publicized him as "the painter of realistic, imbalanced society, full of pain and sufferings, and the dreamer of idealistic society, where all creatures in this universe live in harmony and enjoy the bounties of nature."

Dr. Radhamany Sarma has highlighted the issues such as human rights, nature, multicultural Kerala, child labor, social criticism, religious fanaticism in the poems of Dominic and has shown him as a multifarious personality in Chapter 19, "Philosophical Musings for a Meaningful Life: An Analysis of K V Dominic's Poetry". In Chapter 20, "The Landscape of Kerala in K V Dominic's Poetry", Anisha Ghosh (Paul) has examined the landscape of Kerala, "the multicultural atmosphere as well as various social realities and problems that prevail in the State", in all the three volumes of Dominic and pointed out his ability to integrate society with Nature.

Dr. S. Barathi in Chapter 21, "Eco-critical Perspectives in the Poetry of K. V. Dominic", has investigated the relationship between human activities and the natural world in the poems of Dominic and appreciated the eco-critical consciousness in them. In Chapter 22, "Ecological Issues Reflected in the Selected Poems of K. V. Dominic", Rincy Mol Sebastian has captured the environmental consciousness of Dominic and the address of major environmental problems that disturb the relationship between God, Man, and Nature.

Dr. Arbind Kumar Choudhary in Chapter 23, "Ecological and Social Issues in K. V. Dominic's *Multicultural Symphony*", has declared that Dominic's "intense passion for the burning social and national ailments makes him a disciple of Ezekielean School of poetry in Indian English literature" and his "poetic passion for the natural beauty, animal world, rural landscape, and imaginative poetic approach keep him beside the Romanticists in Indian English poetry." The twenty-fourth chapter contains Kavitha Gopalakrishnan's paper "Holistic Musings: K. V. Dominic as a Poet with Purpose", in which she has analysed all the three collections of Dominic to identify the vision and mission of Dominic who announces "man's exploitation of biosphere, the apathy shown toward fellow beings and other living creatures" and who tries to "wake them to their heinous indifference".

Elisabetta Mariono's interview with Dominic forms the twenty-fifth chapter of the book and it portrays Dominic as a philosopher and a social critic who can bring comfort to all the suffering souls.

Let me wind up the preface expressing my deep gratitude to Modern History Press for its willingness to publish this book. I am also indebted to all contributors who made this book a reality. With this book, I hereby wish all the readers across the world a mental feast.

Dr. S. Kumaran<br>
Editor

## About the Editor

Dr. S. Kumaran is working as an Assistant Professor in the PG & Research Department of English, Thiruvalluvar Government Arts College, Rasipuram. He has received his doctorate from Anna University and has obtained PGDTE from English and Foreign Languages University, Hyderabad. Further, he has qualified both State Eligibility Test and UGC-National Eligibility Test. He is actively engaged in research work and his research contributions include: thirty journal publications, three books, forty paper presentations, eight papers in various anthologies, and guidance to doctoral students. Moreover, he is the Treasurer of Guild of Indian English Writers, Editors and Critics (GIEWEC); Associate Editor of two refereed international biannual journals, *Writers Editors Critics* (WEC) and *International Journal on Multicultural Literature* (IJML); and a Member of the Editorial Boards of various journals from India and abroad.

# About the Poet

**Dr. K. V. Dominic,** English poet, critic, short story writer, and editor is a retired professor of the PG & Research Department of English, Newman College, Thodupuzha, Kerala, India. He was born on 13 February, 1956, at Kalady, a holy place in Kerala where Adi Sankara, the philosopher who consolidated the doctrine of Advaita Vedanta, was born. He got his PhD on the topic "East-West Conflicts in the Novels of R. K. Narayan with Special Reference to *The Vendor of Sweets, Waiting for the Mahatma, The Painter of Signs,* and *The Guide*" from Mahatma Gandhi University, Kottayam, Kerala. In addition to innumerable poems, short stories, and critical articles published in national and international journals, he has authored/ edited twenty-four books so far. The titles are:

- *Postcolonial Readings in Indo-Anglian Literature*
- *Selected Short Stories in Contemporary Indo-Anglian Literature*
- *Pathos in the Short Stories of Rabindranath Tagore*
- *Reason and Fantasy: A Collection of Poems and Short Stories*
- *Winged Reason: A Collection of Poems*
- *Stephen Gill's Poetry: A Panorama World Peace*
- *Discourses on Contemporary Indian English Poets*
- *Studies in Contemporary Canadian Literature*
- *Critical Studies on Contemporary Indian English Women Writers*
- *Write Son, Write: A Collection of Poems*
- *Critical Perspectives on the Poetry of R. K. Singh, D. C. Chambial, and I. K. Sharma*
- *Discourses on Five Indian Poets in English: Keki N. Daruwalla, Shiv K. Kumar, Pronab Kumar Majumder, Syed Ameeruddin, and Aju Mukhopadhyay*
- *Concepts and Contexts of Diasporic Literature of India*
- *Changing Face of Women in Literature: The Flaming Spirit*
- *Studies on Six Indian Poets in English: Jayanta Mahapatra, Hazara Singh, P. C.K.Prem, Gopikrishnan Kottoor, Manas Bakshi, Chandramoni Narayanaswamy,*
- *Multicultural Consciousness in the Novels of R. K. Narayan*
- *African and Afro-American Literature: Insights and Interpretations*
- *Critical Evaluation of Contemporary Indian Poetry in English*
- *Multicultural Symphony: A Collection of Poems*

- *Multicultural Literature of India: A Critical Evaluation of Contemporary Regional Literatures*
- *World English Fiction: Bridging Oneness*
- *Jayanti M. Dalal: Select Stories*
- *Sarojini Sahoo's Feminine Reflections*
- *Indian Literatures in English: New Directions, Newer Possibilities.*

Prof. Dominic is the Secretary of Guild of Indian English Writers, Editors, and Critics (GIEWEC), a registered non-profit having more than two hundred members mainly consisting of university/college professors, research scholars, and professional English writers. Prof. Dominic has conducted several national seminars and workshops all over India. He is a SAARC writer and participant of SAARC literary festivals. He is the editor and publisher of the international refereed biannual journal *International Journal on Multicultural Literature* (IJML) and Editor-in-Chief of the Guild's international refereed biannual journal *Writers Editors Critics* (WEC). Both the journals are abstracted and indexed by Literary Reference Centre Plus, EBSCO Host, USA for Worldwide reference. He is also the publisher of the international refereed annual on fiction *New Fiction Journal* (NFJ).

Dr. Dominic has been interviewed by the reputed Italian Professor, Prof. Elisabetta Marino, and it appeared in the renowned Italian journal *MOSAICO* in Italy and Brazil as well as its English translation in the international refereed quarterly journal *Labyrinth* from Gwalior. He is in the Advisory and Editorial Boards of several leading journals in India. The International Poets Academy, Chennai, conferred on him its highest award—Lifetime Achievement Award—in 2009.

He can be contacted at: prof.kvdominic@gmail.com,

His website www.profkvdominic.com, or blog www.profkvdominic.blogspot.in.

# Chapter 1 - Introduction: Poetic Mind of K. V. Dominic by P. C. K. Prem

Dominic considers multiculturalism or unity in diversity as the essence of existence, the real beauty of oneness. The symphony and harmony in nature are symbols of unity in diversity. Multiculturalism is visible everywhere—from microcosm to macrocosm, from individuals and families to the entire world. The human organism certainly displays diversity, but still, wide-ranging organs work for the whole in perfect harmony. If a man upholds harmony in each wing of life, a meaningful synthesis will work for a dignified cause. Like many poets, he affirms that materialism distorts, rather kills principles, values, family, and social relations. Corruption is the hallmark of contemporary life where poets, as prophets, must perform social duties, he exhorts at many places. And the advent of terrorism and religious fanaticism disturb him. He calls it an irony that a man does everything in the name of God.

K. V. Dominic has published three poetic collections: *Winged Reason* (2010), *Write Son, Write* (2011), *and Multicultural Symphony* (2014) so far, and each volume exhibits the poet's anxieties for the little aspirations of an ordinary man who works in the fields and factories and who does not live a comfortable life.

## *Earthly Realities*

Dominic's *Winged Reason* is a collection of poems of earthly imagination. Lofty thoughts and ideas are not the areas of his poetic forays. Dominic is worried about the social life of man. If a man is happy in a society and earns his livelihood, he makes a wonderful world. *Winged Reason* conveys a definite message. His second collection of poems *Write Son, Write* carries the thought process forward, and again the poet raises issues concerning man, life, and god. He is truly realistic and down-to-earth in the sense that the words with the tonal values do not distract the readers with multi-faceted meanings. In *Multicultural Symphony*, thoughts of love, fellow feelings, social anxieties, and compassion present universal feelings of human sentiments. He attempts to recognize pains, sufferings, and anguish of men, who work hard, live a miserly life but contribute to the building of vast empires, nations, and rulers. However, no one really thinks of the wellbeing of the poor and hardworking people.

The poet believes in simple, straight, and unadorned language while displaying genuine anxiety for the socially neglected segments of society. He is more interested in conveying feelings, thoughts, miseries, and the little joys of life rather than the craft and style of poetry. He is genuinely interested in life of men and considers it a poetic forte when he says:

> A poet should be responsible to his own conscience. Otherwise, he cannot be called a poet. I do agree with Jayanta Mahapatra that the craft and style of language are only frills of poetry. A poet is a creator, a representative of the Almighty Creator. His duty is to recreate the world in the minds of the readers with added beauty. He has to present before his fellow beings an ideal world. Let me make a criticism of my poems, as Seamus Heaney, the Nobel Laureate, has always been doing to his poems. As a poet, I am responsible to my own conscience and I want to convey an emotion

or a message often through social criticism.... poetry should be digestible as short stories and novels are. I adopt a conversational style in poetry, which again attracts the ordinary readers. Here I am influenced much by the Victorian poet Robert Browning.

I believe what he says, and he proves it. Poetry, if serves humanity, will make a permanent impression, he feels. He concentrates on the miserable conditions of the poor and feels emotional attachment. He constructs a philosophy of life worth emulating. In the sufferings of man, he finds hidden zest and meaning for life. The relation between God, Nature, and Man is the theme in Dominic's poetry. The poet believes that Man learns many things from Nature and non-human beings. Unfortunately, human beings break the flow or rhythm of a system. Dominic's poetry appeals to reason and feelings rather than imagination. Dominic's poems 'instruct' and 'delight'—the twin purposes of poetry—and thus, social thoughts predominate his poetry.

## Disease and the System

He is ruefully conscious of the rampant corruption whether political or religious. Whatever concerns a man's life, living, and society is the theme of his poetic creation with minimum use of similes, metaphors, and images. In a long preface, the poet makes a statement about poetic morality, theme, and philosophy of life in totality while underlining the miserable conditions of the poor in the world. In the background of each poem, the otherwise invisible and unobserved existence of obtrusively stark realities of life of hard working poor people, and the utter darkness they confront around, challenges a sensitive mind and makes a powerful and permanent impact, and thereafter, eloquently speaks of the power of poetry, its beauty, and strength. Intensity of experience and sincerity in depiction beautify social realism in Dominic's poetry. Out of curiosity, when I probed further, he wrote to me:

> The major theme of my poetry is the eternal relationship between Man, Nature, and God. Though baptized a Christian, I am primarily an Indian. It is my duty also to propagate noble values to the rest of the world. *Advaita* seems to me more reasonable and acceptable than *Dvaita*. I find the eternal affinity between Man, Nature, and God. Man is not given liberty to kill other beings nor is he allowed to uproot plants and trees for his luxuries. The Creator has given man permission to use plants just for his survival. That is the law of Nature. Are all creations—plants, animals, planets, stars—created solely for man? I have respect for Hinduism and Buddhism as they believe in Ahimsa.

Dominic is deeply aware of the hiatus between the rich and the poor and the degree of prejudice, injustice, and exploitation that governs the lives of the poor. He the agonies and sufferings of women, old men, and the downtrodden with aching intensity and depth. Rural life is ideal, simple, and innocent, where no evil ever enters, but urbanites appear cruel and unsympathetic, materialistic and avaricious.

One may find it difficult to agree with the poet but deep down, truth reveals hard realities of life, where the cultured and the civilized dictate principles of life. In fact, life in totality without philosophic nuances is the subject matter of Dominic's poems and through an objective and realistic evaluation in social perspective, if efforts are sincere, a man's life can be happy and meaningful, the poet asserts.

## Man and the World

Dominic is fundamentally a poet of humanity and his subject is 'man' and 'society'. His compassion and sympathy are concentrated on man and this quality makes Dominic special. His humanism is transparently perceptible, the moment one goes into the emotional areas the poet's verses create. A journey into the heart of the poems is an experience of not only unique stillness but also one feels a terrific eruption of feelings, volatile stirring of suppressed emotions, and restrained but transcendent creation of an affectionate and rich world.

The poet does not take the reader to regions beyond sky or probes into the depths of heart. He is definitely not worried about the other world. Ideas of love, birth, and death do not create ripples in the poet's mind and heart. Intellectual strength, capacity, and physical limitations of Dominic try to understand the known and required essentials of life of a poor man. He wishes to explore the realistic needs of man and wants to share a few moments of joy and happiness with the neglected segment of the society.

He experiments with multifaceted experiences and incidents of life, and the itch drives the poet to the heart of the society where a man lives, flourishes, and suffers. At this moment, the poet intellectualizes life where facts and truths in little fragments surface. Life turns out an indefinite mystery. Bereft of philosophic undercurrent, the little verses of Dominic are highly subjective with an objective outlook. He may appear personal in the depiction of life of a particular section of the society, but if understood properly, he speaks for the whole humanity and invokes sentiments of love for humanity. In one of the lyrics, he asks: "My dear fellow beings/when will you learn/the need for/multicultural existence?"

In beautiful and subtle words, he talks of unity in creation:

> The creator made no divisions
> except man and woman
> he made the division
> to continue creation
> In truth they are one
> two sides of the flow

In the third stanza, he says:

> Multiplicity and diversity
> essence of universe
> From atom to the heavens
> multiculturalism reigns
> This unity in diversity
> makes beauty of universe.
>
> ("Multicultural Harmony", *Multicultural Symphony* 15)

At times, he interprets a man's life from experiences gathered after conscious and careful understanding of man and life.

Many poems indirectly deal with societal setup and man's behavior and attitude in the collective endeavor to make society a better place to live. The wretched and desolate living conditions of the poor disturb the poet and he tries to hold the rich responsible for the sufferings of the subjugated and the poor. It appears the objective of the poet, wherein he makes genuine efforts to look at the issues in the contemporary context and tries to find relevance. It is quite appropriate to recall the words of the poet:

> Poor people are strangled through taxes and their governments do nothing for their welfare. The government is always with the rich, caring for their comfort and luxury. The rich can evade taxes, exploit the weaker sections, torture and kill anyone they like; they get the protection of police; can escape legal punishments…It is the duty of the rich as well as the developed countries to alleviate the miseries of the poor. (Preface, *Winged Reason*, 13)

Unending worries of getting a loaf of bread and shelter occupy the poet's attention and lead him to a calculated, perhaps even manipulated criticism of society. He says, "Very sorry ma / I will never waste / any food in future / Ma, we shall keep / a portion of our food / and send it to / those hungry mouths" ("Hungry Mouths", *Multicultural Symphony* 50). A greatly personal indictment of the rich, whom he finds morally responsible for the injustice perpetrated on the poor and the helpless, might appear unjustified to many, but beneath the surface, the poet's genuine anxieties for the well-being of the vulnerable section of society cannot be underestimated. He talks of the universal problem of hunger. ailing many countries, and the exploitation of the rich, perhaps the rulers.

## Anguish of Eroding Social Values

Injustice, exploitation, and poverty are the recurring themes of many poems while he quite earnestly talks scathingly of the dirty politics and degeneration of value-system. Interestingly, Dominic says it in simple words with straight meaning, but an inherent irony underlines the essence of social thought. One, at times, wonders whether one is reading about the miserable plight of the poor or it is an appeal to humanity to look below and ameliorate the pathetic conditions of the poor class. An element of insightful sarcasm with an integral sense of ridicule shocks a discerning mind. The poet, at times, appears unrealistic and unaware of the truth of life, a bitter and unkind truth.

Social criticism in lyrics provokes a sensitive man to deliberate on the injustice and inequality prevailing in the society. A poet often sings through lyrics a long and continuous song of pain and anguish and attracts a man, who empathizes with the poor and the exploited. Such lamentations appear jarring and monotonous, for ostensibly the poet delineates a poor, exploited, and crippled society because it finds no solution to the problems of livelihood and the need for a comfortable and happy life. Materialistic aspirations mostly remain unfulfilled. The strong in the society flourish and appear to relish rampant corruption and greed.

One is constrained to observe that none speaks for the rich, who, one ought to agree, at one point of time in the not very distant past, must have worked hard to earn and amass wealth so that posterity lives a happy life. Instances are many if one throws a glance outside.

Another inherent flaw in such poetry is a lopsided understanding of issues of hunger and poverty, exploitation and political corruption, which lead many poets to view life differently without invoking critical thinking faculty. At times, the poets genuinely try to find solutions to the depressing situations, but many a time, evaluation and scrutiny of social and economic spectrum is incomplete and consequently results in unwarranted criticism of the rich and the powerful. The poets appear maudlin in approach to grueling conditions in which people spend lives and die slowly. Even a hardcore socialist would not agree that there is some ideal situation where poverty is non-existent.

## Emerging Gulf – The Rich and the Poor

An awful gulf between the rich and the poor is eternal and despite efforts of the saintly rulers and sages, or rulers with average intelligence, the gap remains. Poets are inveterate optimists and, many a time, aspire for something unattainable and wish others to do so. Therefore, the rich, the powerful, the elite, and the sophisticated are the target of criticism and ridicule. It is the predicament of the poet that regardless of true sensitivity and a genuine desire to alleviate the sufferings of the poor and the neglected segments of the society, he is incapable of translating sublime thoughts to a reality of life.

Like any true human being, he is legitimately distressed and impatient. The squalor and extreme deprivation appear to hurt not only the poor man's soul, but it is also physically torturing. He thinks of the poor and goes through a nightmarish experience of unrelenting anguish. In straight words, like 'an obese boy' and 'a bony child', he vividly describes a sense of prevailing hunger on one side, and immediately, he talks of nauseating richness. In "A Nightmare", when he tells us poetically of 'a wedding feast, ragged girls, garbage bin, public school, legacy of the west, liquor and leper', an inherent agony upsets deeply. In sleep even, the poet feels the heat, and the picture he conjures up is a commentary on the poor man's life. Horrible dreams at night create distress in the tranquil mind of the poet who gets up as:

> The siren sounded at five
> And I woke up from the nightmare
>
> ("A Nightmare", *Winged Reason*, 23)

Thoughts of miseries continuing for generations upset and fill heart with disgust. If one looks at the realistic scene he paints about the poor and the downtrodden, one notices that life for generations has been a continuous journey of hardships:

> Not far away were the slums of the city;
> Three generations lived in each hut;
> Grandpa, grandma, their sons and their wives,
> And their little kids sleep in a room!
>
> ("A Nightmare", *Winged Reason*, 23)

The truth that "I had a nightmare the overnight; / I was a hawk hovering in the sky" stuns and reveals a shattering situation inside. The poet's anxiety about the contemporary issues confronting the country is quite genuine, but it is heartening that the teacher's mind of the poet also shows the way to serious problems facing the nation and he alerts a man to the handicaps. In another verse, "Harvest Feast", the poet hints at the effective education system the nation ought to adopt. He is enthusiastic and believes that if the future generation gets appropriate education, it can definitely prove effectual, and one can manage and take care of the perennial shortage of essential commodities, and then indirectly, he tells of the utility of vocational activities and agriculture-related work.

## Instinctive Possessiveness

Practicable efforts to curb the tendency of the hoarders to create continuous shortages in food grains will prove effective if rulers take strong measures. If dignity of labor finds favor and definite plans emerge, the measures would encourage constructive thinking and humanity can hope to live happily:

> how education can be vocational;
> and the beauty and dignity of labour;
> a lesson too to the adult world:
> the way to solve the food crisis,
> and save the world from poverty.
>
> ("Harvest Feast", *Winged Reason*, 35)

The poet tries to draw parallels and comparisons but rarely hesitates. The words like 'obese', 'bony' and 'wedding feast' need deep understanding. A commentary on the present day's deplorable scarcity of food grains shocks and entails fall in the quality of life and morals. A reflection on the government's apathy in managing surplus in food grains tells a different story of bureaucratic and political ineptitude and the lethal role of deep-rooted self-interest. One often hears assertions that no scarcity of food items exists but the masses remain hungry, for sufficient food stuff does not reach the right people. A dreadful parallelism between the rich and the poor exists, and ironically, it takes place in a country where moral values are often much flaunted, the poet bemoans. He is critical of present politics and politicians. One wonders if a man will ever realize the objective of real socialism. In "A Nightmare", a sensitive poet is extremely sarcastic where emotions and pathos disturb. A hint at queues speaks more than what the words say. He has a dig at the permit-oriented and rationed living, a fashion in a democratic set up.

## Sufferings – A Measuring Principle

Sufferings determine the fate of the poor and the deprived. The poor keep working hard but get nothing. He observes a man's life from different perspectives. Each incident occurring in the life of the poet carries an inherent generalization where an insightful and compassionate heart connects it with the humanity. Alas, all socialists do. Nothing escapes keenly observant eyes as he looks at men and society from various viewpoints, but an ironic indictment is an inseparable part of deeply felt anxiety. The poet philosophically laments that the creator never thought of any division among men. Whatever divisions exist, man created for serving self-interests. Nature feeds everyone but a man eats up even nature, creates a vacuum and a disruption in the perennial flow of life.

If a man acts well, he is also destructive. Despite lofty achievements, millions die of hunger. A strange phenomenon in a civilized world raises questions of social obligation and moral responsibility. The poet regrets that division speaks of inherent injustice, and at this stage, he airs socialistic thoughts with ironic parallels. maybe, the poet keeps in mind the great split a man attempts to bring about in the society and divides it not only into classes but castes, religious sects, "man-made categories; / never in creator's dream." (*Winged Reason*, 36). Consequently, regional and fissiparous tendencies dominate the society and man, a penchant for predictable dissolution and conflict.

> What right has the mortal man
> to divide and own this immortal planet?
> What justice is there for the minority
> to starve the majority?
> . . . . . . . . . . . . . . . . .
> Capitalism rules the day;
> Have-nots number swell.
> Shattered and smashed
> are their dreams
> of health and happiness.
>
> ("Haves and Have-nots", *Winged Reason*, 37)

In *Multicultural Symphony* (37), he again speaks of 'Caste Lunatics' and he observes:

> "The Dalits have no right to ride motorbikes
> in presence of high caste men"
> My country, the greatest democracy,
> When will it be freed from
> Lunatics of caste and religion?

He touches a moot point that defies solution despite solemn proclamations in the statements of leaders, powerful men, and the Constitution. Any discerning mind would be sharp, curt, and sad at the movement of time in the destiny of poor people.

## **Workers, Farmers, and Builders – A Mere Infrastructure**

The poet is a hardened promoter of workers, and "Lal Salaam to Laborers" is a tribute to workers. Workers build a society and it lives happily. He reinforces a belief in the basic honesty of man. He feels animated and praises workers. An emotional outburst keeping with the ideology and the poet espouses the cause sincerely and elicits sympathies of apathetic people. He advocates a communistic philosophy with the precise dictum that only workers are the backbone of society and humanity. The poor is noble, virtuous, and works for the well-being of the society, the poet believes, but appears not very reasonable:

> They build houses
> Where they never rest,
> And there we live and snore.
> They sweat in factories;
> Produce numberless goods;
> And we use and enjoy.

(Winged Reason, 44)

Perhaps, it would be better to look into the past of the rich, so that one gets at the truth. Realities must guide man to attain objective through genuine efforts, honesty and sincerity. The world has rich men, who began with a penny and built great empires, if we just ignore a few unscrupulous politicians and men in power. It is a sad commentary that very few among the powerful live an honest life.

"Write My Son, Write" is a very long poem and one finds consolidation of poet's thoughts, feelings, and ideas in the lyric, which teases, provokes, and encourages an activist. The poet acts as a messenger of God, fortifies a mission, and then spreads the message of eternal values. He takes up the task of enlightening human souls, and leads men to enjoy the wonders of nature, or perhaps, he offers a prayer and therefore, asks everyone to participate. He observes: My son, / I have a mission / in your creation, / God spoke / to my ears. /. . . . / Write, my son, / write. / Write till / I say stop. (*Write Son, Write*, 21)

It is a statement of the poet's belief and faith in the eternal principle that efforts bring success. The poet talks with a little anguish when he says, "Intellectual mafia / assumes omniscient; / exploits innocent people; / detracts them / from their Creator; / makes them pessimists; / imposes their / obsolete philosophies. / No different at all / between religious / and intellectual mafias; / twin sides / of the same coin." (*Write Son, Write*, 37) and reveals a naked truth a man promotes, and thus, contaminates life. God reminds human beings how they prefer to act against the will of the Creator, then, ill-treat and exploit nature and non-human beings. He emphasizes the concept of multiculturalism and speaks of conservation, eco-friendly relations, and clean environment. He underscores the danger of tumbling the balance of nature.

The thoughts are new but the anguish is ancient, and man refuses to learn. It is an intellectual dishonesty, a failure of a leader espousing the cause of humanity but occupied in the promotion of self-interest.

Humanitarian considerations often impede a correct appreciation and evaluation of society and its behavior. A society thrives on challenges, competitions, subjugating the weak, and unending conflicts. A struggle continues and only the fittest survive. A socialistic mind probably ignores the fundamental latent truth a society loves to live with, and therefore, a confrontation lives on as a truth, and if a man comprehends correctly, the creativity will have a different shape.

When asked, Dominic writes rather poignantly, "...a thorn that thrusts my heart is the corruption done by the politicians and government officials. Why? Because they have money. In fact, my country as well as the world as such is ruled by a few multimillionaires who constitute not even one percent of the world population. It is a shocking truth that a thousand million people live in this world without a square meal a day when raw and cooked food in thousands of tons is wasted every day. How can we justify this luxury? One can become rich only at the exploitation of the poor. It is the duty of the rich as well as the developed countries to alleviate the miseries of the poor" in a personal communication perhaps; yes perhaps, the poet wants all to listen to him. Well, Vedic Truth it is but it also speaks about the truth of other religions that speak for the poor and the exploited.

Who is responsible for making good and healthy citizens? Who makes a man meaningful? Is education worthwhile? Are teachers sincere? Do academicians work honestly or believe in fat salaries? Do teachers pursue ethical values? Questions are many. In the above questions, one has to find answers.

## Freedom and Exploitation of Man

A man boasts of ability and skill of living an independent life and believes that he lives because he is strong, wise, and intelligent. However, it does not happen. A man follows the past, imitates its total psyche, and drafts a personal agenda. It has been happening since ages but alas, a man is a wonderful cheat, one must reason out and understand. The poet appears to pay sincere tributes to men, who contributed to ameliorate the poor (social, economic, and political) health of the people or who appear to have served the nation befittingly. To recognize the greatness or nobility is a charitable virtue very few harbor. An elegy on the death of E. K. Nayanar is singing of paeans in praise of a socialist pattern of society where workers get dues without any exploitation. The poet observes, "No rain could stop them; / no sleep could retreat them; / Thus mourning with the Nature, / your people swarmed round your body, / bidding "Lal Salaam, Lal Salaam." ("Long Live E. K. Nayanar", *Winged Reason*, 19). Yet, the enigma of a great divide remains engraved.

A socialist pattern will remain a dream or turn into a reality is yet not clear when he makes another pathetic and repulsive comparison between the city dwellers and the villagers. The poet finds rural people an epitome of virtues and compassion where urbanites are egotistic and impassive and warmth in human relations means nothing. He says, "Man is a wonderful work; / Unimaginable his achievements; / . . . . / Achievements prove beneficial / only to Haves a minority." ("Haves and Have-nots", *Winged Reason*, 36)

If one looks at different verses, one finds a derisive ironic vein running through each word, making it more authentic. The poet's intention is not to advocate the cause of the poor, but he is emphatic that wealth does not make society a better place to live as exploitation of the weak continues and it persistently widens the disparity between the rich and the poor. Here, another brilliantly emotional poem attracts attention. In "Tsunami Camps", the poet is callous in telling the unresponsiveness of the government machinery engaged in lessening the anguish and miseries of people facing lethal assaults of nature's fury that spread destruction, death and unparallel devastation. When the state machinery brought suffering people to the newly established camps, the life became more miserable, for in testing moments, self-interest ruled supreme and the so-called well-wishers failed to deliver social duties. Even the suspected people with leftist philosophy failed to deliver duties properly and contributed to the collapse of socialistic thought.

*Philosophical Musings for a Meaningful Life*

In hours of crisis, a man is not sincere. He is selfish and callous. People suffer in camps but exploitation continues. To render help in a crisis becomes a device to strengthen political roots. Terror and dread walk into the refugee camps.

> How dreadful the life in a Tsunami camps!
> People burnt in man-made hells;
> God's crazy seeing their sufferings.
> Money is hoarded in the government exchequer
> Or diverted for some other purposes.
>
> ("Tsunami Camps", *Winged Reason*, 33)

Corruption, dishonesty, and cruelty determine the mindset of people engaged in relief operations.

If one deeply examines the implied meaning of Onam, a great festival of Kerala, one enjoys and cherishes joviality, gay abundance, and a feeling of exuberance one witnesses among the people on Onam festival. The festival is a sign of paying genuine tributes to the hardworking people, who work and water fields, plough and sow seeds in the fields, toil hard, and reap rich harvest so that fellow brethren do not go hungry. A system is born where equality is pervasive, and values of life enrich each mind and heart. A sense of sacrifice and public weal governs the psyche of people. The poet stands aloof and appears to evince belief in an indistinguishable force that provides hope:

> Onam has a legend:
> a remembrance of
> the golden rule of Maveli
> an icon of the just king.
> Equality prevailed in society
> no lies, no crimes, no deceits,
> and no cheat
>
> ("Onam", *Winged Reason*, 54)

At another level, "Old Age" (*Winged Reason*, 51) heightens an inbuilt irony and pessimism amidst hopes of a vibrant life and the "The monarch of yesterday, / feels humbled today. / Imprisoned amidst unripe ripeness; / utterly helpless." And a sadistic pleasure continues to overwhelm.

## *Wistfulness – Peace and Harmony*

If one enquires into the reality of life, an ultimate perception of equality, where happiness and joy triumph, frequently fascinates the poets. An irony of circumstances overruns and nothing concrete happens despite pious sentiments. Shortage of money, ethics, hope, and joy is a persistent theme of Dominic's lyrics and even if he does not refer, a disturbing and perturbing thinking pervades lyrics and keeps teasing. Lyrics constitute an entreaty and make appeals to the wealthy to get up and make a solemn pledge to help vulnerable segments so that they get freedom from a ghostly dominance of exploitation, poverty, and sufferings.

In a similar strain, the poet narrates an incident where the "sacred ornaments of Krishna are stolen" and elsewhere "golden rosary" disappears. Ironically, one cannot catch hold of the culprits. Does he hint at the land of thieves or corrupt people? Furious faces of gold-crazy gods and the golden robes of the priests, offer a pathetic but irritatingly sardonic and laughable picture. Pleasures and pains dominate and it appears a huge void with little joys.

At another level, the scenario is vast where a man indulges in intellectual exercise, and forgetting anguish of life, hopes to live in peace and harmony. The poet goes beyond national borders:

>     Dear my fellow beings
>     Break away all fences and walls
>     Fences of your petty minds
>     Compound walls of your houses
>     Walls of your religions and castes.
>                 "Multicultural Harmony", *Multicultural Symphony*, 22)

If it happens, quite genuine desires of a peace-loving person will bring meaning in life. A true man wants no cultural, linguistic, historic, regional, religious, national, or individualistic ambitions to survive, for universal love will flourish when humanity lives as a family. A teacher stands up and takes us to a primary school.

If hard work becomes the ruling passion of everyone, it brings health, wealth, and prosperity. If one notices rich people around, one ought to go back to past and find out the truth. The rich of today must have worked hard as the poor of yesterday. It is also possible that the rich of today. if do not work hard, may become the poor of tomorrow. Therefore, the rich and poor continue to move in a vicious cycle. The poets, who write so passionately and painfully about the poor, ought to evaluate past, present, and future to arrive at a correct picture. Undoubtedly, the pre-dominance of miseries in life often give trouble but somewhere, the poet keeps the flame of hope alive and conceivably, he says obliquely that a spring of inspiration flows out to invigorate drooping spirits when experiences anguish.

## Man, Nature, and God – A Thematic Concern

The poet avers that his areas of concern are 'Man, Nature, and God', and truthfully, it encompasses life in entirety with no derivations. Around the three dimensions, the total life of a man moves and it defines limits of various conscious and unintended acts. He concentrates on 'Man' with intensity and each word, even if he uses the theme inadvertently, focuses on the anxieties and predicaments of human life. In "Old Age", the poet is vivid, realistic, and harsh when he talks that "Human life is a cycle." The verse is a true portrayal of a journey from pains to pleasures, and then from pleasures to pains it continues. The sequence is uninterrupted and the meaning of life is obvious.

At another level, the poet's anxieties appear perceptible when he observes that only strenuous work makes a man's life meaningful and that the workers are the true custodians of a life of meaning and truth. Such patterns of thoughts continue to flow in the verses of Dominic. The poet appears a little idealist and, ignoring truths, remains occupied with the thoughts of the poor. He often forgets to assess the dynamics of life and its various dimensions, whether philosophic or otherwise. He tries to define the life of a worker from various aspects. In "Why is Fate So Cruel to the Poor" (72), he raises similar issues when he takes us to the plight of workers in Jharkhand.

>     Landlessness and graft in public schemes
>     Compel the villagers every year
>     To compel the villagers every year
>     To migrate to neighbouring Bihar
>     . . . . . . . . . . . . . . . . . . . .
>     Twenty five labourers and ten children
>     Died suffocated under heavy sacks
>     They struggled hard for the grain
>     And the grain led them to their graves
>     Why is fate so cruel to the poor?

Workers in different areas of life disturb the poet and the pains travel to *Multicultural Symphony*, a latest offering of lyrics.

A socialistic thought process primarily determines the humanism of the poet in Dominic. A humanitarian thought awakens the poet and he gives a clarion call to the man to turn all ornaments into food and 'Gods will be Pleased' and it will bring contentment and affluence. Possibly, thoughts of widespread hunger and scarcity pester the poet. Food and food only appears to be the panacea for all ailments in the world:

> Take all ornaments
> from temples and churches
> turn them into food
> and serve
> to hungry mouths
> AND GODS
> WILL BE PLEASED.
>
> ("Gods will be Pleased")

Genuine hard work makes a man's life meaningful and only the workers are the true custodians of a life of meaning and truth. Such patterns of thoughts continue to flow in the verses of Dominic. The spirit of work is a prayer in itself, and the poet is adequately vivid when he speaks through the words of a parish:

> ("You are right, my son,"
> whispered God to my ears,
> "I've never asked my children
> to waste a day flattering me.)

And again he says:

> My dear son, live in Karma,
> love all creations,
> for I am in everything.")
>
> ("Work is Worship", *Write Son, Write*, 95–96)

The teachings of the men of wisdom and great men, who often exhort a man to work hard, apparently attract the poet. However, one notices that in such situations, sensitive people often forget to evaluate critically the contemporary situation in historical perspective and therefore, often indulge in wishful deliberation.

## Unhealthy and Deformed System and Karma

All religions tell men to work honestly and ardently with faith and dedication, for hard work gets adequate reward. The poet puts emphasis on the theory of *Karma* of *Gita* in the true sense of the word, and possibly irrevocable and deep belief, encourages him to hold the workers in high esteem. At times, he appears to digress and touches other themes, but the idea of a man's contentment continues to occupy idea of life. Elected representatives govern the people in a democratic system and one thinks it is the gist of themes of governance. When the poet speaks of common persons, workers, and the masses, he does not forget to talk of the rich and the powerful.

However, in different perspectives, he spells out that the rich are the products of an unhealthy and deformed economic system where the concept of equality in social, economic, and political life is utopian. As a theory, it is good to talk about and it seems enriching as a sublime thought; but when translated into reality, it is a burden because a man cannot accept equality when he is poor and the elites and the advocates of egalitarianism must understand the truth, an unpleasant fact. Socialism and a democratic form of government are developing a system where perfection is still a mirage. Even communism has failed and democracy is not a noble and virtuous structure entirely to govern society. The poet talks of Communism and Socialism or a socialistic pattern of society, and now, in "Indian Democracy", he takes a pessimistic view of life in such an organization.

> Secularism butchered;
> caste and religion
> raise their hood;
> Regionalism and parochialism
> devour
> nationalism and patriotism.
> . . . . . . . . . . . . . . . . .
> Gullible people
> they vote them again and again;
> no other options.
> Still democracy shall prevail
> or tyranny will
> sit on the Chair.

("Indian Democracy", *Winged Reason*, 60–61)

...and in the recurring state of disturbed mental frame elsewhere, he affirms the origin of sufferings and prays to God for relief.

> "God, save us
> From this extreme heat;
> Save us from the drought;
> Merciful and Almighty God;
> grant us rain
> save our land."

("God is Helpless", *Write Son, Write*, 63)

He talks of the filth man has spread through toxic gases and thus contaminated the environment. One finds man's ruthlessness creates havoc where man tortures plants, animals, water, and air; and thus, the created beings suffer from lack of food, water, shelter, and air. The poet, a communist, is sad and stands defeated as he requests an invisible force to help man and the world. The change in poet's thoughts baffles.

One finds a subtle journey in the thought process of a sensitive poet. Sufferings and lethal way of life in crushing situations distress the poet, and suddenly, he probes into 'identity' and 'self' when questions like "Who am I?" come up; and again, he goes to workers and farmers and expresses sympathy where he finds lack of appreciation shown toward life:

> An illiterate farmer is greater than you;
> His service is greater than your scribbling;
> Labourers' sweat is dearer than your ink;
> If they strike, your writings will cease,
> and ultimately you yourself will disappear.
> Hence support them and write on them;
> Proclaim to the world the noble
> service they render to the humanity.

("Who am I?", *Multicultural Symphony*, 64)

Thoughts of inherent defeat force the poet to surrender to hands that work and feed humanity. Highly sentimental attitudes in difficult times when emotions are futile overwhelm a tender heart.

## A Hesitant Message

It is quite apparent that the observed attitude of selfishness torments the poet. How to fight against such evils ailing the society is the worry of many poets. Still, hopes survive. Religious, political, and intellectual mafias continue to reign over the world-structure and promote vices of self-perpetuation and greed. If media and means of communication (print and electronic media) play significant roles in purging and shaping the minds of people in a more effective and selfless way, the world would be a better place. He reveals the inner wish of each noble and realistically ideal man.

Instead of alleviating the sufferings of the masses, efforts of man have failed miserably. It happened because man has destroyed the bases of a democratic system. The virus of voting pattern in reality divides not just man, but society and the nation as well. India is a vast country with a wonderful parliamentary system but it is also 'a stage of heinous means'. Unfortunately, the politicians in the country exploit sentiments of people, raise non-existing issues of communalism, and thus divide the people. Once unknown, communalism is now eating into the vitals of people's energies and faith. Religions are no more a sustaining force but split and segregate men, based on caste, creed, class, and region/geography. In such circumstances, what should one expect from workers, who suffer, cry, and fight for rights?

Now, if one examines the issue, one observes a painful truth that even the workers live divided in feelings, thoughts, and warmth. For many people, their loyalties remain within their own class and so discrimination and exploitation continue. While the 'gullible people' suffer, violence and terrorism thrive. The very existence of man is meaningless. The life of a man can be happy and full of optimism in any system. Happiness and prosperity of people is the objective of good governance and if it does not happen, the system needs burial. The poet is disillusioned because the people do not get relief from the system. The present system and the governance crush and kill the spirit of man despite vociferous claims to the contrary.

> What right has the mortal man
> to divide and own this immortal planet?
> What justice is there for the minority
> to starve the majority to death?
> How pitiable
> that religions give no solace and hope
> to the miserable multitudes.
>
> The Have-nots found a haven
> in socialism and communism;
> no private property;
> state-owned wealth;
> selfless work for the society.
> But power corrupted;
> leaders turned tyrants;
> the philosophy failed.
> Equality to man utopian.
> Capitalism rules the day.

("Haves and Have-nots", *Winged Reason*, 37)

With a slight tilt in thoughts, he looks at his shoes and symbolically finds relations with the attitude of a rich man toward workers, farmers, and laborers when he observes:

> Same is the plight of proletariat
> They are shoes worn by the rich
> Service being complete
> They are spat out like curry leaves
> Women too are often treated like shoes
> Mothers and wives when old and weak
> Become burden to sons and husbands
> ("Musings on My Shoes", *Multicultural Symphony*, 58)

The poet appears quite callous and ungenerous but truth forces him to write so curtly.

While going through the poetry of Dominic, it is obvious, he conveys a certain message and is sure of it, and the quality constitutes a singular exquisiteness and power of social lyrics. When he thinks of Man, Nature, and God, he is more concerned about the synthesis among the three, and the harmonious concord is the cause of tranquility and synchronization on earth. He tries to establish a deep relationship between the objects of nature and experiences that nature is essentially magnanimous and liberal. Man brings disharmony in life. He hints at the frightening cracks in relations and integrity among men. Ferocious and wicked inconsistencies among the rich, the powerful, and the poor and the weak look understandable whereas nature does not differentiate. For all the acts, a man tries to involve God and justifies the existing break between man and man.

A thoughtful man—the social animal—erects walls of separation and conflicts, as animals and plant life appear as symbols of peace and prosperity. Dominic is definite and optimistic at times, when he indirectly exhorts men to show compassion and sympathy. His philosophy is a search unending where he must rest only when true happiness visits everyone. The poet is not only inclined to a socialistic thought, but also deep down the philosophy of Mahatma Gandhi and John Ruskin vastly determines his thoughts. Undoubtedly, the poet is distinctively modern, and is worried about the system and its mechanism.

Dominic has an obsession for the workers and so he writes about the workers and farmers, and irritates frequently. However, one needs to offer an authentic ear, true sympathy, and appreciation, for he speaks of a historical truth. A person committed to an ideology can feel and say with precision and conviction. Dominic is an advocate of a socialistic pattern, and the value system he espouses implicitly borders on principles that care for the poor and the exploited.

The poetic art of Dominic shifts focus from one issue to another. He tries to emphasize an economic view of life in society, and at times, falls in abstractions temporarily. He creates a structure of words where he provokes intellectual deliberation, and at this point, a perception of decentering disturbs, for unity suffers. He intellectualizes on social and economic issues and creates a post-structural approach to the understanding of man, life, and society.

Dominic's social perception is quite evident in many verses. A continuing movement within and without is a fact and it affects the life of man. A humanitarian and philosophic approach to man gives him strength. He looks at man closely. He does not make efforts to find themes for lyrics. Even a little news, an insignificant incident, an important or petty person, a simple lie or a truth inspires him to write. Workers, farmers, laborers, and the exploited encourage him to write and write. He aspires to live in an idealistic society but fails to find a fulcrum. He constructs a lyrical structure, dismantles it, and again reconstructs it with a subtle transformation in feelings and thoughts, but continues to prolong a humanistic perception.

## Chapter 2 – Humanism in K. V. Dominic's *Winged Reason* by Dr. S. Kumaran)

The 7th edition of the *New Oxford Advanced Learner's Dictionary* defines humanism as "a system of thought that considers that solving human problems with the help of reason is more important than religious beliefs. It emphasizes the fact that the basic nature of human is good" (Hornby 2005). Corliss Lamont, the author of *Humanism as a Philosophy,* states that "Humanism, in brief is a philosophy (religion) the guiding principle of which is concentration on the welfare, progress, and happiness of all humanity in this one and only life" (Lamont 1997). This paper explores K. V. Dominic's *Winged Reason*, a collection of poems, to bring out the humanistic values expressed in it. The poems found in the collection are an ardent expression of the poetic soul to witness peace and harmony in the Universe. They proclaim the poet's faith in the humanistic values and his belief in the inherent worth and intrinsic value of non-human others. Further, the poems reveal the poet's anguish at the evils and the inhuman attitude prevalent in the society and necessitate harmony of existence.

In this modern and busy world, people have lost their respect for human values and lead insular lives. Empathy is often neglected for convenience and for selfish gains. The poet proves to be different from the rest by his sympathy and concern for others. "In Memoriam George Joson," the first poem in the collection, the poet declares his sorrow on the death of his colleague in a car accident and expresses his concern for the welfare of the family. According to Lamont (1997), "Humanism simply means 'human being-ism', that is, devotion to the interests of human beings, wherever they live and whatever their status" and the poet's ability in bringing out the pathos is beyond comparison; and it reveals his genuine grief:

> When your youngest kid,
> not knowing what has happened,
> kissed your face
> again and again
> and plucked flowers
> from your wreath;
> tossed them to her sisters weeping and screaming
> What a game He plays!
>
> ("In Memoriam George Joson", *Winged Reason*, 17)

Most of the humans in this world are confused about the activities of the world and its functioning. As a fellow being, the poet shows the path of divine knowledge and illuminates the minds of humans with the knowledge of the universe. The poet accepts and informs humans about the role of fate in the lives of humans but establishes faith in the divine play of the Supreme Being and urges humans to surrender unto the will of the ever-lasting soul. He avers that:

> As the great poet sang:
> We are all puppets in His hands,
> dancing to the tunes He plays.
> The best is to resign

>  to what He ordains
>  in time and out of time
>
>  *(Winged Reason*, 18)

As the success of a nation depends on politics, humans cannot isolate themselves from it. A good deal of knowledge and interest in politics is necessary for every human so as to ascertain their contribution to the glory of the nation. The poet's interest in the politics of his times is commendable. Unlike Abbey who wanted to find an alternate place, i.e., Abbey's Country to place himself away from the reach of people, the poet discloses his interest in politics and also points out the good qualities of a politician through "Long Live E. K. Nayanar." He commends E. K. Nayanar:

>  You were a true Communist;
>  a comrade to the core of your being,
>  a rare species,
>  compassion and love
>  an epitome of Socialism
>
>  ("Long Live E. K. Nayanar", *Winged Reason*, 19)

The poet upholds Indian democracy and reveals its lapses through "Indian Democracy". He feels that Indian democracy is the largest on the planet and is considered a wonder by the world. At the same time, he does not fail to point out how it is made ugly by the selfish politicians who fail to fulfill their duties. He remarks:

>  National parties play
>  trump cards with communalism;
>  bow their heads before priests.
>  The real issues of the country
>  never discussed among people.
>  Election campaigns:
>  fireworks of lies and abuses
>
>  ("Indian Democracy", *Winged Reason*, 80)

The poet extols peace and condemns violence in all forms. He does not approve the brutal attacks made on the people by authorities for power, selfish gains, and false beliefs, and questions the rationality of their inhuman actions. He addresses the sad plight of the people and reveals his interest in human values. In "A Blissful Voyage", he avers that:

>  I wish I had the claws of a vulture
>  to fetch the skeletons from Iraq
>  and build a bone-palace
>  to imprison Bush in it!
>
>  ("A Blissful Voyage", *Winged Reason*, 21)

In fact, the poet is ready to sacrifice his life for the sake of the country and desires to explore a distant legion. As he believes in the transforming power of humanism, he is determined to inspire humans to be aware of it and to adopt it. In this regard, Kurtz (1973) feels that "Humanists have a moral commitment to free thought, to the fulfillment of human potentialities and the democratic ideal of humanity as a whole." Dominic also brings out the unfulfilled attempts made by the great personalities to establish humanism and points out their ever-remaining dream:

>  If I could fly like an angel,
>  would plead all prophets

*Philosophical Musings for a Meaningful Life* 17

>to inspire and instill humanism
>in millions' communal minds.
>I would meet Gandhi too
>who is weeping at his shattered dreams.
>
>("A Blissful Voyage", *Winged Reason*, 21)

Humans long to have a sense of belongingness to a place and are ready to die for their homeland. On the other hand, its absence questions the meaning of their lives and puts them at the mercy of others. Further, the lack of mercy leads to mental trauma and inexplicable woes. In "Tsunami Camps", the poet brings out the unhealthy atmosphere of Tsunami camps. He feels that even gods will become crazy seeing the sufferings of the refugees. Though many days are over since their arrival on the camps, their status has not been improved a bit. Further, the poet mourns that they are not given basic amenities for their living and vehemently remarks:

>"Where have gone the crores
>collected for our relief?"
>Money is hoarded in the government exchequer,
>or diverted for some other purposes.
>"It's better to kill us than torture like this."
>"We don't have sufficient food,
>we don't have pure water"
>
>("Tsunami Camps", *Winged Reason*, 33)

The division among the people is the result of their contaminated minds and it makes the world an unsuitable place for living. The poet shows how humans have brought division among themselves ignoring the purpose of God's creation in "Haves and Have-nots." He reveals that God had no idea of Have and Have-nots when he created humans and they are purely 'man-made categories.' He finds Nature is bountiful enough to feed with its resources but 'selfish man disrupts Mother Nature's feeding. Further, he questions:

>What right has the mortal man
>to divide and own this immortal planet?
>What justice is there for the minority
>to starve the majority?
>
>("Haves and Have-nots", *Winged Reason*, 37)

Humanism has become an integral part of the poet. Even in his dream, he thinks of humanity. He brings out the existence of quite contrary things in the society and questions the rationality behind incongruous actions in "A Nightmare". He finds a mother forcing her obese child to eat more and juxtaposes it with the description of a bony child who was crying for a crumb. Further, he notices people relishing feast and also observes 'two ragged girls outside struggling with the dogs in the garbage bin'. The poet points out the desertion of aged people by their children and the sufferings of the parents in "Gayathri's Solitude". He tells that the children leave for foreign countries, ignoring their parents at the hometown. They think that the money they send could make their parents happy. The irony is that:

>Poor, miserable mother,
>she has no hunger,
>she has no sleep.
>An old lily flower
>pale and faded.

> Dawn to dusk,
> sitting in an armchair,
> looking at the far West,
> longing for her children's calls,
> she remains lonely.
>
> ("Gayathri's Solitude", *Winged Reason*, 31)

The poet brings out how human values are violated under the pretext of religion. In "In the Name of God", the poet exposes how the name of God is used to cover illegal actions and to practice evils. He also thinks that 'criminal actions' taken in the name of God outnumber the good things done in His name. He observes:

> Terrorists butcher thousands
> in the name of God.
> Teens become terrorists
> in the name of God.
> Sexism prevails
> in the name of God.
> Higher castes exploit
> in the name of God.
> Secularism is nullified
> in the name of God.
>
> ("In the Name of God", *Winged Reason*, 69)

The poet believes in the beauty of village life and encourages humans to learn humanism form it. The poet compares city life with village life in "City Versus Village" and elucidates the greatness of village life. According to Pragg (1973), humanists deem "creating conditions for free development of individuals and groups in the form of prosperity, equity, legality, participation, and self government," and Dominic addresses the same. He finds people in the city live in their 'own island' without caring even about the death of their neighbors. They do not exercise humanism and confine themselves to their inhuman actions. On the other hand, village is a place:

> where all live
> in harmony and love.
> They are gullible-
> so fooled and cheated
> and looted by the townsmen.
>
> ("City Versus Village", *Winged Reason*, 72)

The poet's exposure of the loss of human values is commendable. He points out the evils of kidnapping children in "Anand's Lot" and ascertains the mental trauma of the kidnapped children who are made to beg for the kidnappers. Readers could not help shedding tears when the persona of the poem, after having immersed his eyes on the pupils in 'tempting uniforms' remarks:

> How happy were those days!
> Mummy gave me kiss and ta-ta;
> like butterflies flew to the school
> with Rajesh, Praven, and Smitha
> chattering, singing, dancing, running.
> Alas! Like a vulture came the car then;
> picked me in and dashed away.

*Philosophical Musings for a Meaningful Life*

("Anand's Lot", *Winged Reason*, 26)

Humans should treat non-human others on par with them. In "A Sheep's Wail", the poet expresses his love for animals and exposes humans' lack of attention to them. The Sheep, persona on the poem, reveals how humans ignore the rights of animals and butcher them mercilessly. It blames humans, for shearing its fur given by God, for sucking and draining the milk for its lamb, and for killing it along with its kith and kin. Further, it censures humans as the cruelest and the most ungrateful of God's creations and questions:

> Nothing can be more absurd!
> Aren't we His children?
> How can He forgive you?
> If a heaven is there
> We will reach there first
> And pray to God to shut you out.
>
> ("A Sheep's Wail", *Winged Reason*, 25)

In "Ammini's Lament" and in "Ammini's Demise", the poet reveals his tender nature and his acceptance of non-human others as his constituent part. In "Ammini's Lamnet", he pictures how his pet cat Ammini could not stop its 'incessant cry' over 'the loss of her darlings' that had been sold by the poet in a 'weak moment' when 'troubles increased'. The poet and his wife shared the sorrow of their dear Ammini and 'the pangs of' his heart was a 'laughing-stock' to his guests. Kurtz (1988) opines that "There is a deeper aspect to the ethical life, however: moral awareness is rooted within our nature as human beings. There is a built-in dependency relationship based on socio-biological roots and cultural conditioning, and this reflects itself in our emotions" and the same is expressed by the poet. In "Ammini's Demise", the poet captures his sorrow over the loss of his poisoned Ammini and questions:

> How could that fiend
> poison this angel?
> What harm had it
> done to him?
>
> ("Ammini's Demise", *Winged Reason*, 65)

Humans should revere Nature and abstain from looting its resources. The poet informs humans about the sanctity of Nature through "I am Just a Mango Tree". He asserts that humans could learn from a tree. He also pictures how the Mango tree has fulfilled the plan of the Creator by serving others. It shelters the student-friends, gifts people with its fruits, and offers its lap to sleep. Further, the poet exposes the selfish nature of humans. As the humans desire to construct a waiting shed, they want to cut the Tree. The Tree is perplexed and for its prayer, God replies:

> 'My child, I created him
> in my own Image
> but he's gone astray;
> My agony is endless.
> That's the fate
> of the Father everywhere.
> I shouldn't have created this human species;
> But how can a father kill his sons?'
>
> ("I am Just a Mango Tree", *Winged Reason*, 41)

The poet announces how humans have lost even their sleep, owing to their unnatural ways of life in "Sleepless Nights". The poet feels that birds sleep peacefully all through night as they obey the norms of nature whereas humans have lost all their peace and spend their nights without sleep.

The poet's philosophy on the various aspects of human life is par excellence. In "Beauty", he exalts inner beauty as real and terms physical beauty temporal and unworthy. He assures that nothing on this earth is ugly as all things are created by God. Further, he says physical beauty fades like a flower's and is forgotten once its life is over. On the other hand, achievements of humans earn them eternal beauty and "only spiritual beauty gives eternal joy" ("Beauty," *Winged Reason*, 28). The poet reveals the bliss of married life in "Connubial Bliss". He declares that male and female are made for each other and none can reject pains and pleasures as they are 'God's own gifts'. Further, he ascertains that marriage brings heaven on earth and it helps humans to fulfill the plans of the Supreme Being. The poet captures the true nature of old age and warns the youth who neglect old people in "Old Age". He reveals that life cycle of humans becomes complete with old age and it humbles the 'monarch of yesterday'. Further, he points out the apathetic attitude of the children toward their aged parents and warns:

> Ageism is contemptible;
> unpardonable too.
> Today's torturer tomorrow's victim;
> we live with ironies.
>
> ("Old Age", *Winged Reason*, 52)

In "Pleasures and Pains", the poet considers pleasures and pains as a part of human life and avers that:

> Pleasures and pains:
> two sides of a coin.
> We toss it early morning;
> majority gets the pains side.
> pleasures come like sprinkles,
> while pains fall like a deluge
> and continue like monsoon.
> Happiness is a mist
> while sorrows shower like snow.
>
> ("Pleasures and Pains", *Winged Reason*, 68)

The poet acknowledges the greatness of women and asserts their dignity and independent nature in "International Women's Day". He considers women as the harbinger of all lives and commends them for their service to humanity. At the same time, he exposes the cruelties imposed on them and reveals the narrow mindedness of patriarchal society. He exposes patriarchy thus:

> Woman is the game!
> Birth to death,
> an instrument of lust
> and hot-selling sex!
> Her very birth ill omen:
> an unwelcome event.
> No guilt in foeticide;
> foeticide is matricide;
> no life without mother.

("International Women's Day", *Winged Reason*, 42)

Humans should not usurp the property of other humans and should live by their own labor. The poet emphasizes the dignity of labor in "Lal Salaam to Labour." He considers laborers as the 'backbone of the country' and believes that the service they render to the society cannot be repaid. Moreover, he feels that people live because of the labor of the laborers and they should not ignore their plight. The poet finds that the laborers build houses but have no home to stay. They clean roads and markets but are avoided by the common men. Further, he calls:

> Let us not be unjust
> when we pay them wages,
> for we can't do what they do.
>
> Give them at least their due;
> the more we give, the more we get;
> Put charity in humanity
> a spiritual bliss that never dies.

("Lal Salaam to Labour", *Winged Reason*, 45)

Thus, the analysis reveals how the poet declares his faith in humanism through his treatment of human life, divine play, politics, Indian democracy, poverty, natural calamity, division in society, religious hypocrisy, Nature, village vs city, kidnapping, love for animals, independence of women, and dignity of labor. Moreover, the analysis reveals the poet's faith in didactic poetry and ascertains the relevance of his writing to the present-day world.

## Works Cited

Dominic, K. V. *Winged Reason*. Delhi: Authorspress, 2010. Print.

Hornby, A. S. *New Oxford Advanced Learner's Dictionary*. Ed. Sally Wehmeier. Oxford: Oxford University Press, 2005. Print.

Kurtz, Paul. *Forbidden Fruit: The Ethics of Humanism*. New York: Prometheus Books, 1988. Print.

---. "Humanism and the Moral Revolution." *The Humanist Alternative: Some Definitions of Humanism*. By Kurtz. New York: Promotheus Books, 1973. Print.

Lamont, C. *The Philosophy of Humanism*. New York: Humanist Press, 1997. Print.

Praag, J. P. Van. "What is Humanism?" *The Humanist Alternative: Some Definitions of Humanism*. Ed. Paul Kurtz. New York: Prometheus Books, 1973. Print.

# Chapter 3 - An Angel in Flight:
## A Critique of K. V. Dominic's *Winged Reason*
## by Dr. Sudhir K. Arora

Though K. V. Dominic (b. 1956) in his debut poetic collection, titled *Winged Reason* (2010), claims to be much influenced by Jayanta Mahapatra for the cause of poetry that lies in a "bad heart" and Robert Browning for his conversational mode, he is neither difficult like the former nor ambiguous like the latter. He is a poet with feelings and nothing else. As plain and simple in living, he breathes poetry in an unsophisticated fashion that offers an outlet to his conscience that articulates "an emotion or a message often through social criticism" (*Winged Reason*, 12). For him, the content is more important than the style. He himself admits that his poems "lack much imagery and other figures of speech" (*Winged Reason*, 12). It does not mean that he does not know how to adorn a poem but it is simply because of his poetic agenda that "poetry should be digestible" (*Winged Reason*, 12) so that an ordinary reader may also grasp the meaning and make his life worth living with an idea that developed because of "arrows and thorns" that pierced his heart, resulting in the gushing of the blood, which filled his pen that penned the agony on the paper. He likes to call poetry "cuckoo" and feels proud of himself that in his mature years the bird made her nest from where she sings to the extent that his mind that wishes for wings begins to sing songs of man, nature, and God.

The poet in Dominic knows well that "pains and pleasures" are "God's own gifts" (*Winged Reason*, 29) though pleasures "come like sprinkles" (*Winged Reason*, 68) while "pains fall like a deluge" and "continue like monsoon" (*Winged Reason*, 68). He is in love with the Sun, which becomes the symbol of knowledge and virtues and, hence, advises the lass to "be like the sun" so that she may brighten the dark world with her "inner beauty", which is true and worth longing in comparison with the "bodily beauty", which is "all subjective and relative" (*Winged Reason*, 28). What God has created is beautiful. It is cuckoo that inspires man to love and labor for making life meaningful. It is she who lives "singing and loving" while "man exists / sweating and moaning" (*Winged Reason*, 30). He is shocked to learn that "criminal actions" are committed, "superstitions survive", "Communalism is strangled", "Terrorists butcher thousands", "Sexism prevails" (*Winged Reason*, 69) in the name of God. Why does "worm-like man" challenge "the creator"? Om, a word with three letters in Hindi or Sanskrit "representing Vishnu, Shiva, Brahma" (*Winged Reason*, 66) is not only a "key to all problems of the world" but also "a tonic to mind and body" (*Winged Reason*, 66). He wishes for peace and prosperity in the world and so wishes to go on a blissful voyage. He longs for:

> If I could fly like an angel,
> would plead all prophets
> to inspire and instill humanism
> in millions' communal minds.

(*Winged Reason*, 21)

The poet's heart cries when he sees injustice and exploitation done to woman who, for a man, remains a game throughout her life right from her birth to death. It is tragic that in spite of claim for women empowerment, she is still considered "an instrument of lust / and hot-selling sex" (*Winged Reason*, 42). How ironical is that her birth becomes "ill omen"! She is "chained in kitchen" (*Winged Reason*, 42) and remains dependent because of no education. She is "born to be dictated" (*Winged Reason*, 43). She "bears the pangs of child-bearing; / endures the rearing of her children" but "her love and sacrifices / remain unrewarded" (*Winged Reason*, 43). As she is treated as 'Other' in spite of her female heroism, which is neglected by patriarchy, the poet favors her and so becomes the champion for her cause as she is an angel—the angel that plays different roles successfully —roles of being mother, sister, wife, guide, teacher, and nurse. He shows his sympathy for a mother who appears at the examination but feels restless because of the cries of her baby that she hears. The problem with her is that she fails to concentrate on her examination in spite of the fact that she knows all answers to the questions. Though she has graduated, she is unemployed. Her husband, who has to support the family of seven members, is the "sole earner of the family" (*Winged Reason*, 73). She does not know what to do—whether she should quit the exam and feed her child or not. Her story brings tears in the eyes of the poet as well as the reader.

No doubt, God has created all equal but it is man's evil mind that has categorized man into "Have and Have-nots". It is man who, for his selfish motives, has uprooted nature and disturbed the plan of nature. He has made "deadly weapons" which have become "a great threat / to life itself" (*Winged Reason*, 36). It is tragic that the minority 'Haves' enjoys "at the cost of majorities' necessities" (*Winged Reason*, 36). Religions offer "no solace and hope / to the miserable multitudes" (*Winged Reason*, 37). Equality is merely a utopian ideal for the Have-nots that take shelter in "socialism and communism", which believe in "no private property; / state-owned wealth; / selfless work for the society" (*Winged Reason*, 37). But, unfortunately, it is capitalism that dominates the Have-nots and crushes "their dreams of health and happiness" (*Winged Reason*, 37). Corruption that has entered politics has paralyzed Indian democracy, which has become a mockery in spite of being the largest in the world. Democracy is not bad, but the politicians have defiled it with crimes for their personal gains. Secularism is butchered; casteism is in the air and "regionalism and parochialism / devour / nationalism and patriotism" (*Winged Reason*, 60). Election campaign is nothing except "fireworks of lies and abuses" (*Winged Reason*, 60). Those who have criminal records stand in the election and get victory with the help of muscle power. Even politics is played in the name of help to Tsunami camps where "Government gave kits and boxes" without "essential things" (*Winged Reason*, 33). It is sad that the money worth crores collected in the name of relief is "hoarded in the government exchequer / or diverted for some other purposes" (*Winged Reason*, 33). The people in the camps cry for food and pure water but remain unheard by the authorities.

What makes Dominic extraordinary is his love for juxtaposing the contrasts. He puts diametrical points of view, keeps mum, and leaves the reader to ponder over the situation. He does not believe in imposing his opinions or viewpoints; rather he offers choices to the reader. He sees a nightmare in which he becomes a hawk. He sees a fat boy being beaten by his mother, who is forcing him to eat more while on the other side, there is " a bony child" who is "crying for a crumb" (*Winged Reason*, 22). He sees a boy in tears, standing on the verandah in the hot weather of forty degree because of "a punishment for not wearing his tie" (*Winged Reason*, 22). The poet makes the reader think over the "slavish mimic" of wearing a tie which is simply "a legacy of the West" (*Winged Reason*, 22). Does it not sound strange that there is a long queue of men, including queue jumpers, for getting liquor from a government liquor shop while on the other side, there is a long queue of "poor women" who "wait for their rations" (*Winged Reason*, 22). He sees a water tap making "the road a black river" (*Winged Reason*, 22) while on the other side, he sees "a waterless tap / laughing at the hopeless wait /

of all the pots of the neigbourhood" (*Winged Reason*, 23). He sees a double-storeyed edifice equipped with modern amenities, where an old man with his wife sits "at the phone with sighs and moans" longing "for the calls from the sons abroad" (*Winged Reason*, 3) while on the other side, he sees the slums where "three generations live in each hut; / grandpa, grandma, their sons and their wives, / and their little kids sleep in a room" (*Winged Reason*, 23). He offers *lal salaam* to labourers who "sow the seed; / reap the corn" (*Winged Reason*, 44) not for themselves but for others who "eat and sleep" (*Winged Reason*, 44). How ironic it is that they "build houses / where they never rest" (*Winged Reason*, 44)! Without them, it is impossible to think of life. Hence, in a moralistic tone, he asks man not to be "unjust" in giving wages to them. He should not forget that "the more we give, the more we get" (*Winged Reason*, 45) and, hence, it is better to "put charity in humanity" which is "a spiritual bliss" (*Winged Reason*, 45). The poet sees the people of the city who remain "busy and selfish, / devoid of humanity" (*Winged Reason*, 71) to the extent that they are lost in their own islands. But, the people of the village who "live in harmony and love" (*Winged Reason*, 72) are "fooled and cheated / and looted by the townsmen" (*Winged Reason*, 72). The poet puts the city and village side by side and leaves the reader to reflect.

The poet lives in Kerala, a state known as "God's own land". Onam is a national festival celebrated with zeal and zest for ten days, beginning with a harvest festival Atham. Regional fragrance can be felt when "children run for flowers, / make pookalams" (*Winged Reason*, 53), people wear new dress, relish "ceremonial food", take pleasure in Onam songs, Onam plays, and Onam dances and participate in competitions. The sight of boat racing becomes "a pageant of rare beauty" (*Winged Reason*, 54). The festival of Onam is associated with Maveli, a just king who comes to visit Kerala on this pious day. The poet loves nature that is adorned by God with the brush. The beauty of "snow-capped mountain" and "multi-coloured sky" fills his heart with love and wonder. He weeps over the selfishness of man who disturbs "the earth's balance" (*Winged Reason*, 41). The mango tree complains against man's materialistic attitude urging God to withdraw him so that the planet may turn into a paradise. It bears "fruits for others" (*Winged Reason*, 40), provides shelter to birds, drops "mellow yellow fruit" (*Winged Reason*, 40) to the beggar friend and feels happy because of "the fruit of service" (*Winged Reason*, 41).

But, it is man who, out of material gains, thinks of cutting the mango tree who cries: "Don't I have feelings and pains / though I endure in silence! / Haven't I the right to live? / God, why is your Man so selfish and cruel" (*Winged Reason*, 41)? Not to talk of nature, man also exploits animals for his selfish motives. A sheep complains that what is given to it by God is taken by man who has conquered because of "some special powers" (*Winged Reason*, 24). It is man who shears its fur to make himself cosy, sucks the milk, and grows "fat and cruel". The sheep calls man "the cruelest" and 'the most ungrateful / of all God's creations" (*Winged Reason*, 25) and wishes to enter heaven first so that it may pray to God for closing the gate for him. The poet leaves his teenage hobby of catching the fish when he imagines that he is himself a fish that has been "pulled from the sky" (*Winged Reason*, 48). He now feels that catching the fish is merely a "sadistic pleasure" (*Winged Reason*, 48) and, hence, spends most of his time in "reflections on life" (*Winged Reason*, 48). He becomes conscious so much that he thinks that "man has no right / to torture any other being" (*Winged Reason*, 76) because of the same father God. He becomes a vegetarian and follows the Gandhian way of life. He becomes sad over the demise of the cat named Ammini, who was poisoned to death by some wicked man. It is also tragic that thousands of such fiends "inhabit this planet" and turn "the earth to a big slaughter house" (*Winged Reason*, 65). The poet's heart prays to God to make the fiends "humane".

The poet in Dominic is sympathetic to Anand who was kidnapped and forced to begging. When Anand sees the pupils "in tempting uniforms" (*Winged Reason*, 26), he remembers his mummy, who used to give him a kiss and ta-ta. But, the kidnapping incident has changed his fate and made him a beggar. It is an incident of past when he left his mom, dad, and Smitha. He wonders whether they recall him or not. When he is lost in his past days, he is slapped by the bearded man, who threatens him to go to the shops for begging. The sight of the blind Helen pierces the heart of the poet, who lectures for the Rasa theory through "the analogy of the lamp and the pot" (38) to make the students understand "how the lamp reveals the pot" (*Winged Reason*, 38). But, Helen's eyes search for the lamp and the light. She is a brilliant student, who has read a lot through her brother's eyes. It is a paradox that light that sees all cannot see itself. She is "the light of the class" (*Winged Reason*, 39) fighting against "darkness".

The poet presents the case of Laxmi, who is still not married while her colleagues are married. She is an able girl fit for being "a lamp to any house" (*Winged Reason*, 46) but this lamp is "destined to burn out" because of dowry, which she fails to provide. She has to support her family with her meager salary of two thousand. She has pricked her "bubble of dreams" and wishes none to dream for her. The poet also sympathizes with Rahul who is turned out from the class by the teacher because of his failure in completing homework. He fails not because of his own fault but because of his drunken father, who beats his mother and him. For him, the world seems to be cruel by virtue of "cruel father / cruel teacher" and, hence, "longs for love" (*Winged Reason*, 55). The poet is much impressed by Vrinda, who turns "her challenge to strength and success" (*Winged Reason*, 57). She is a girl with one leg but in spite of that, she dances like "a peacock to Hindi film tunes" (57). The poet's heart starts aching and interrogates: "Why is destiny so cruel" (*Winged Reason*, 57)? This is the world full of ironies. One who tortures today becomes a victim tomorrow. For him, "ageism is contemptible" (*Winged Reason*, 52).

Gayatri, who became a widow at thirty-five, is now eighty-two years old. She lives alone in "the palatial house" equipped with modern facilities. The children think that she lives happily but the reality is that she has become "an old lily flower / pale and faded" (*Winged Reason*, 31). She longs for "her children's calls" and remains "lonely". The thing that is striking in his poetry is that he uses the name just opposite to its meaning. Anand begs, though his name suggests pleasure or happiness. Helen means the brightening or shining one, but in the poem, she is blind. Laxmi is the goddess of wealth but here she has no amount for her dowry, the result of which is that she is unmarried. Rahul, the meaning of which is 'capable', is also the name of Siddhartha's son, but here Rahul is incapable of doing his homework. Vrinda, whose name suggests 'cluster of flower' and also symbolizes 'virtue and strength', is a girl who dances with one leg. The name of Gayatri, who is the consort of Brahma, means hymn or song. But here, Gayatri, the widow, lives alone. Hence, Dominic has used the names for the characters that are antithetical and different to what their names indicate.

The poet in Dominic is also much influenced by some characters, who played a significant role in his life directly or indirectly. He writes in memory of his friend George Joson, who died in a car accident on May 14, 2004. The poet's heart feels grief and pain when he sees Joson's youngest kid kissing his face and plucking flowers and tossing them to her lamenting sisters. Jonson proved himself fast in everything, even in death. He finds that "life is uncertain" (*Winged Reason*, 17) and "we are all / bound by His will / to be here / or to be away" (*Winged Reason*, 18). As he becomes stoic, he thinks that "the best is to resign / to what He ordains / in time and out of time" (*Winged Reason*, 18). He does not believe when he comes to know about E. K. Nayanar's death. People come even in rain to pay homage to Nayanar, "a true communist" bubbling with "compassion and love" (*Winged Reason*, 19). He was a true fusion of "rhetoricians and statesmen" with "no foes, only friends" (*Winged Reason*, 20). It was he who "championed the cause of the denied / and the deprived" (*Winged Reason*, 20). The poet does not forget to pay his regard to the teacher Kaumudi, who remained "a lone fighter, a role model; / a single woman to fulfil her mission" (*Winged Reason*, 74).

In her teens, she joined the politics and followed Gandhi, who was much impressed when she offered her ornaments. She passed an unassuming life and taught Hindi. She is a rare gem that "dimmed / the dazzle of all other women in jewels and ornaments" (*Winged Reason*, 75). The poet loves Michael Jackson, who challenged the white in dance and staked his health "for the fulfillment of art" (*Winged Reason*, 77).

The poet in Dominic is an angel who searches for the angelic qualities in men and when he misses, he motivates them through his poems offering choices by displaying the two contrasting pictures. It is his heart that realizes the importance of Keats' line "a thing of beauty is a joy forever" and, so, values the beauty of mind and beauty of character. He makes others believe that the loss will result in "sorrow forever" (*Winged Reason*, 64). He wishes that no other Bush may kill the people in Iraq. Hence, he likes to have "the claws of a vulture" so that he may "fetch the skeletons from Iraq" and "build a bone-palace" in order to "imprison Bush in it" (*Winged Reason*, 21). On the winged reasons, he makes a flight of his imagination but does not soar high because he knows the reality of life that he has to live on this very earth, which is "the home for all" and, so, "all should hear the heartbeat of others" (Blurb).

## Work Cited

Dominic, K. V. *Winged Reason*. Delhi: Authorspress, 2010. Print.

# Chapter 4 -
# K. V. Dominic's *Multicultural Symphony*: A Critique
# by Dr. Sudhir K. Arora

In a churchyard Gray
releases anonymous poems
fiction blows the candle.

(Khatri, 69)

    This Haiku from C. L. Khatri's *Two-Minute Silence* reveals the truth about the fate of poetry in the present-day scenario, which favors fiction that has dominated the scene and brought poetry from the centre to the periphery. Notwithstanding this miserable state of poetry, many poets continue to light the candle with the hope that one day the world will understand them and apply what they have recommended through their poems, which is the rich storehouse of knowledge and wisdom.

    K. V. Dominic is one of the poets who believe in poetry and its capacity to impart values to the world. He finds poetry as "the best and easiest medium to impart messages and values to the people" (*Multicultural Symphony*, 7). He discovers the world, dotted with the colors of evil, alienation, separation, disease, selfishness, wickedness, and oppressions. He cries to see the miserable plight of his countrymen and so wishes to do something for them but "the tragic irony is that none listens to the poets nowadays" (*Multicultural Symphony*, 7). People have developed the materialistic attitude, which has changed the way of seeing and living life. The poet in Dominic holds media and internet responsible for the lack of interest in serious thinking. People avoid intellectual and metaphysical discussion for the sake of the materialism. Matter matters. In spite of the fact that "The tragic fate of poetry is universal and the poets are ignored worldwide" (*Multicultural Symphony*, 7), he continues to pen the pain that he feels when he sees the miserable plight of his countrymen, who do not hesitate even to interfere the world of birds, animals, fauna, and flora.

    What matters for Dominic in composing poetry is content, not form. He believes in the authority of content over form and thinks that form will take care of itself and open naturally its arms to take content within. He himself admits: "Since the content of the poem is most important to me, I don't mind if the lines lack the luster of style" (*Multicultural Symphony*, 10). Searching for the fusion of feelings and thoughts in the garb of images is useless because he attempts to pack every line with matter so that the reader may forget the form under the influence of the matter. To some extent, his poetry results from the newspaper reports and this habit of penning poems out of them makes him a poet ready with the news to awaken the consciousness of the people toward the evils so that they may have feelings in the hearts, suffering with the disease of materialism, which makes them selfish to the extent that they do not hesitate to kill their fellow beings for the sake of their material benefits. Hence he is a poet with contents, not with poetic style.

    His poetry is a beautiful combination of soft words that have the power to evoke feelings. He knows the art of saying with poetic touches which penetrate the heart, if not the mind. He writes to convince with what he offers. He does not intend to make the reader visualize the idea, which comes out of the amalgamation of the images and the figures. He misses it on purpose because he knows that today the reader has no time to go into the depth of the philosophical and the metaphysical ponderings. He offers poetry—the poetry for a common man, who cannot perform the mental gymnastics with the images and the figures. He writes with a message—the message of cosmopolitanism, which makes every being to live in harmony. To him this universe seems to be "a big concert or symphony, a harmony of diverse notes" (*Multicultural Symphony*, 8). The multicultural symphony present in the vast universe justifies the title of this poetry collection.

In India there is unity in diversity. Diversity leads to multiculturalism, which is a positive term. Multiculturalism is new wine in the old bottle of diversity. But this term is more misused or ill-used than used in positive mode. It is the right term for promoting and acknowledging multiple cultures. To acknowledge diversities and differences results in a healthy relationship among the people who are free to promote their cultures without encroaching on others' space. Various cultures are the bunch of variety of flowers in the bouquet of multiculturalism.

Multiculturalism does not force to cook various ingredients in order to turn them into one kind of food. Rather, each ingredient seems to have its own uniqueness. Its uniqueness is its beauty. Language communicates; communication makes interaction possible with different cultures resulting in acknowledging the differences, which finally give birth to multiculturalism. The concept of multiculturalism is favored not because of diversities but because of its being a possible way of protecting the local culture of a particular place or nation, which certainly is a promoting factor in making the global cultural diversity rich and safe. Cultural diversity is not a sin; rather it has become a virtue. One can learn what is best in other cultures and leave what clashes with the basic cultural structure. Multiculturalism provides multiple approaches to life and vision and helps in understanding the extremes—cultural interface and cultural seclusion. What translates justice into reality is not the yardstick from one culture but cultural communications via dialogs among multiple cultures. The magic is done by the idea of multiculturalism, which offers possibilities to several different cultures for coexisting peacefully and fairly. (Arora, 9–10)

The poet in Dominic believes in multiculturalism and considers it a harmony of diverse notes. He asks his fellow beings to realize the need for multicultural existence. He attempts to make them understand thus:

> The entire system
> is a grand concert
> composed by the Sole spirit
> As matter and spirit
> animate and inanimate
> visible and invisible
> tangible and intangible
> audible and inaudible
> movable and immovable
> are instruments multitudinous
> of His perfect symphony.
>
> (*Multicultural Symphony*, 15)

For him the diversity is the very essence of universe and this essence is present in every atom. The beauty of the universe lies in its diversity. All human beings are participatory beings, participating in the execution of this beautiful creation—the Universe of God, who is none other than the Being of all beings. The poet is no doubt a Christian, but he believes in the Advaita philosophy as he sees the part of 'Being' in all his fellow beings. He recommends to flow with the system without interrupting or encroaching on the animal world, flora and fauna, because they have their value and without them existence will be an impossibility. The poet sees the presence of multicultural beauty everywhere and in every object—animate or inanimate.

> Multicultural instincts
> exist in all creations
> Inanimate beings know
> how to flow with the system
> Plant world too is
> well aware of the system
> Look at the woods
> Look at the wild
> Look at the birds
> Look at the fish
> Multicultural beauty everywhere.
>
> (*Multicultural Symphony*, 16)

The poet does not differentiate and so asks his fellow beings not to create or make differences. Differences may lie on surface, but there is somewhere interconnection or unity that binds all objects together in one thread. A cow is a cow. Why does a man differentiate a cow on the basis of nationality? This is Indian cow and this is American cow. It is the human being who creates the difference while initially a cow is a cow and vice versa. The poet has firm faith that the part of Being (God) is present in every participatory being. Hence, there is no use boasting of one's culture or language. It is better to respect all cultures and give space to each one for its growth and progress. One's culture or language is not pure as it takes the good ingredient from other cultures as well. Hence there is possibility of it being hybrid in essence.

> Is there any culture
> which is not hybrid?
> Is there any language
> which is not mixed?
>
> (*Multicultural Symphony*, 22)

The poet is grieved when he finds that millions of people are killed in the name of culture for claiming one's supremacy or superiority over others. He simply asks these people, who call themselves Indian: how much are they Indian?

> How many millions have been killed
> in the name of culture?
> Look into the pages of history
> Most of the wars have been waged
> for the supremacy of culture
> Conquest of cultures over cultures
> amalgamated to multicultural world
> How much Indian is an Indian?
>
> (*Multicultural Symphony*, 22)

What the poet dreams is unity—the unity that fuses all the people and all the nations into one. THE WORLD is the only one nation which he recommends because only then every participatory being will be able to live in harmony with the harmonious relations. Mark the excerpt, which reveals the poet's utopia, which promotes THE WORLD as one nation:

> Let there be no India, Pakistan, or China
> America, Africa, Europe, or Australia
> But only one nation THE WORLD
> where every being lives in perfect harmony
> as one entity in multicultural world
>
> *(Multicultural Symphony, 23)*

What makes the poet a participatory being in this universe is his philosophy of advaita. He sees the image of being in all—birds, animals and vegetation. He recalls the past when the participatory being used to be in harmony with all—be they cats, dogs, cows, goats, or fowls. But today the cycle moves in the reverse direction. He is grieved when he sees man differentiating not only among men but also among the birds and animals. Man becomes worse than animal when he kills them and does not allow others to live with parity. Mark the lines which reveal the poet's pain through questions:

> When will we begin to love
> kites, eagles, bats, owls
> as we long for parrots, cuckoos,
> skylarks and nightingales?
> When will we stop the massacre
> of animals, birds and fish
> and learn to respect
> other beings and their right to live?
>
> *(Multicultural Symphony, 51)*

Man comes alone and goes alone when he dies. This is with all the people who fail to understand that even their inhaling also depends on the exhaling of the plants. Here is an excerpt which reflects the gist of the life of man, who returns empty-handed to the place from where he comes:

> He fails to learn
> and millions fail to learn
> that God is the sole owner
> Empty-handed we come
> Empty-handed we go
> We inhale what plants exhale
>
> *(Multicultural Symphony, 28)*

The poet explores his identity. When his superego asks him who he is, his Id responds with the feeling of pride, saying that he is Prof. Dominic and besides this, he is an English poet, critic, and editor. But the superego makes him realize that even an illiterate farmer is greater than him. Sweat is preferred to scribbling. His life depends on the ordinary beings, like a farmer or a laborer. Hence it becomes his pious duty to write on them and support them.

> Labourers' sweat is dearer than you ink;
> If they strike, your writings will cease,
> and ultimately you yourself will disappear.
> Hence support them and write on them;
> Proclaim to the world the noble
> service they render to the humanity.
>
> *(Multicultural Symphony, 64)*

The poet's heart cries when he sees discrimination against the fair sex. He himself admits: "Sexism or discrimination shown to woman as part of patriarchy is another wounding thorn, which forces me to react through poetry" (*Multicultural Symphony*, 9). Why does a human being discriminate male or female while the animal world does not know even the word 'discrimination'? The birth of a female child becomes an omen to the extent that they are "butchered / before they are born" (*Multicultural Symphony*, 18). Parents also take them not as dear ones but as "burden to family" and so are confined to home, particularly kitchen, where she is compelled to work from morning till late at night. She sacrifices her 'self' and desires in the name of the family. In the kitchen, she "fights with utensils", cries within and dies while crying. Crying is her destiny.

> She is born with a cry
> goes on crying and crying
> till she reaches
> her destination death.
>
> (*Multicultural Symphony*, 19)

No doubt she is "the lamp of house" but this lamp becomes a victim of sexism, "a product of patriarchy" (*Multicultural Symphony*, 19), which never allows their entries in certain places like churches, mosques, and temples where they cannot choose their career to serve despite their longings and interest. A woman is created out of Adam's bone. Why is she not taken as counterpart? Today she is no better than a product in the global market where her beauty is for sale. She has her body to which she owns the sole right. The poet conveys a message to the people so that they may respect a woman as a woman, not a woman as merely a body or a commodity for commercial benefits.

> Why is she viewed
> as a consumer product?
> Why do you look at her
> with lascivious eyes?
> Hasn't she right over her body?
> Why do you dictate her apparel?
> Why do you forget
> that she is your mother
> she is your wife
> she is your sister
> or she is your daughter?
>
> (*Multicultural Symphony*, 20)

The poet feels humiliated when he sees women treated no better than shoes, which are thrown away when they become useless. He fails to understand why mothers and wives, in their old age, become a burden to their young relatives. Mark the poet's musings on the plight of women who are no better than shoes in the patriarchal society:

> Women too are often treated like shoes
> Mothers and wives when old and weak
> Become burden to sons and husbands
>
> (*Multicultural Symphony*, 58)

Religion has done more harm than help in the lives of men. It is tragic that man becomes a puppet in the hands of certain religious masters, who make him dance to their tunes. The poet refers to marriages that are arranged according to the horoscopic tallies with the intention that they may be successful. If it is so, why there are cases of divorces. He finds the deceit in the name of horoscope.

He considers that these religious masters or pundits exploit the common people and their faith. He does not find the way out of this vicious circle meant for trapping people in the name of religion. He is not against religion as he is a devout Christian. But he is against all kinds of superstitions and malpractices done in the name of religion. Ponder over the excerpt exposing the reality of these religious mafias:

> Do horoscopic matches bring happiness and peace?
> Why then cases of thousands of divorces?
> Peace and happiness are fruits of Karma
> Horoscope is the product of religious mafia
> A means to exploit laity's ignorance
> Millions are trapped in this vicious circle
> No sign of redemption in near future (*Multicultural Symphony*, 25)

The poet in Dominic sometimes becomes so innocent that he wishes to enter the memory lanes while sitting on Time's shoulder. He wishes to return to the days of his youth when he was quite happy with his real friends, who showered pure love on him. But when he returns to the present time, he finds that his friends are not as innocent and pure as the friends of his youth. Mark the excerpt which reveals the poet's longing for the friends of yore because they were not selfish like today's friends:

> I wish I could sit on Time's shoulder
> and fly back to my youth
> I could then be jolly
> with my friends and colleagues
> who bathed me with pure love
> which flowed from their surging hearts
> I do have friends today
> who are selfish, fake and fraud (*Multicultural Symphony*, 44)

The poet's heart weeps when he sees the condition of the poor people, who do not have enough to eat. He finds a monstrous gap between 'Have' and 'Have-not' and its tragic consequence, which makes poor poorer and rich richer. The poet admits: "The fast widening gap between the poor and the rich—the vast majority deprived of food and shelter, indirectly caused by the greed of the two or three percent rich—bleeds my heart and results in several poems" (*Multicultural Symphony*, 9). The greed is responsible for such a miserable plight. The truth is that even today there are thousands of children who are famished, not in India only but in the other countries also. The poor sustain themselves on the leftover of the rich. It is a tragedy that the ten percent rich rule the rest of the ninety percent. What an irony!

> Leftovers of the
> ten percent Haves
> can sustain
> ninety percent Havenots
> and make this hellish world
> a blissful heaven.
>
> (*Multicultural Symphony*, 49)

The poet thinks of shoes and relates them to the plight of the proletariat. They have their labor for sale and the rich people have capital to buy. They are in work as long as they are useful. The moment they are not useful, they are thrown away.

> Same is the plight of proletariat
> They are shoes worn by the rich
> Service being complete
> they are spat out like curry leaves

(Multicultural Symphony, 58)

The poet is in a dilemma and does not know what to do because he has taken an oath that he will love all the creatures. He sees the part of his being in them. In his bathroom, he finds a spider, which lives on mosquitoes that bite him. How can he kill the spider when he loves all creatures? The spider is also a creature and so he should love him. Here is his short poem "A Spider in My Bathroom", which reflects the mental state of the poet.

> A spider in my bathroom
> To smite or spare?
> Lives on mosquitoes
> who inject me
> The creator has sent
> it along with mosquitoes
> Being a poet vowed
> to love all creations
> what shall I do?

(Multicultural Symphony, 52)

He simply asks what he should do to keep his vow. It is true that man should love all creatures, but when they become a danger to the existence, it is better to kill them. Santiago in *The Old Man and the Sea* loves fish but he kills in order to keep himself alive. There is no harm in keeping such creatures as long as they do not harm; but the moment they become danger or create a sense of fear, it is better to keep them away because it becomes a question of existence.

The poet reviews life from morning till evening—the moment when he comes into and the moment when he departs from this world, leaving everything behind. When he is in the morning of his life, he does not find anything that may disturb or puzzle him. The lone open shop becomes the only shop for his guidance and sharing. His home becomes the only shelter where he feels at ease. When it is evening, he hears the din and bustle from all the opened stalls. Now he becomes confused because of the noise of opinions and reviews. He is on his journey with this surety that one day he will achieve the goal, but the moment he enters, he becomes astonished because of the darkness, which makes him see nothing and resulting in a mystery. Quoted below is the short poem "Sail of Life", which makes the reader ponder over the stages of life:

> My morning walk takes me
> to a tea stall
> The lone opened shop
> at the still Gandhi Square
>
> I am astonished
> by the din and bustle
> that comes out
> from all opened stalls
> in the evenings
>
> My boisterous sail will reach

>     its harbour one day
>     I will be astonished
>     by its stillness and darkness (
>
>                                      *Multicultural Symphony*, 55)

The poet does not close his eyes to the contemporary scenario, colored with corruption, selfishness, oppression, and the like. He reflects over the problem and comes to the conclusion that the media are responsible to a great extent. He is shocked when he finds teenagers indulged in crimes. Media and its associates dish out venoms before the teenagers instead of bringing the correcting forces to light. It is shocking that they make terrorists heroes, and heroes terrorists. Mark the lines which reveal the harmful role of the media and its associates in adding fuel to fire:

>     Media, print and visual
>     forget ethics they are bound to follow
>     Instead of being a correcting force
>     to all subjects and other estates
>     filling minds with eternal noble values
>     they inject venoms of violence
>     communalism and superstitions
>     They focus terrorists and anti-heroes
>     Arch corrupters and human deities
>     And no wonder, tender minds
>     are bewitched by their illusion
>
>                                     (*Multicultural Symphony*, 56)

What will the people do when their representatives become corrupt? Once the leaders were the models for the nation because they never hesitated sacrificing their lives for the sake of the nation. The interest of the country was far above their self-interest. But today, politicians are quite opposite the image of the past.

>     Once politicians were apostles
>     their selfless service to the nation
>     lauded gratefully by the people
>     Now people look at them with dubious eyes
>     for corruption is stamped on their brow
>
>                                     (*Multicultural Symphony*, 78)

The poet weaves all the pieces of his themes in order to make his poetry collection "a symphony". He creates a collage—the collage that displays multicultural Kerala, global warming's real culprit, martyrs of the borders, Thodupuzha Municipal Park, the images of Sakuntala Devi, the Siachen Tragedy, the pathetic plight of Dhanalakshmi, the heinous crime of slashing the nose of Prakash Jaatav by the high caste, the exploitation of Beena in the Mumbai Hospital, celebration of girl child's birth, Women's Cricket World Cup 2013, ACTS—Saviors on the Roads, Beach Beauticians, protest against sand mafia and the like. He is a poet with headlines because he composes poems on the incidents that took place, and to give them a real shape, he mentions the incident's date or year, or both, with the name of the newspaper in which the report was published. Simply any painful incident that occurs anywhere pierces his heart, which feels the pain of the sufferers to the extent that it shows empathy with them and spreads its pain on the white sheet.

The poet's ideal is Swami Vivekananda whom he pays a glowing tribute because of his substantial contribution that he made in making religion, a science of consciousness and "a universal experience

/ of transcendent Reality" (*Multicultural Symphony*, 79). He promotes religion, which leads to "Supreme Freedom, Supreme Knowledge and Supreme Happiness." Here is an excerpt showing his contribution in the field of spiritual humanism:

> He laid foundation for spiritual humanism
> which makes life meaningful and worth living
> He taught world man should be pure
> for purity is our real nature and soul
> We should love and serve our neighbours
> for we are all one in the Supreme Spirit (*Multicultural Symphony*, 79)

Swami Vivekananda is a spiritual saint, who is no less than a cultural ambassador because he taught the people "how to master Western science / based on Indian spirituality" and "how to adapt Western humanism / to Indian life and culture" (*Multicultural Symphony*, 79). The poet wishes to retrieve the past of India when she was a "fertile land for free and secular thoughts" and "people lived in multicultural harmony" (*Multicultural Symphony*, 78). He is grieved when he sees the present India that has now become "a hell of intolerance and religious fundamentalism." Even then he never thinks of flying away from this fruitful land. He belongs to India, and India is in his blood. Hence he is a poet of Indian landscapes—the landscapes which, despite the dark shades, have the bright colors of hope. This hope makes the poet so confident that he thinks that one day people will sing multicultural symphony and live happily while respecting each other, and then the universe will become one nation—THE WORLD, where all human beings will become participatory beings, who will be thankful to the 'Being of Beings'. Such are the feelings that flow with the flow of system from the pen of K. V. Dominic, who is determined to win the hearts of the reader by virtue of his 'content' because 'form' is not his strength.

## Works Cited

Arora, Sudhir K. "Culture, Multiculture and the Case of India." *International Journal on Multicultural Literature* (IJML) 2.2 (July 2012): 8-15. Print.

Dominic, K.V. *Multicultural Symphony*. New Delhi: GNOSIS, 2014. Print.

Khatri, C. L. *Two-Minute Silence*. New Delhi: Authorspress, 2014. Print.

# Chapter 5 -
# K. V. Dominic—A Humanitarian in Conception and Socio-Consciousness: An Analytical Study of *Write Son, Write* by Dr. D. C. Chambial

K. V. Dominic's second poetic collection, *Write Son, Write* is a collection of 31 recent poems. The poems have cartoon illustrations by Mr. K. K. Anas.

## *Love for God's Creation*

"Write, My Son, Write", the first and title poem of the book, is a long poem in 21 parts: Part One exhorts the poet to write because He has created him with this purpose. In Part Two, the God asks him if he doesn't feel "the symphony / of the universe" and tells him that while animals and plants dance to His music, man doesn't. Part Three tells that all creatures and objects live in harmony with Nature. Part Four tells that as all parts of human body work in harmony, so do all creations. Part Five informs about man's "discordant notes" with nature. Part Six is about the harmonious existence of all animate and inanimate things in this world while man's mind makes all the difference. Part Seven implies that God has created other things—plants animals and nature—for man's company but man is bent upon destroying them. Part Eight tells about man as God's latest and intelligent creation. Part Nine exhibits man's folly in considering himself "the master / of all wisdom". Despite his celestial qualities, he prefers to foster "hate and violence", and shows "no mercy / to animals and plants".

Part Ten tells that man, for his jovial festivities, kills animals to devour them and feels happy. While Part Eleven again exhorts man to learn from nature to live in harmony, Part Twelve tells him to expose human deficiencies and imbibe God's "symphonies". Part Thirteen is about God's love for man; even thunder is not his wrath. Part Fourteen is about God's granting man His "reason / [not] to learn / my [His] plans". Part Fifteen is about God's love for man like all other creatures and things of this universe, but asks the poet to tell man that he "needs humanity". Part Sixteen is about man's position in this world: he is one among other creations to live happily and harmoniously and not exploit and mislead others. This part introduces readers to three types of existent mafia: religious, political, and intellectual. Part Seventeen is about "religious mafia" that misguides common men that He loves flattery, hymns, money, and jewellery that men offer in their places of worship. Instead, "karma is the best prayer" and service unto humanity the best service of God. Part Eighteen is about vegetarianism: God has created man as herbivorous but he kills animals living on land, sky, and in water for his food. Part Nineteen is about political mafia that "exploits masses; / dictates strategies / and makes them slaves".

Part Twenty tells about intellectual mafia that "assume [to be] omniscient," deludes and diverts common man's mind from God, the Supreme Creator, and imposes his pseudo philosophies on them. Here the poet also shows that religious and intellectual mafias are one and the same without any difference. Part Twenty-One is the crux of the poet's "views and philosophy" of life in this poem: if and only if man learns to live in harmony with nature and His creations, he has the possibility of

## Elegy

The second poem, "An Elegy on My Ma" (*Write Son, Write*, 38-41), is based on his emotions for his mother after her death on 14th October, 2010. It is a poem that tells about mother's suffering in her old age when she suffered from "old age ailments" accompanied with breathing problem. He tells about her life that she brought up her brothers and sisters, about the death of her parents, and hard labor in farm from "Dawn to dusk". Mother's life is all pure without any dross: "Truly mother's love / is the purest love." In her acute suffering, she often cried: "Why doesn't God / call me back?" Ultimately she is confined to bed and lives without food. The poet also laments that, because of his job responsibilities, he could not be by her side when she called for her children and wanted them to sing. Now he feels deserted after her death. The poem ends with complete surrender to Him: "Surrender unto Him / who created you." The poem is replete with tragic pathos.

## Poems about India

There are two poems, "Victory to thee, Mother India!", and "Rocketing Growth of India", that tell about India. The first one (*Write Son, Write*, 42-43) sings praises for fostering unity in people of varied cultures, religions, races, and speaking different languages: it sings of unity in diversity. But now divisive forces sadden Mother India: "Patriotism, nationalism, secularism / give way to / terrorism, communalism, and regionalism." He asserts the cause: "Matha, I know the cause of your tears: / Religious, political, intellectual mafias / tear thy heart and drink your blood." In these lines, the poet's concern for the country as one being weakened by its own people is also manifest. The Indian virtue of harmony in diversity seems at stake at the face of some shenanigans and multi-faceted mafias jeopardize not only her unity but also her very nature.

Despite present dismal image, the poet is hopeful that many great men like Tagore, Gandhi, and Nehru will be born to redeem her of her present sorrow. The second poem, "Rocketing Growth of India" (*Write Son, Write*, 77–78), is a satire on the government's statistics showing growth vis-à-vis development in India, while the truth is quite contrary to these statistics: "First in population growth; / first in number of poor; / top in ignorance and illiteracy; top in superstition and fundamentalism." It is the rich, who, in fact, are growing. The death of the poor, at the collapse of a gate of an ashram, who had swarmed there for food is the stark reality that our rulers are averse to see. The poet's jibe comes alive when he writes:

> Had the government granted
> half the amount when they were alive;
> had the government shown half the love
> they shower to the rich,
> many such tragedies be averted. (*Write Son, Write*, 78)

## Poems about Animals

The poems like "Massacres of Cats" (*Write Son, Write*, 44–46), "A Cow on the Lane" (*Write Son, Write*, 47–48), "Crow, the Black Beauty" (*Write Son, Write*, 57–58), and "To my Deceased Cats" (*Write Son, Write*, 97–98) are about animals. "Massacre of Cats" is about the cats that met their death when they were poisoned by the neighbor. It not only teaches the lesson "to love other beings / as fellow beings. The poet compares the killing of cats to the killing of albatross in S.T. Coleridge's *Ancient Mariner* and pleads for a similar expiation from the killer of cats. "A Cow on the Lane" is adamant to occupy its space on the road, which leads to the railway station through which the person wants to drive and reach the station on time before the trains leaves. The cow doesn't budge; the person has to take another route to reach the station.

The poet beautifully uses an allusion from Mahabharata when Bhimasena—the great and powerful Pandava—is unable to move the tail of Hanuman across on his path. "Crow, the Black Beauty" is about a bird that is always detested. None wants to hear its caw-caw. The poet exclaims that crow is also His creation and should have the same love and laudation of the people that cuckoo and dove and such other birds enjoy. He laments: "When will we behold God's creation / with impartial eyes / and find His beauty in all forms?" (*Write Son, Write*, 58) "To my Deceased Cats" describes the pain and suffering that the cats, after being poisoned, suffered. It relates its story of previous birth the cat was a human being, a doctor, he had also poisoned a cat that also suffered the same pangs of death. Now the cat thinks its present fate is only the result of its action in previous life. Indirectly the poet teaches the altruistic theory of karma—as you so, so shall you reap; if not in this birth, but must in the next. It concurs with the Hindu view of karmic retribution.

## Poems on Hero Worship

Poems like "Aung Sun Suu Kyi: Asia's Lady Mandela" (*Write Son, Write*, 53–54), "Bravo Katie Sportz!" (*Write Son, Write*, 55), "Tribute to Mohammed Rafi" (*Write Son, Write*, 87), and "Wolfgang, the Messiah of Nature" (*Write Son, Write*, 93–94) imply the poet's hero-worship. In all these poems, the poet sings the glory of these persons in their respective fields. Aung Sun Suu Kyi has been eulogized as the Mandela of Myanmar. She suffered a lot at the hands of military junta there and spent most of her life in jail. Her suffering didn't deter her from her crusade to free the country from military junta [now she has been released from jail and won the recent election, held in March 2012, in Myanmar].

Katie Sportz, a 22-year-old, is dauntless in her courage and rowed alone in her boat for 4,534 km in sun and rain, braving the sea storms, all on her own in a bid to raise US $70,000 fund for the project "Blue Planet Run Foundation, / supplying drinking water round the globe." The poet is all praise for her and prays: "Let your race fill this planet." It is his greatest encomium to the "valour of women".

Mohammed Rafi has been a prodigy of Indian singing. When he sang, his notes touched the very cords of heart and mind alike. He died some 30 years back but his music is still alive; nay, it will survive till eternity. The poet/persona likes his songs very much and feels as if Rafi is with him. He feels "his melodies raise us to heaven." Indeed his voice in his songs has immortalized him. In "Wolfgang, the Messiah of Nature", the poet sings of Wolfgang, a German by birth, who came to Kerala at the tender age of twenty and since has lived here for more than forty years in the forests of Kerala, teaching people how to live in harmony with nature. He lives in the company of dreaded snakes, animals, and lovely birds. They do not fear him nor do they cause any harm to him or to his children. Such is his intimacy with Nature. The poem, while singing Wolfgang's glory, also teaches that God created everything to live in harmony. It gives not only peace and joy but also brings heavenly bliss for both Man and Nature. The poet calls Wolfgang "Nature's Christ/ born to redeem Nature". All human beings should learn a lesson from him on how to live in harmony with Nature and save not only earth but also humanity from destruction.

## Poems on Nature/Poems on Other Themes

Poet's love for Nature is contagious. While reading his poems, one loves to live in Nature. It is difficult to shift Nature from his poems, yet "Coconut Palm" (*Write Son, Write*, 56), "Nature Weeps" (*Write Son, Write*, 71), and "Wagamon" (*Write Son, Write*, 88) are two typical poems that describe Nature in two different shades. "Coconut Palm" is a short poem and tells the rapid growth of the tall slender tree. Its "sparkling leaves and alluring nuts" mingle the visual and gustatory senses beautifully. Its tall, thin stem bearing tons of fruit appears like a "marvel to all architects". Every part of this tree is used for human welfare. The poet wonders at its mysterious nature. "Nature Weeps" speaks about the havoc that man and his industrialization has brought upon Nature. All trees serve humanity in one or the other way, yet man cuts them to denude earth. Ecological imbalance leads to scarcity of rain: fields turn dry, no crops grow; if it rains, it is full of acid due to emission of poisonous fumes from factories that cause air pollution; flowers wither; birds fail to sing; temperature rises very high; man encroaches upon the land meant for wild beast, so they move toward settlements... In fact, the ecology is totally disturbed. All beauties of Nature have become things of past. Nonetheless, the poet presents a heaven of natural beauty in "Wagamon". Here God's omnipresence appears in natural beauty: full of greenery, cataracts falling "like white curtains", uneven texture of land--"mounds after mounds", clouds, moon, and stars seem to abound in "the therapeutic / power of Nature".

> The beautiful
> Pine valleys of Wagamon
> an exotic wild beauty.
> Tall and thick pine trees
> support firmament
> from falling.

(*Write Son, Write*, 89)

Really the tall pine trees present a look of pillars supporting the sky. Here the sun is "always gentle", evening full of "nocturnal music" and "resounding hymns of angels", and the "semi darkness" that falls here at dusk lifts "our minds / to an eternal / abode of repose." Will there be some other place so beautiful, so soothing and so lively to live on earth? Certainly not.

## Tragic Poems

The poems entitled "Teresa's Tears" (*Write Son, Write*, 81), "To My Colleague" (*Write Son, Write*, 83), "Train Blast" (*Write Son, Write*, 85), "Water, Water, Everywhere..." (*Write Son, Write*, 91) picture human tragedy in various moods. Teresa is a labor-woman who sweeps floors in a school to earn her bread; she is given wages after a year but taken back as donation to the institution as per the condition laid down in the agreement. Her eyes are suffused with happiness to see currency but, at the same time, tears represent her helplessness, for she has to give them and she is left penniless. The poet calls "such forced donation / a canker of Kerala."

The poem "To My colleague" is manifestation of irrational religious fanaticism: the poet's colleague's [Prof. T.J. Joseph's] hand and leg are hacked, rather severed from his body, on 4th of July, 2010. None come to his help. Only crocodile tears are shed. The poem is an attack on the right of liberty to do anything that may cause others' death: "Largest secular state! / Equality, fraternity, liberty. / Liberty to do anything?"

In the poem 'Train Blast,' he pleads that "diabolic means" should not be used to achieve "Utopian ends". Though those who are killed in such blasts are spared of the pains of this world, those left behind are subjected to endless suffering. The poet, here again, with an allusion to Mahabharata, tries to show his doubt in the existence of the all-protecting and merciful God: "How can I ease in / sambhavami yuge yuge?"

Still there are poems that have not been mentioned, for space restriction, but equally important and charming that exhibit the poet's understanding of the life around and lend weight to his humanitarian philosophy steeped in contemporaneous societal consciousness, making him an advocate of the downtrodden and human values. It is a must read for all those who want to enjoy a good read with some social sanity.

## Work Cited

Dominic, K. V. *Write Son, Write*. New Delhi: GNOSIS, 2011. Print.

# Chapter 6 -
# K. V. Dominic's *Winged Reason:*
# Poems of Man's Earthly Life and Painful Realities
# by P. C. K. Prem

*Winged Reason* is a collection of poems of earthly imagination. Deep down, Dominic conveys the anxieties of human life, not just lofty thoughts and ideals. Dominic's poetry is a document of social concerns in lyrics, beautiful and rhythmic. *Winged Reason* enshrines a definite message. Perhaps it is a rare collection of poems in Indian English Poetry that is realistic. Here, the words with the tonal values do not distract with multi-faceted meanings. The poet believes in simple, straight, and plain language while showing genuine anxiety for socially neglected segments of society.

He is ruefully conscious of the rampant corruption whether political or religious. Whatever concerns man's life, living, and society is the theme of his poetic creation with minimum use of simile, metaphors, and images. In a long preface, the poet makes a statement about poetic morality, theme and philosophy of life in totality while underlining the miserable conditions of the poor. Each poem exhibits invisible and disregarded existence of obtrusively stark realities of hardworking poor people, and the sheer obscurity they confront around; and this challenges a sensitive mind while leaving a powerful and enduring impact and here lie the poems' beauty and strength.

Dominic is profoundly conscious of the hiatus between the rich and poor; and the degree of bias and exploitation governing the life of the poor. He, with aching intensity, experiences the agonies and sufferings of women, old men, and the downtrodden, as if to him rural life is ideal, simple, and innocent where no evil ever enters, but urbanites are cruel and unsympathetic, materialistic and avaricious. In fact, life without philosophic nuances is the subject matter of Dominic's poems and through objective and realistic social evaluation, if efforts are sincerely made, man's life can be meaningful, the poet asserts.

Dominic is a poet of humanity and speaks of man and society. His compassion is concentrated on man. His humanism is patently perceptible, when one goes into the lyrics' emotional areas. This journey into the heart of the poems is an experience of stillness, terrific eruption of feelings, volatile stirring of suppressed emotions, and subdued but sublime creation of a loving and rich world. Here, the poet does not take the reader to the regions beyond sky or probes into the depths of heart. He is also not worried about the other world. The ideas of love, birth, and death do not worry him. But what occupies the entire intellectual strength and physical borders of the capacity of Dominic are the explored and still-to-be-explored dimensions of man's worldly needs.

His experiments with multifaceted experiences drive him to the heart of the society where man lives, flourishes, suffers, and intellectualizes life and this truth, in little fragments, is revealed through an indefinite mystery. Bereft of philosophic undercurrent, these poems are greatly subjective but with an objective outlook. He interprets life from experiences gathered after conscious understanding of man. Many poems indirectly deal with societal setup and man's behavior and attitude in a collective endeavor to make society better. The poor's miserable living conditions disturb the poet and he tries to hold the rich responsible for the sufferings of the downtrodden, and here an attempt is made to look at issues in the contemporary context and relevance. Thus, the collection is a social document.

Worries of bread and shelter disturb and lead the poet to a calculated criticism of society. It is a personal indictment of the rich who, he observes, are morally responsible for the injustice done to the poor and the helpless. Injustice and poverty are the recurring themes of his poems while he does talk scathingly of the dirty politics and degeneration of value-system. Interestingly, in simple words with straight meaning, the poet underlines an inherent irony. At times, the poet appeals to mankind to look below and ameliorate the pitiable conditions of the ignored segment.

It is a predicament of the poet that despite a genuine desire to alleviate the sufferings of the poor, he is unable to translate sublime thoughts to reality of life. Squalor and extreme deprivation appear to hurt not only the poor man's soul but it is physically torturing, the poet says. Genuinely thinking of the poor, he goes through a nightmarish experience of unrelenting anguish. In straight words, like "an obese boy" and "a bony child", he vividly describes prevailing hunger and nauseating richness. In "A Nightmare", he tells poetically of a wedding feast, ragged girls, garbage bin, and public school; and this intrinsic agony simply upsets. Even in sleep, the poet feels the heat of these words and the pictures he conjures up are a commentary on the poor man's life.

> Tears streamed down my cheeks
> I could see nothing more;
> Nor did I wish for it;
> The siren sounded as usual
> To disturb my nightmare!
>
> ("A Nightmare", *Winged Reason*, 23)

In "Harvest Feast", the poet hints at an effective education system, which can serve the country better. In strident words, he exhorts that the coming generation, if imparted education in agricultural-related activities, can definitely make a dent in the perennial shortages of essential commodities and food grains. If dignity of labor finds favor, mankind will be happy, he observes.

> Their teachers taught them the great lessons:
> how education can be vocational;
> and the beauty and dignity of labour;
> a lesson too to the adult world:
> the way to solve the food crisis,
> and save the world from poverty.
>
> ("Harvest Feast", *Winged Reason*, 35)

The poet tries to draw parallels and comparisons here and there and does not falter. The words like "obese", "bony", and "wedding feast" need to be deeply understood. It is a commentary on the deplorable present-day scarcity of food grains or lopsided allotment system through controlled channels. It is also a reflection on the government apathy in the handling of surplus food grains. It is often claimed that there is no scarcity of food items but the masses are not properly fed or are deprived. It is an appalling parallelism between the rich and the poor and ironically, it is happening in a country where moral values are often much flaunted.

For the poet, the sufferings determine the fate of the poor, who work hard but get nothing. Man's life is seen from different perspectives. Each incident observed around is infused with meaning and this shows the poet's inherent strength to generalize logically. The insightful and empathetic mind and heart of the poet connect the sentiments and thoughts with humanity. Nothing escapes his ardently vigilant eyes. He views man from various thought-processes but the sardonic indictment remains an inseparable part of the poet's anxiety. The poet philosophically laments that the creator

*Philosophical Musings for a Meaningful Life*  47

never had thought of any division among men. Whatever disintegrating factors there are, these have been created for serving self-interests. Nature feeds all but man eats up even nature and crafts a vacuum, a disruption in the perennial flow of life, and thus the very oxygen of life is exhausted. If man has done magnificently well, he is equally destructive. Despite lofty achievements, millions are dying of hunger and it appears a strange phenomenon but murderous truth. The poet's painful regret is that division is injustice, and here he gives bent to his socialistic thoughts with sarcastic parallels. Perhaps the poet has in mind the great divide man is attempting to bring about in the society by splitting it into not only classes but castes, religious sects, and regional and fissiparous tendencies predominating the society and man.

> But power corrupted
> leaders turned tyrant;
> the philosophy failed.
> Equality to man utopian.
> Capitalism rules the day;
> Have-nots number swell.
>
> ("Haves and Have-nots", *Winged Reason*, 36)

This thought horrifies as the revealed truth frightens man when the poet further says, "Shattered and smashed / are their dreams / of health and happiness." Irony hurts as even plants and animals do not behave in a partisan's manner, the poet avers. The poet is an inveterate advocate of workers and "Lal Salaam to Labours" is tribute to the workers. It is because of the workers that society lives and survives. The working class makes humanity happy. Excitement is apparent when he praises workers. It is an emotional outburst which also highlights socialistic thought and ideology the poet espouses. It is a communistic philosophy, he appears to advocate with the precise dictum that only workers are the backbone of society.

> Let us not be unjust
> When we pay them wages,
> for we can't do what they do
> Give them at least their due;
> the more we give the more we get;
> Put charity in humanity
> a spiritual bliss that never dies.
>
> ("Lal Salaam to Labour", *Winged Reason*, 45)

An elegy on the death of E. K. Nayanar is singing of paeans in praise of socialist pattern of society where labor class gets reward for the hard work without being exploited. A pathetic and repulsive contrast is also apparent between the city-dwellers and the villagers. The poet finds rural people an epitome of virtues and compassion whereas urbanites appear selfish and impassive with no reverence for human relations. If one looks at these poems, one observes a scathing vein running through each word, which makes it more authentic. The poet's intention is not advocating the cause of the poor, but he is emphatic that riches do not make society a better place to live in as exploitation and the gap between the rich and the poor widens. Another beautifully poignant poem "Tsunami Camps" attracts but the poet is ruthless in describing the apathy of the government machinery engaged in mitigating the miseries of the people who suffered natural calamity when a terrible "Tsunami" brought about unparallel devastation everywhere. When people were brought to the newly established relief camps, their life seemed more miserable. Even the so-called people with leftist philosophy failed to fulfill duties properly.

In hours of crisis, man is essentially self-seeking and it is the rich who gain. The lamentations of the refugees living in the camps are unbearable and speak volumes of the indifference and cold-hearted attitude of man to man.

> We don't get any help
> either from the Right or from the Left.
> Unending wails and unending sobs;
> not even gods listen to their cries.
>
> ("Tsunami Camps", *Winged Reason*, 34)

If one deeply examines the implied meaning of Onam, a great festival of Kerala, one is attracted to the sheer sense of joviality, gay abundance, and feeling of cheerfulness among the people of Kerala on the occasion of Onam festival. It is a tribute to the hardworking people who work and water, till fields, sow seeds, and reap rich harvest so that fellow brethren do not go hungry. Here, a system is born where equality is all pervasive and values of life enrich every mind and heart. A spirit of renunciation and sacrifice is quite visible among the people; and it appears the poet, though a communist, holds faith in an undefined and invisible force. It is interesting to read these simple poetic lines:

> the golden rule of Maveli
> an icon of the just king.
> Equality prevailed in society;
> no lies, no crimes, no deceits;
> no poverty, no child death.
> All were happy
> heaven cannot be different
>
> ("Onam", *Winged Reason*, 54).

An ideal concept of equality, where happiness and joy triumph, usually fascinates poets. It is an irony of circumstances that nothing concrete happens despite pious sentiments. Poverty is a recurring theme of Dominic's poems and even if he does not make a reference, the disquieting thought runs invariably in the poems. This collection is a prayer and a petition to the rich to come forward and eliminate the ghostly phantom of poverty and sufferings from this earth. In the same strain, the poet narrates an incident where the "sacred ornaments of Krishna are stolen" and elsewhere the "golden rosary" is missing but there is no trace of thieves. The anger of the gold-crazy gods and the golden robes of the priests present a hilariously pathetic picture. Slightly different, he speaks of pleasures and pains in life. To the poet, it appears sufferings and pains dominate the life of a man whereas there are very few moments of joy and happiness.

> Pleasures and pains:
> two sides of a coin.
> We toss it early morning;
> majority gets the pains side.
> Pleasures come like sprinkles,
> while pains fall like a deluge
> and continue like monsoon.
> Happiness is a mist
> while sorrows shower like snow.
>
> ("Pleasure and Pains", *Winged Reason*, 68)

Undoubtedly, the poet is often troubled by the predominance of miseries in life but somewhere, he does keep the flame of hope alive and perhaps he indirectly wishes to say that from such pains, a spring of inspiration flows out to invigorate sagging spirits. It is only possible if a man has positive attitude to life.

The poet avers that his areas of concerns are Man, Nature, and God and truthfully, this encompasses life in entirety with no derivations. Around these three dimensions, the total life of a man moves and defines limits of acts. He concentrates on Man with intensity and each word, even if he uses it inadvertently, focuses on the anxieties and predicament of human life. In "Old Age", the poet is vivid, realistic, and harsh when he talks that "Human life is a cycle." This line is a true portrayal of life. It is a journey from pain to pleasure and then again from pleasure to pain; this cycle is perpetual and from here, the meaning of life has to be derived, the poet appears to say with an innate irony:

> Old age begins to play its colour –
> The monarch of yesterday,
> Feels humbled today.
> Imprisoned amidst unripe ripeness:
> Utterly helpless.

("Old Age", Winged Reason, 51)

At another level, the poet's anxiety is apparent when he observes that only strenuous work makes man's life meaningful and only workers are the true custodians of a life of meaning and truth. Such patterns of thoughts continue to flow in the verses of Dominic.

All great religions tell man to work sincerely and devotedly with faith and he will be rewarded suitably. Here, the poet emphasizes the theory of Karma in the true sense of the word and possibly because of this irrevocable and deep conviction in work that he holds the workers in high esteem. At times, he appears to digress and touches other themes but the idea of man's life and happiness continues to occupy his philosophy of life. People governing themselves through the elected representatives is the primary theme.

When the poet speaks of a common man, a worker and the masses, he does not forget to talk of the rich and powerful. But in different perspectives, he spells out that the rich are the product of an unhealthy and deformed economic system where the concept of equality in social, economic, and political life is quite utopian. In theory it is good and enriching. As a sublime notion, it harmonizes distressing thoughts. But when translated into reality, it is a burden as man can't accept equality even when he is poor; and this truth and fact of life must be understood properly by the elites and advocates of equality. Socialism and democratic system of government is a developing system where perfection is still a mirage. Perhaps, even communism has failed and democracy is not entirely a noble and virtuous system to govern man and society. In many of his poems, the poet talks of communism and socialism or socialistic pattern of society and now in "Indian Democracy", he takes a pessimistic view of life of people and one can see the consequences:

> Secularism butchered;
> caste and religion
> raise their hood;
> Regionalism and parochialism
> Devour
> nationalism and patriotism.
> . . . . . . . . . . . . . . . .
> Gullible people
> they vote them again and again;
> no other options.
> Still democracy shall prevail
> or tyranny will
> sit on the Chair.
>
> ("Indian Democracy", *Winged Reason*, 60–61)

One is stunned when sufferings and agonies of the hungry do not elicit an iota of charity from the Haves and in the recurring state of disturbed mental frame elsewhere, he reaffirms the origin of sufferings:

> Man is a wonderful work;
> Unimaginable his achievements;
> Equally heart-rending his destructions
> Achievements prove beneficial
> only to Haves a minority.
> When millions die of hunger,
> thousands compete for delicacies.
>
> ("Haves and Have-nots", *Winged Reason*, 36)

Instead of alleviating the sufferings of the masses, the democratic system has failed miserably. It is bound to happen because the bases of the democratic system have been damaged beyond recognition. The virus of voting pattern has in reality divided Man but to talk of society and the nation. India is a vast country with a wonderful parliamentary system; but it is also "a stage of heinous means". Unfortunately, the politicians in the country exploit sentiments of the people by raising the non-existing issues of communalism, and thus divie the people. Once unknown, communalism now is eating into the vitals of people's energies and faith. Religions are no more a sustaining force but these are splitting men on the basis of caste, creed, class, and region/geography. In such circumstances, what is expected of workers who suffer, cry, and fight for rights? But these too are segregated on the above lines of various divisions. Thus, while the "gullible people" suffer, violence and terrorism thrive. Here, the very existence of man is meaningless; whereas in a system which has people's welfare in the heart, it is life of man and how it should be made optimistic and happy that should be the objective. Presently, this noble idea has lost credence. Though the poet is disillusioned with the kind of governance people get despite vociferous claims to the contrary, yet hopes sustain faith in the spirit of man. The poet observes in another context:

> What right has the mortal man
> to divide and own this immortal planet?
> What justice is there for the minority
> to starve the majority?
> The Have-nots found a haven
> in socialism and communism;

no private property;
state-owned wealth;
selfless work for the society.
But power corrupted;
leaders turned tyrants;
the philosophy failed.
Equality to man utopian.

("Haves and Have-nots", *Winged Reason*, 37)

While going through the poetry of Dominic, it is obvious that he conveys a certain message and he is sure of it and that is the singular exquisiteness and power of his lyrics. When he thinks of Man, Nature and, God, he is more worried about the synthesis among the three only, it would appear, which again to the poet's mind is the fountainhead of peace and harmony on earth. He tries to establish a relationship between the objects of nature and finds that nature is fundamentally kind and generous. It is man who brings disharmony in life. He hints at the formidable gaps among men. There are ferocious and brutal disparities among the rich, the powerful, the poor, and the weak whereas nature does not differentiate. For all these acts, man tries to involve God and justifies the prevailing differences between man and man. It is the thinking man, the social animal, who erects walls of separation when animals and plant life are symbols of peace and prosperity. Dominic is definite and optimistic when he indirectly exhorts men to show compassion and sympathy to men in distress. His philosophy is a search unending where he must rest only when true happiness comes to everyone. It appears the poet is not only inclined to a socialistic thought but deep down, he is vastly influenced by the philosophy of Mahatma Gandhi and John Ruskin. He, without directly making a mention, hints at the ethical values determining the life of man. Here, the poet is uniquely contemporary and yet a bit ancient while he is apprehensive about the value-system in economic and social life, a rare commodity indeed.

Dominic's social concerns are genuine and he is forthright in unequivocal condemnation of the rich. This is possible only for a person who is committed to an ideology. Dominic is an advocate of a socialistic pattern and the moral system he champions implicitly borders on values that care for the poor and downtrodden. Dominic's social perception is quite evident in many poems and he is aware of the continuing process of change in values of life that transforms the mindset of people, keeping in view the movement of man in time and space, for he is unwittingly susceptible to outside influences. As a teacher, he feels deeply about men and matters and takes, philosophically, a humanitarian view of men in distress. He believes that words sublime and true, sincere and forthright cannot provide happiness to the downtrodden but definite and positive efforts are needed so that they get all the essential things of life necessary to live and so food, shelter and good hygienic conditions must be provided which also include water and functional infrastructure to make lives comfortable.

## Work Cited

Dominic, K. V. *Winged Reason*. New Delhi: Authorspress, 2010. Print.

# Chapter 7 -
# Social Criticism in the Poetry of K. V. Dominic
# by Prof. T. V. Reddy

K. V. Dominic is a writer with social consciousness and his poems often express his impressions and views on contemporary social situations and problems. He writes in the Preface to his first collection, "As a poet I am responsible to my own conscience and I want to convey an emotion or a message often through social criticism." So far he has authored three collections of poems: 1. *Winged Reason* (Delhi, Authors Press, 2010), 2. *Write Son, Write* (Delhi, GNOSIS, 2011), and 3. *Multicultural Symphony* (Delhi, Access, 2014).

*Winged Reason* happens to be his first collection of thirty-nine poems covering a wide range of subjects from childhood to old age, from pleasures and pains to cats, birds, and animals, from feasts to singers, from politics to economics. Unquestionably, this book is a social document presenting his social concerns in lyrical lines and reflecting his active participation in the fabric of social life at large. His poetry is an expression of his sympathy for the suffering sections of our society, for the poor and the downtrodden, for the helpless women, and the aged. In clear terms, he attacks corrupt politicians and government officials and the callous apathy of the government to the poorer sections. He emphatically says: "Poor people are strangled through taxes and their governments do nothing for their welfare. The government is always with the rich, caring for their comfort and luxury." Though a Christian by birth in Kerala, known from ancient days as God's own land, Dominic says, "I have respect for Hinduism and Buddhism as they believe in Ahimsa," and his poems are a direct expression of his unbiased and balanced attitude and catholicity of outlook.

As the book opens, the first poem, "In Memoriam: George Joson", an elegy written on his colleague, who died in a car accident, speaks eloquently of the writer's spirit of intense humanism. While he feels haunted by his absence, he reconciles himself with the inevitable and ends with the lines –

> The best is to resign
> to what He ordains
> in time and out of time.

(*Winged Reason*, 18)

In sharp contrast with the opening poem, the next poem "Long Live E. K. Nayanar" is politically inspired. Like most of the Keralites, Dominic too comes under the influence of the communist ideology and he is very much moved by the death of E. K. Nayanar, the thrice Chief Minister of Kerala, who is still remembered as the man of the masses. The writer bids "Lal Salaam" to the leader, a true communist and patriot, and an "epitome of socialism", who championed the cause of the denied and the deprived and the downtrodden:

> You are our polestar
> who saves us from Darkness.

(*Winged Reason*, 20)

The next piece, "A Nightmare", is a vivid picture of the present social situation, which is indeed a nightmare to any observer with a feeling heart. It is a picture of terrible contrasts and anomalies and horrible gaps that refuse to be bridged so easily—an overfed boy whose mother beats him to eat more and a bony child crying for a crumb, a lavish wedding feast in the town hall on one side and on the other side, two starving girls in rags struggling with the dogs at the garbage bin, two long queues—one at the liquor shop, where beggars too compete and the other at the ration shop, two-storeyed edifices with luxury rooms and swimming pools on one side and on the other slums and huts. "A Sheep's Wail" is an interesting piece running into a dozen three-lined units giving an autobiographical picture of a typical sheep whose piercing cry is in the nature of a plea and a complaint:

> Man, you are the cruelest,
> you are the most ungrateful
> of all God's creatures.
> . . . . . . . . . . . . . . . . .
> If a heaven is there
> we will reach there first
> and pray to God to shut you out.
>
> (*Winged Reason*, 25)

While the piece "Anand's Lot" is a sympathetic narration of the heart-piercing cries and sufferings of the kidnapped child Anand, a school-going boy, who was beaten and forced to beg and give the collected earnings, the poem "Gayatri's Solitude" is a moving description of the eighty-two-year-old widowed mother Gayatri, who is fated to live a lonely life in an old age home, though well-furnished, in India although she is the mother of three sons and two daughters as all of them live in the US:

> The depth of maternal love,
> and the pangs of separation
> no child can gauge.
>
> (*Winged Reason*, 32)

In "Tsunami Camps", he narrates the untold miseries of the victims of the natural disaster who "lost their dear ones / and fight against destiny." Though the Government gave kits and boxes, they did not contain essential things and their plea for boats and fishing nets and their unending wails became a futile cry in wilderness; their piercing cry—"It's better to kill us than torture like this" (*Winged Reason*, 33)—failed to reach the deaf ears of the government.

Now the poet tries to harp on his favourite subject of the widening difference between haves and have-nots in the verse piece of the same title "Haves and Have-nots". This is a world where capitalism rules and communism fails and it's a pity that even the so-called champions of socialism and communism do not put their principles in practice. As such the writer says:

> But power corrupted;
> leaders turned tyrants;
> philosophy failed
>
> (*Winged Reason*, 37)

In the poem "I am Just a Mango Tree", the writer succeeds in painting the man in true colors and even the tree complains to God regarding the inhuman nature and unlimited greed of man:

> God, why is your man so selfish and cruel?
> Did you create him

to disturb this earth's balance?

The God sincerely regrets His thoughtless action of creating this cruel man and expresses His bitter feelings with pain and remorse:

> My child, I created him
> in My own image
> but he's gone astray;
> My agony is endless.
> That's the fate of the Father everywhere.
> I shouldn't have created this human species;
> But how can a father kill his sons? (*Winged Reason* 41)

"Indian Democracy" is a stark presentation of the sordid reality of the existing state of our democracy. Though ours is the largest democracy, "regionalism and parochialism devour nationalism and patriotism"; election campaigns overflow with "fireworks of lies and abuses"; holding of Parliament elections is "a several billion business"; 'Criminal MPs are brought from jails to prove majority on floor." The result is that we have "Corrupt Governments / draining the blood of people" (*Winged Reason*, 60–61). "In the Name of God" is an interesting piece presenting the bitter truth of all anti-social activities committed in the name of God; the name of God is unnecessarily dragged into all unethical acts. Criminal actions are done in the name of God and history is a witness to the killing of millions in crusades in the name of God. Now democracy gets diluted in the name of God. In the name of God superstition survives, poison of communalism spreads, terrorists butcher innocent people, teens are transformed into terrorists, higher castes indulge in exploitation, secularism is destroyed and corruption gets promoted:

> God is dethroned
> in the name of God.
> And human gods are crowned
> in the name of God.
>
> (*Winged Reason*, 70)

The poet pays high tribute to the woman teacher Kaumudi who is now no more and who is a role model and a guiding spirit for all other women with her glowing spirit of patriotism, revealed in her early age of sixteen when she donated all her golden ornaments to Gandhi for the freedom struggle when he addressed a meeting at Vadakara in Malabar. She was so deeply influenced by Gandhi's message that she pledged to wear no ornaments, followed in his footsteps, taught Hindi in Malabar schools, and led a simple life till her death at ninety-two:

> Kaumudi's dazzle dimmed
> the dazzle of all other women in jewels and ornaments.
> Let's bow our head to this rarest gem.
>
> (*Winged Reason*, 75)

His second collection *Write Son, Write,* published a year later in 2011, has thirty-one poems with a Preface and a Foreword by the contemporary poet P. C. K. Prem. In this second volume, the writer seems to continue his favorite theme of social reform and justice aiming the shaft of his satire on corruption that has grown to monstrous size. Finding fault with all-embracing materialism, his sensitive heart grieves at the loss of moral values in all walks of social life. The first poem, which happens to be the title poem "Write, My Son, Write", is a lengthy piece of verse divided into twenty-one parts that run over seventeen pages with pictorial presentation. Dominic declares in his Preface that "The opening poem 'Write, My Son, Write' is indeed the manifesto of my views and philosophy." Divided into twenty-one parts, it declares my views on God, Man and Nature." God created man with a purpose and a mission and not for fun or to fill the vacuum. As such this poem starts on a solemn note with God's words:

> My son,
> I have a mission
> in your creation,
> God spoke
> to my ears.
>
> *(Write Son, Write*, 21)

God asks his son to look at the tip of his pen and tells him that he is the ball of his pen, the ink that flows on the paper and asks him "Write till / I say stop". He asks him to feel the symphony of the universe and it grieves Him to see that his species seldom feels His rhythm and they have become insensitive, and in this respect, plants and animals are better than human beings. Part three elaborates the rhythm and harmony, present in every molecule and in every atom. It is present in the majestic tramp of elephant, in the dart of deer, trot of tiger, race of rabbit, lope of leopard, swoop of swine, scud of squirrel, canter of kangaroo, tear of bear, gallop of horse, bound of bull, dash of dog, dart of cormorant, plunge of kingfisher, flit of swift, swoop of kite, plummet of eagle, buzz of bee, wing of mynah, drone of mosquito, motion of snake, march of centipede and millipede, and movement of worms and insects. He says: "Rhythm is there / everywhere / and creates / the perpetual / harmony" (*Write Son, Write*, 23). Part Six speaks of the importance of co-existence and cooperation and states the core of the message:

> Your existence
> depends on others;
> all my creations,
> useful and beautiful.
>
> *(Write Son, Write*, 25)

Part Ten finds fault with the cruel and violent nature of man: "Who gave you right / to kill my creation?" (*Write Son, Write*, 29). The writer is against the killing of animals, fowl, and fish for their taste and food, for their sport and fun. Part Fourteen deals with the limitations of man; what we hear, see, and know is very little: "What you hear / is little; / much more lies / beyond your ears." (*Write Son, Write*, 32). While Part 16 gives a brief sketch of different types of mafia, religious, political, and intellectual, Parts 17 &18 deal with religious mafia, Part 19 with political mafia and Part 20 with intellectual mafia. The last part, i.e., part 21, is more or less a summation of the lengthy verse reiterating the message that human beings can survive in this world only when they allow other creatures, plants and animals to live in harmony:

> If they heed
> they will be saved;
> other beings
> will be saved;
> plants will be saved
> and the universe
> as such will be saved.
>
> *(Write Son, Write*, 37)

*Philosophical Musings for a Meaningful Life* 

The lines of the next poem "An Elegy on my Ma" are written in memory of his mother, who passed away on 14th October, 2010 and in this context, it is good to remember that this book is dedicated to his beloved mother. His mother was a symbol of the purest love, selfless service and sacrifice, and a source of inspiration, and the poem has an appropriate ending:

> Ma, we will go ahead
> boosted by your divine words.
>
> (*Write Son, Write*, 41)

After a poem, it is followed by another piece "Massacre of Cats", which is a sad reference to the poisoning of his four favorite cats by his neighbor, a man of high rank in the society, and in the poet's words, the death of his cats was as shocking to him as his mother's death. His materialist neighbors go to church every day, read the Bible every day, but they have not learnt "to love other beings as fellow beings." The next poem "Aung San Suu Kyi – Asia's Lady Mandela" pays a glowing tribute to the patriotic leader and champion of democratic rights in Burma, whose name bears the title of the poem:

> Suu Kyi, the epitome of valour,
> showed her people through her life
> liberty is born from the ashes of fear.
> Her twenty years of political life,
> more than fourteen in solitary cells.
>
> (*Write Son, Write*, 53)

Now Dominic the poet is enchanted by the captivating sight of coconut trees, which are seen in abundance in Kerala, and in fact, Kerala and coconut trees go together; the result is the short piece "Coconut Palm":

> A marvel to all architects.
> No human hand can build
> such a parallel pillar.
> Kudos to the Architect of architects.
>
> (*Write Son, Write*, 56)

It is followed by an interesting poem "Crow, the Black Beauty" and the writer wonders why the black crow is neglected even by poets while the white dove is extolled by all. The writer's sympathetic heart does not approve of this color discrimination:

> When will the Black and the White
> dwell in the same house
> and dine from the same plate?
>
> (*Write Son, Write*, 57–58)

The verse piece "For the Glory of God" narrates an incident reported in a local newspaper *The Malayala Manorama* Sunday Supplement on 25th July, 2010, which is an instance of communal harmony of Hindu and Muslim women in the midst of communal rancour, clashes, and killings. Chellamma, a seventy-five-year-old helpless Kerala Brahmin woman receives help and shelter from a Muslim lady, Resiya Beevi, at a time when religious extremists hacked off a Professor's right palm with the intention of killing him in that region. The verse "Hunger's Call" is more communistic in tone and tenor and it is a plea to support the sinking life with soup and fight poverty the logical result of "hyperinflation and economic mismanagement" the result of "the impact of globalization, / liberalization and privatization" (*Write Son, Write*, 66). "Rocketing Growth of India" is a strong satire upon our Government and at our so-called much boasted progress, which in reality is an eyewash. Of course the rich are growing richer and poverty is growing and the gap between the rich and the poor is enormously growing. The lines of the poem "To My Colleague" are really heart-rending as the piece refers to a shameful incident of religious fanaticism when the right palm of a Professor of Newman College at Thodupuzha, a colleague of the writer, was hacked off while he was returning home after Sunday Mass on 4th July, 2010:

> India, my motherland.
> Land of corruption, terrorism
> and religious fundamentalism.
>
> (*Write Son, Write*, 84)

The poem "Train Blast" is a description of the poignant train blast, a heinous act of the Maoists, causing the tragic death of a hundred and fifty innocent people. They think that:

> End justifies the means;
> Utopian ends,
> Diabolic means.
>
> (*Write Son, Write*, 85)

Now the poet asks Lord Krishna why He is so indifferent, and questions:

> Can't you punish
> these terrorists
> as you punished
> Asuras?
>
> (*Write Son, Write*, 86)

"Work is Worship" is the last but one in this volume and the writer rightly states the good old saying and reiterates it by strengthening the message with good instances. God is with the person who works and does his duty without wasting his time and idling. He says God whispers in his ears:

> "My dear son, live in Karma,
> love all creations,
> for I am in everything."
>
> (*Write Son, Write*, 96)

The book closes with the piece "Lines Composed from Thodupuzha River's Bridge" which is a picturesque description of the river with the bridge across it that merges at last into the sea and the lines reveal the influence of Wordsworth, the famous Romantic poet of Nature since his description of nature grows imperceptibly into philosophical reflections:

> Invigorating cool water gushing through your vein
> overflows my mind with eternal realities.
> Every second passed in our lives
> is irredeemably lost for ever.
> Invisible Time flashes in meteoric speed;
>
> (*Write Son, Write*, 99)

In his third collection, *Multicultural Symphony* Dominic deals with a wide range of topics embracing multiculturalism, global warming, environmental problems, and other social problems such as poverty and unemployment, child labor, and dignity of labor, the deep-rooted system of caste—which is the root-cause of all the social problems—and superstitions, like blind belief in horoscope etc.

Thus Dr. Dominic is a poet with social awareness which fills almost all the lines of his poems and it is no exaggeration to say that his profound concern for the marginalized sections of the society forms the life force and breath of his poetry. He tries to dissect corruption at all levels, political or religious, social or academic, and presents it in its true colors with all the ugliness and monstrous greed. He says in his Preface, "Corruption has become the hallmark of these leaders, and influenced by them, the masses also deviate from the right track to the evil track. And who will save this society? My answer is: writers, particularly poets who are like prophets." Thus it is quite clear that Dominic is a poet of the suffering masses and oppressed sections of the society; moreover his poems are a strong testimony to his socialistic ideas, to his leanings toward communistic ideology, and to his earnest zeal as a social reformer. His poems in general are more descriptive and narrative than suggestive; though he does not make use of imagery, he is richly imaginative.

## Works Cited

Dominic, K. V. *Winged Reason*. New Delhi: Authorspress, 2010. Print.

---. *Write Son, Write*. New Delhi: GNOSIS, 2011. Print.

# Chapter 8 -
# Concurrent Predicaments and Urge for Philanthropy in the Poetry of K.V. Dominic
# by Dr. Sugandha Agarwal

This research paper endeavors to present the theme of the three fantabulous poetic collections *Winged Reason*, *Write Son, Write*, and *Multicultural Symphony* by K. V. Dominic, which highlights major social, political, ethical, and environmental issues of the world. K. V. Dominic is one who searches life and beauty in nature and seeks the interconnectivity betwixt human beings and Nature. Most of his poems reveal to us that he never writes to express beauty, spirituality, or aesthetic pleasure. He said in the preface to *Winged Reason*: "I give priority to the content of a poem than to its style. That is why my poems lack much imagery and other figures of speech... Poetry should be digestible as short stories and novels.... I adopt a conversational style in poetry, which again attracts the ordinary readers (*Winged Reason*, 12).

His poems are related to the social issues as he wants to bring awareness in the thinking of common men about the plight of the environment or nation. He is the bursting voice of Indian English poetry that has enlightened the poetic scenario from a decade with his harmonious poetry, lofty ideas, and luminous thoughts. K. V. Dominic's first collection *Winged Reason* is replete with the humanistic values and the poems are fervent expression of the literary soul, which reflects Peace and Harmony in the world. His poems reveal the heartache and grief at the inhuman attitude existing in the society. In this newfangled world, people have forgotten their reverence for human values and ethics. Empathy is an alien word and people are more focused on their own convenience and wish to fulfill selfish motives. The poet established himself to be different from the others by his empathy and concern for others. His way of expressing ideas is really remarkable; he takes us to the world where we also seek Love, Peace, Empathy, and Compassion. He has the power to ignite the flame of the sense of responsibility among the readers. He is not the poet who composes poetry for appreciation; he is not the poet who writes to please others; he is the poet who pens down his emotions, his feelings, his sentiments for the prevalent disturbances in the nation and in the world.

There are thirty-nine poems in *Winged Reason*, which describes several themes, such as poverty, human suffering, ecology, corruption, terrorism, nature, communalism, downtrodden, women, old age, workers, social evils, animals, birds, politics, and religious discrimination etc. The main theme of his poetry is the eternal relationship between Man, Nature, and God. He believes in the concept of *Jeevatma* and *Paramatma* (individual soul and universal soul) and the Indian concept of *Aham Brahmasmi* (I am the God). *Advaita* seems to him logical and acceptable than *Dvaita*. Dominic's poetry clearly shows him as a realist and torch-bearer of the down-trodden. This collection starts with two elegies, one on his friend George Joson and the other on E. K. Nayanar, Chief Minister of Kerala. Most of his poems have the theme of social disparities, which he has experienced in his life. "A Nightmare" is a heart moving poem figuring out the neglected daily tortures at school. His other poems like "Beauty", "International Women's Day", "Lal Salaam to Labour", "Vrinda", "Kaumudi Teacher is No More", "Luxmi's Plea", and "Old Age" are the poems revealing the shortcomings of the concurrent time, but some poems like "What A Birth", "Om", and "Pleasure and Pain" have a philosophical touch that inspires man to comprehend the true meaning of the existence of human beings on this planet called Earth. Dominic left no stone unturned to show the true picture of our social and political and human life, i.e., inequality, poverty, corruption, pollution, greed, suffering, and plight of women.

Humanity and Ethics have a special place in his poetry. Corruption indulged in by politicians and government servants pierces his heart like a thorn. His outburst can be seen in these words: "Poor people are strangled through taxes and government is always with the rich, caring for their comfort and luxury. The rich can evade taxes, exploit the weaker sections, torture and even kill anyone they choose; they get the protection from the police and can escape legal punishments. Why?" (*Winged Reason*, 13) These thoughts are like the arrows and thorns that pierce his heart every day and blood spills through his pen onto paper. His earnest request for humanity can be viewed here:

> If I could fly like an angel,
> would plead all prophets
> to inspire and instill humanism
> in millions' communal minds
>
> ("A Blissful Voyage", *Winged Reason*, 21)

He really wants to punish the brutal terrorists himself in the below-mentioned passionate words:

> I wish I were a bullet
> and shoot into the chest of that terrorist
> who compels that teenage boy
> to explode and kill that innocent mob
>
> ("A Blissful Voyage", *Winged Reason*, 21)

The poet depicts the mental trauma and agony of kidnapped children in "Anand's Lot". He remarks:

> How happy were those days!
> Mummy gave me kiss and ta-ta;
> like butterflies flew to the school
> with Rajesh, Praven and Smitha
> chattering, singing, dancing, running.
> Alas! Like a vulture came the car then;
> picked me in and dashed away.
>
> ("Anand's Lot", *Winged Reason*, 26)

K. V. Dominic unveils the situation of old age homes—how the parents are ignored in their old age by their own children. He tells of the plight of woman discarded by her own family members. The poet shows the negligence of aged people by their children and the sufferings of the parents when their children leave for foreign countries, leaving parents at their hometown. They opine that the monetary assistance they are providing could make their parents happy:

# Philosophical Musings for a Meaningful Life

> Poor, miserable mother,
> she has no hunger,
> she has no sleep.
> An old lily flower
> pale and faded.
> Dawn to dusk,
> sitting in an armchair,
> looking at the far West,
> longing for her children's calls,
> she remains lonely
>
> ("Gayatri's Solitude", *Winged Reason*, 31)

He is the ecological poet as he composed poems on animals and birds. He wrote the wail of sheep in his painful words:

> The fur God gave me,
> mercilessly you shear
> to make you cosy.
>
> The milk for my lamb
> you suck and drain
> and grow fat and cruel
>
> ("A Sheep's Wail", *Winged Reason*, 24)

Dominic is a true realist with immeasurable social feelings. Agony of any kind, caused either by destiny or people or animal, makes his heart bleed like a brook. The poet shows the unpleasant atmosphere of Tsunami camps. The poet wails that the victims are not provided basic facilities for their livelihood:

> "Where have gone the crores
> collected for our relief?"
> Money is hoarded in the government exchequer,
> or diverted for some other purposes.
> "It's better to kill us than torture like this."
> "We don't have sufficient food,
> we don't have pure water"
>
> ("Tsunami Camps", *Winged Reason*, 33)

His poem "International Women's Day" narrates that on the one hand we celebrate women's day and on the other hand, we exploit them:

> Woman is the game!
> an instrument of lust
> and hot-selling sex!
>
> ("International Women's Day", *Winged Reason*, 42)

The poet urges to maintain the decorum and dignity of women. He writes:

> Venerable is woman,
> for she is your mother;
> she is your sister;
> she is your wife;
> she is your guide;
> she is your teacher;
> she is your nurse;
> and above all,
> she is your angel
>
> ("International Women's Day", *Winged Reason*, 43)

He pleads for the equal rights for women as she is the person who serves her family as a daughter, sister, wife, and mother. So she deserves all the joys of this world but it is a matter of agony that we are providing her only dishonor which is highly unjustified.

The next poem of this collection "*Lal Salaam to Labour*" highlights the value of labor. He draws the attention of the readers at the well-known truth that without labor, nothing can be done properly as it is required in fields, factories, construction, or we can say, everywhere. He writes:

> Lal Salaam to Labour
> the backbone of the country!
>
> They sow the seed;
> reap the corn;
> and we eat and sleep.
> . . . . . . . . . . . . . .
> Let us not be unjust
> when we pay them wages
> . . . . . . . . . . . . . .
> Give them at least their due;
> the more we give, the more we get;
> Put charity in humanity
> a spiritual bliss that never dies ("Lal Salaam to Labour," *Winged Reason* 44-45)

In "Ammini's Demise," the poet reveals his pain over the death of his poisoned cat, Ammini:

> How could that fiend
> poison this angel?
> What harm had it
> done to him?
>
> ("Ammini's Demise", *Winged Reason*, 64)

The poet's philosophy on the various aspects of human life shows wonderment. In "Beauty", he admires inner beauty as original in comparison of physical beauty which is temporary. He reminds that nothing on this planet is ugly as all the things are formed by God. He says physical beauty fades like a flower and is forgotten when it disappears whereas the accomplishments and attitude of human beings fetch them eternal beauty and "only spiritual beauty gives eternal joy."

K. V. Dominic's second poetic collection *Write Son, Write* is a collection of thirty-one poems, which displays his worry for the missing human values and ethics in the world and among human beings who do not hitch to display their cruelty towards human beings and the animal world.

*Philosophical Musings for a Meaningful Life*

According to K. V. Dominic, poetry is the shortest form of literature, most captivating and didactic; he believes that in this busy and hustling world, people should have a special attraction to poetry. Since reading habits of modern man have diminished considerably and she/he takes to watching TV and such visual media, he believes that it is his duty as a writer to promote poetry at any cost. He has already published four edited books consisting of innumerable critical articles on the poetry of established and emerging contemporary Indian poets in English. This anthology consists of 31 poems on several themes of expressing significance of mercy, nature, and his compassion for his mother, work, fellow beings, and international personalities, like Aung San Suu Kyi, Mother Teresa, and Mohammad Rafi. Dominic feels that in the present scenario, people are crazy after materialism, and the qualities of divinity and holiness in them are vanishing so they give no importance to principles, values, family, and social relations. They are trying their maximum to exploit their fellow beings, other human beings, and the planet itself. Dominic said about this situation in the preface of his second poetic collection:

It is the duty of the religious leaders, political leaders and the intelligentsia to inject the lost values into the masses and thus preserve this planet and its inhabitants from imminent devastation. Instead, majority of these leaders become mafias and inject communal and corruptive venom into the minds of the masses. Corruption has become the hallmark of these leaders and, influenced by them, the masses also deviate from the right track to the evil track. And who will save this society? My answer is: writers, particularly poets, who are like prophets. (*Write Son, Write*, 8)

In *Write Son, Write*, K. V. Dominic is articulating truth with delicate treatment, which moves our sensitive and emotional hearts. He laments at the heartlessness and cruelty of people toward other human beings. The poet is concerned about human life as he experiences brutal, unsympathetic, and violent attitude of man toward nature and human beings. K. V. Dominic is a true humanitarian; he cannot detest Almighty's creation, so his love for the animal world is immense. He truly loves birds, insects, and every creature of this earth. The poet has deep faith in love, sympathy, and non-violence. These are the most powerful forces and man lives harmoniously if he learns to implement these forces in life. Today people blame, condemn, and even kill each other in the name of injustice. Our biggest enemies are our ignorance, poverty, ego, unemployment, etc. The dreadful atomic and destructive weapons are made in the name of security, humanity, and prosperity. The feelings of mercy and compassion for others are disappearing day by day. He expressed his feelings in one of his poems:

> . . . teach my neighbors
> and millions of my brothers and sisters
> to show love and mercy
> to all non-human beings ("Attachment", *Write Son, Write*, 52)

K. V. Dominic's poetry is full of social realism; he is a writer with social consciousness and his poems often express his impressions and views on concurrent social conditions and problems. Undoubtedly this anthology is a social work presenting his social concerns in the form of rhymes and reflecting his devoted participation in social welfare. His poetry is an articulation of his sympathy for the downtrodden, suppressed, or aged women. He criticizes corrupt and greedy politicians and government officials for their discrimination between rich and poor. The very first poem of *Write, Son, Write* is a lengthy poem with twenty-one parts that lasts to seventeen pages with pictorial presentation. Dominic himself declares in his Preface that the opening poem "Write, My Son, Write" is indeed the manifesto of his views and philosophy which declares his views on God, Man, and Nature. God created man with a particular aim and a mission and this poem starts on a grave note with God's words:

> My son,
> I have a mission
> in your creation,
> God spoke
> to my ears.
> Write, my son,
> write.
> Write till
> I say stop
>
> ("Write, My Son, Write", *Write Son, Write*, 21)

The poet is replete with the thoughts of honesty, truth, nonviolence, social welfare and kindness, so he speaks about the sufferings of the poor; he also develops a desire within, where man should curb misusing national property or wealth. He pleads to eradicate hunger and destitution with the same dangerous weapons that man creates to attack enemies. His poems are soul-stirring for readers as he innocently raises questions on the existence of poverty:

> Isn't poverty the greatest enemy?
> Why not fight against it
> and wipe out destitution,
> pointing guns, rifles and missiles
> at the chest of the poor?
>
> ("Hunger's Call", *Write Son, Write*, 66)

His affection for his mother is clearly shown in an elegy he composed in the memory of his mother. He declares that the love of mother is most divine and the purest of its kind. He once again reminds this to his readers that in the lap of mother, all sorrows can be forgotten. He says:

> Ma, that smile on your face
> ripples down
> to a Tsunami of
> grief in my mind.
> The glow in your eyes
> darts like lightening
> to my burning heart...
> Truly mother's love
> is the purest love
> and divine love
>
> ("An Elegy on My Ma", *Write Son, Write*, 38–39)

Dominic is a true and honest poet, so he portrays people's feigned and dual character. In the poem "Massacre of Cats", he relates a story of his cat that was poisoned by the poet's neighbors. He explains their pretense in these words:

> My materialist neighbours
> go to church everyday
> read the Bible everyday
> but never read the part
> to love other beings
> as fellow beings
> . . . . . . . . . . .

*Philosophical Musings for a Meaningful Life*

> God, instill in them
> thy creation's purpose;
> the need to love
> other creations--
> animals, plants
> and the planet itself
>
> ("Massacre of Cats", *Write Son, Write*, 45–46)

His poem "Aung San Suu Kyi – Asia's Lady Mandela" is a memorable tribute to the renowned leader and winner of democratic rights in Burma:
Suu Kyi, the epitome of valour,

> showed her people through her life
> liberty is born from the ashes of fear.
> Her twenty years of political life,
> more than fourteen in solitary cells.
>
> ("Aung San Suu Kyi – Asia's Lady Mandela", *Write Son, Write*, 53)

Dominic's love for nature is immense and immeasurable; his art of portraying the beauty of nature is really commendable. He beautifully gives the pictorial description of the coconut palm in one of his poems:

> Tall and majestic coconut palm
> shot like a rocket to the sky
> with a brilliant view of
> sparkling leaves and alluring nuts ("Coconut Palm", *Write Son, Write*, 56)

His poems show that human beings have the superior opinion of being the best creation of God, so they think that they have a right to spoil nature and use animals as they like. The poet attacks racism and expresses his anger at how man can be so brutal and stone-hearted. The poet sorrowfully writes:

> Why is white attractive
> and black disgusting?
> When will the Black be
> kindred to the White?
> When will the Black and the White
> dwell in the same house
> and dine from the same plate?
>
> ("Crow, the Black Beauty", *Write Son, Write*, 57)

Dominic's concern and tension on the burning or current issues of the society and the world show in his poetry. His writes through his poem about the scarcity of water and the problem of global warming, which is the cause of other major problems:

> Water, the source of life;
> Omnipresent and abundant
> like its parent oxygen.
> Free and 'insignificant'
> for millions;
> going to be more precious
> than gold and diamond.

> Absence of rains and trees,
> enhanced by global warming,
>
> ("Water, Water, Everywhere", *Write Son, Write*, 91)

Prof. Dominic pours out his feelings for the commonest bird crow, which is not getting that much praise as cuckoo. He seems to share the opinion of Walt Whitman, who felt that even the most ordinary thing, such as grass, has its own significance and not a single object in this world is waste—every object has its own value. In the same way, Dominic said that most of the poets generally like to compose poems on nightingale, cuckoo, or skylark; but it is he himself, perhaps, the first poet who composed a poem on crow's beauty. He beautifully says:

> When will "crow-crow" be
> Pleasing as "koo-koo"?
>
> ("Crow, the Black Beauty", *Write Son, Write*, 57)

Undoubtedly, the poetry of Prof. Dominic reflects the humanistic values in a commendable way and moves the readers to do self-analysis. His poems are the pure expressions of the divine poetic soul to witness tranquility and harmony on the globe. The poet's heart is so true and child-like as he finds bliss in the smile of the child:

> Infants always
> tempted me
> like bloomed roses.
> Babies—human
> and non-human—
> are embodiments
> of grace and innocence ("Musings from an Infant's Face", *Write Son, Write*, 69)

Dominic is also a poet of Nature and Environment as he comprehends the value of nature and depicts the adverse effects of the exploitation and ill treatment of Nature in his poems. In his poem "Nature Weeps", he presented presents the reason for drooping mango leaves and fading roses; he reveals why tigers are entering in public area and, quite uniquely, he writes that cuckoos or birds sit on Gandhi's statue as there is lack of trees. He drags our attention with his beauty of words toward the prevailing problems related to flora and fauna:

> Mango leaves droop:
> irrational man ill-treated
> gods of summer showers
>
> Tigers started roaming
> seeking food in villages:
> people killed their preys
>
> Gandhi's statue smiles:
> could serve as seats for birds
> longing for a birch
>
> Rainbows appear
> only on papers:
> no moist in the sky

*Philosophical Musings for a Meaningful Life* 69

("Nature Weeps", *Write Son, Write*, 71–73)

Dominic also pens down the condition of the school-going, who are carrying heavy weight on their back, and he uncovers the reality of stone-hearted mentors as well, who welcome the students in the school with stick and give them punishment:

> The child is reluctant
> to go to school:
> teacher welcomes with cane
>
> The boy goes to school
> stooped and exhausted:
> ten kilo books on his back ("Nature Weeps", *Write Son, Write*, 72,74)

The poetry collections of Dominic exhibit his distress at the awkward tendencies and the inhuman attitude prevalent in the society that spoils harmony of existence. In) another poem, he presents the contrast between the growth and drawbacks of developing India:

> Rocketing Growth of India!
> Overtaking America…
> First in population growth;
> first in number of poor;
> top in ignorance and illiteracy;
> top in superstitions and fundamentalism;
> very low standard of living.
> Rocketing growth of the rich;
> express growth of the poor;
>
> ("Rocketing Growth of India!", *Write Son, Write*, 77)

In this modern era, people have forgotten the significance of human values and ethics. Empathy is almost put aside for personal comfort and for selfish motives. The poet established himself to be unique from others by his virtues, humanity, and concern for the downtrodden. The poet describes role of destiny in the lives of humans but requests to develop pure faith in the divine power of God. Dominic deeply expresses his sentiments of love and compassion for humanity, animals, birds, and nature. The poet believes that the true worship is to help the needy; one needs not go to Temple, Church, or Mosque. He writes:

> "Daughter, service to the poor
> is superior to
> prayers and hymns."
>
> ("Sister Mercy", *Write Son, Write*, 79)

Dominic is the all-rounder of human emotions and sentiments; he left no area of feelings untouched in his poems as he knows how to acknowledge talent. So he appreciates renowned bollywood singer Mohammad Rafi and pays a wonderful tribute to him in these words:

> Gandharva of music,
> he was sent by God
> to ease and solace burning minds.
> Greatest of all Indian singers,
> he was modest, dignified and humble.
> Blessed by goddess Saraswati...
> "Immortality, thy name is Rafi."
> ("Tribute of Mohammed Rafi", *Write Son, Write*, 87)

The third collection of K. V. Dominic is *Multicultural Symphony*, which contains 47 poems on concurrent predicaments. The poet feels that poetry is the best medium of passing messages and values to the society. In this cyber age, which lacking in human values, poetry can do wonders in molding civilized society, but the tragedy is that no one listens to the poets in the present scenario. Few people develop reading habit and the wish to establish themselves as good persons. Poetry is the oldest form of literature but the choice of the modern people has changed completely now that they don't want to read or listen to philosophical or serious themes. The addiction of internet has distracted people from reading books and the poetry has suffered much because of this. But even knowing the whole situation, Dominic is not losing hope; he is continuously trying to bring awareness in public for social reform and to curb brutality. His latest collection proves that he is a poet of social issues, nature, and philanthropy. He writes in the preface:

> To me this universe is a big concert or symphony, a harmony of diverse notes. All creations play their role in concordance, but man tries to play discordant notes— stands against the rhythmic flow of the system. The inter-relationship between Man, God, and Universe is the main theme of my poems. To me, science and religion are two sides of the same coin. As man is the latest evolutionary being, he should respect other beings and plants, which have greater legacy to claim in this universe. The intellectual capacity of man is used more for destruction than construction, more for vices than virtues. It is an irony that the more one is intellectual and educated, the more he is vicious and crooked. Illiterate, rural people are more innocent and graceful than educated, urban people. (Preface, *Multicultural Symphony*, 8-9)

The poet is a follower of Advaita philosophy that sees God as a separate entity and believes that that there is a Supreme Power or Energy controlling this universe. Like the American poet Walt Whitman, he feels that God is present in every object of this planet. The poet seeks to bring harmony to this society, nation, and to the whole world, where people can survive with love and peace. I love the lines which he passionately writes and which are the crystal clear mirror of his deep emotions:

> Dear my fellow beings
> break away all fences and walls
> Fences of your petty minds
> Compound walls of your houses
> Walls of your religions and castes
> Boundaries of your native States
> And ultimately borders of your nations
> Let there be no India, Pakistan or China
> America, Africa, Europe or Australia
> But only one nation THE WORLD
> where every being lives in perfect harmony
> as one entity in multicultural world

*Philosophical Musings for a Meaningful Life*                                                                                                                                                                                                                                 71

>                               ("Multicultural Harmony", *Multicultural Symphony*, 22–23)

I think no other diction or locution could more beautifully define these thoughts of Prof. Dominic. His thinking is outstanding and his way of expression is unique. He says that diversity is the main feature of the universe:

> Multiplicity and diversity
> essence of universe
> From atom to the heavens
> multiculturalism reigns
> This unity in diversity
> makes beauty of universe
>                               ("Multicultural Harmony", *Multicultural Symphony*, 15)

K. V. Dominic is a man with lofty views and remarkable approach as he questions the discrimination against women and inquires about their rights. His urge to respect women is again shown in this poetry collection in these words:

> Woman is most venerable
> for she is your mother
> she is nurse and teacher
> and above all
> she is the lamp of house…
> Why can't women be priests
> in churches, mosques and temples?
> Can't she enter and pray
> in her Heavenly Father's abode?
>                               ("Multicultural Harmony", *Multicultural Symphony*, 19)

He continues his anguish toward the disrespect for women and shows it in his next poem on the discrimination against women:

> Why such discrimination to women's sports?
> Why such double standards to women's feats?
> . . . . . . . . . . . . . . . . . . . . . . . . .
> Dear my brothers in India and abroad
> let's appreciate and promote
> our sisters' talents and skills
> rather than looking at them
> with vicious hungry eyes
>                               ("Women's Cricket World Cup 2013", *Multicultural Symphony*, 73)

He also recounts the quality of mother's love:

> Maternal love, love sublime
> Inexplicable, unfathomable
> Noblest of all emotions
>                               ("Mother's Love", *Multicultural Symphony*, 67)

Another different theme in his poem is the increasing importance of matching horoscope for wedding. It is really a wonderful satire on those who believe in it blindly. I think no other poem would have ever been composed on this theme so exquisitely as this one by Dominic:

> Horoscope, bread earner of astrologers
> Arch-villain of Hindu marriages
> Monster who pricked the rosy dreams
> and sucked the blood of thousands of spinsters…
> Do horoscopic matches bring happiness and peace?
> Why then cases of thousands of divorces?
>
> ("Horoscope", *Multicultural Symphony*, 25)

Dominic wrote on numerous issues, especially on environment and nature that are deteriorating day by day. He focused on the increasing global warming and found out some causes of it in his next poem:

> Carbon dioxide produced by
> home appliances of the rich
> room heaters, air conditioners,
> refrigerators, washing machines,
> and the toxic emissions
> from their cars and planes
> plays the major share
> in polluting air and
> resultant global warming
>
> ("Global Warming's Real Culprits", *Multicultural Symphony*, 26)

He is the poet of empathy and compassion; he is very much attached to the birds and animals. He composed many poems in his all three collections about the sudden demise of his cats that were poisoned by his neighbors. He feels that the animals are also created by God and they have the right to live, and that's why the poet is not able to forget the death of those loving cats:

> Souls of the seven cats
> Haunt me and wound me
> Unanimously they ask
> why they were poisoned
> Haven't they right to this planet?
> ................
> I can only vision
> my neighbor will be reborn
> as a mouse to be chased
> by half a dozen cats
>
> ("Cohabitance on the Planet", *Multicultural Symphony*, 28)

Another poem of Prof. Dominic depicts his love for his State Kerela for it natural beauty, literacy rate, and numerous other reasons:

> My native State Kerala
> blessed with equable climate
> and alluring landscape
> crowned by the Sahyas
> ................
> Multitudes of brooks and rivers
> ................
> Thousands of species of flora and fauna

*Philosophical Musings for a Meaningful Life* 73

> Six months long rainy season
> . . . . . . . . . . . . . . . . . . . .
> Autumn and winter fear to enter
> Tourists call it God's own country
> ("Multicultural Kerela", *Multicultural Symphony*, 29)

Dominic is concerned for the well-being of each and everything as in one of his poems, he is showing care to even a piece of paper—which sounds unbelievable but is true. He personifies the piece of paper, which is requesting the poet:

> Though I am a passive sheet of paper
> I have a soul as vibrant as yours
> Please don't vomit your trash
> through your volcanic missile
> The less you write the more we live
> ("On Conversation", *Multicultural Symphony*, 31)

The poet is worried about the social evil of child labor that is spoiling the golden period of life of countless children. He wrote this poem after reading a newspaper report, which raised emotions in his heart for an innocent child:

> Her hellish life from dawn to midnight
> Her tender soft palms
> smooth as petals of lilies
> burnt, bruised, bled
> . . . . . . . . . . . . . . . .
> Poor lass helpless and crying
> None in the world
> to share her sorrows
> . . . . . . . . . . . . . .
> When children of her age
> strolled gaily to their schools
> tears ran like brooks
> ("Child Labour", *Multicultural Symphony*, 35-36)

Some of Dominic's poems are political and truly expose the original picture of society, but the defining feature of his poetry is that he doesn't criticize nor tries to impose his opinion on his readers; he simply presents his thinking and leaves it to readers to evaluate the right and wrong. That is the reason that he has written various poems on concurrent themes after reading the different news in newspapers, which instill in him the current of poetry. His poems like "Siachen Tragedy", "Beena's Shattered Dreams", "Mullaperiyar Dam", " Pearl's Harbour", "Drowned Dreams", "Ananthu and the Wretched Kite", "Mukesh's Destiny", Mahi's Fourth Birthday", "Tears of a World Champion", "Why is Fate So Cruel to the Poor?", "ACTS – Saviours on the Roads", " Beach Beauticians", "Agitation through Farming", and "Protest against Sand Mafia" are the reflections and outcome of his innermost feelings after reading the heart-moving and dreadful news of incidents in the daily newspaper.

Dominic is a versatile personality with numerous shades of thoughts. He is also a poet of imagination who wants to travel on the wings of time to re-enjoy his moments of merriment:

> I wish I could sit on Time's shoulder
> and fly back to my youth

> I could then be jolly
> with my friends and colleagues
> who bathed me with pure love
>
> ("I Wish I could Fly Back", *Multicultural Symphony*, 44)

He stresses noble values and ethics and condemns blindly following westernization. He thinks that we should copy merits and humanity from others but unfortunately we mimic only dress, food, and fashion. He writes:

> My countrymen fail to imitate
> noble qualities:
> industry, perseverance,
> enterprise, adventure,
> equality, fraternity,
> cleanliness, health
> love of nature
> and environment.
>
> ("Dignity of Labour", *Multicultural Symphony*, 47)

His next poem highlights the grave problem of hunger in India where many people are not getting food to fill their stomach, and on the other side, the rich are wasting it in abundance:

> Thousands of children
> are famished
> in our country
> and other countries
> day after day.
> Leftovers of the
> ten percent Haves
> can sustain
> ninety percent Havenots
> and make this hellish world
> a blissful heaven.
>
> ("Hungry Mouths", *Multicultural Symphony*, 49)

In his poems, Dominic throws light on the drawbacks and shortcomings of our education system and the low awareness of media in developing the moral character of today's youth:

> Where does our education
> lead teenage minds to?
> . . . . . . . . . . . . . . .
> Media, print and visual
> forget ethics they are bound to follow
> Instead of being a correcting force
> to all subjects and other estates
> filling minds with eternal noble values
> they inject venoms of violence
> communalism and superstitions
>
> ("Valueless Education", *Multicultural Symphony*, 57)

*Philosophical Musings for a Meaningful Life*

Dominic really deserves a bouquet of everlasting fragrant flowers and admiration for expressing his gratitude toward his shoes. He composed a poem to appreciate the enduring power of his shoes, which are carrying Dominic everywhere, the theme sounds out of imagination and reflects Dominic's attitude, which is down to earth. The incredible lines are:

> Dear my black leather shoes,
> I should prostrate over you
> for carrying seventy kilos
> for more than two years
> You are relieved only
> a few hours at nights
> Yet how little did I
> deem your service
>
> ("Musing on My Shoes", *Multicultural Symphony*, 58)

His next fantastic and stunning poem, which is mind-blowing and appeals to me a lot, is "Who am I?". The poem reveals the attitude of Dominic toward himself, which is full of humility and softness. He considers himself nothing in comparison to farmers and laborers. The lines, which he has composed in this poem, really constitute a commendable, unique, and true homage to farmers and laborers; besides, it clearly displays the transparency of his views and the beauty of his thoughts:

> "Who are you?" my superego asked
> "I am Prof. K. V. Dominic, MA, M.Phil, PhD," my id replied
> "Alright, what else?"
> "English poet, short story writer, critic, editor."
> "Keep that long tail under your armpit," superego exploded.
> "An illiterate farmer is greater than you;
> His service is greater than your scribbling;
> Labourers' sweat is dearer than your ink;
> If they strike, your writings will cease,
> and ultimately you yourself will disappear
>
> ("Who am I?", *Multicultural Symphony*, 64)

Dominic painfully writes about the situation of our soldiers who are deprived of family warmth and he calculated that the total money which is spent on defence can eradicate poverty from this earth:

> Total money spent on defence
> can wipe out poverty from the planet for ever
> Is human species so belligerent and destructive?
> Aren't the masses peace lovers,
> benevolent and compassionate?
> Why then such a huge waste
> for defence unnecessary?
> Why create tension at the borders?
>
> ("Martyrs at the Borders", *Multicultural Symphony*, 66)

His tribute to Swami Vivekanand is also remarkable and memorable one, which highlights the accomplishments of Vivekanand and makes the readers aware about it:

> Swami Vivekananda,
> the morning star of the East
> . . . . . . . . . . . . . . . . . .
> India's greatest cultural ambassador to the West
> taught his countrymen
> how to master Western science
> based on Indian spirituality
> How to adapt Western humanism
> to Indian life and culture
> ("Homage to Swami Vivekanand", *Multicultural Symphony*, 79)

Prof. Dominic has composed his poems on countless themes and it is impossible to mention each and everyone here. He melodiously sings the songs of peace and condemns violence; he is strongly against the brutal attacks made on the people by authorities for selfish gains. The poet is very keen on different aspects of man's cruelty toward all creatures. Dominic has a sharp and very sensitive conscience for the evils like inequality, dishonesty, violence, corruption, terrorism, the plight of women and aged people, the suffering of animals, birds and nature, which pierce his heart and motivate him to compose poetry.

Thus, K. V. Dominic is a poet with social awareness which is visible in almost all of his poems. The poet expresses the need for the coexistence and nurturing empathy for peaceful life on the earth. He seeks God's grace and blessings through service to mankind as he knows the fact that human beings themselves are responsible for their poor condition. Dominic's expressions are very simple in their style and meaning, which can reach the understanding of ordinary readers. He is endowed with a poetic gift by God and so he has written his gems of poetry. His poems address the entire humanity about its prevailing issues and problems in the society. He is very much inspired by Gandhi, Darwin, and Ruskin Bond, and believes that the real wealth of a nation is its citizens. Undoubtedly, the thoughts of Dominic are just like invaluable diamonds elegantly strewn in the golden necklace of his poems.

## Works Cited

Dominic, K. V. *Multicultural Symphony*. GNOSIS, New Delhi. 2014. Print.

---. *Winged Reason*. Authorspress, New Delhi. 2010. Print.

---. *Write Son, Write*. GNOSIS, New Delhi. 2011. Print.

# Chapter 9 -
# Poetry for a Better World:
# A Critical Look at the Poetry of K. V. Dominic
# by Rob Harle

K. V. Dominic recoils at the injustices and unnecessary subjugation of millions of humans. He attempts through his poetry to expose these injustices so as to raise awareness in others with the hope of making the world a better place for all.

He has published three separate volumes of his poetry, all by Authorspress, India, as well as been represented in numerous journals and anthologies. His first book *Winged Reason* was published in 2010; this was followed by *Write Son, Write* in 2011; and most recently his third book, *Multicultural Symphony* came out in 2014. The three books display a remarkable continuity in both style and subject matter. This is a rather interesting point to note, which, from my perspective, establishes Dominic's *unique* style. As he has said, "The content of the poem is most important to me. I don't mind if the lines lack the lustre of style" (*Multicultural Symphony*, 10). Further, he notes: "I adopt a conversational style in poetry, which attracts ordinary readers. Here I am influenced much by the Victorian poet Robert Browning" (*Winged Reason*, 12).

Dominic in the Preface to *Winged Reason* recalls how Seamus Heaney always critiqued his own poems; Dominic does similarly with his poems.

> As a poet, I am responsible to my own conscience and I want to convey an emotion or a message, often through social criticism. I have a commitment to my students as a professor, to the reader, scholars and writers as an editor, and to all human and non-human beings as a poet. (*Winged Reason*, 12)

Dominic suggests that his poems "lack much imagery and figures of speech." This is not altogether true, and whilst it is an excellent poet's attribute—to be honest and ethical enough to critique one's own work—it does not always mean it is an accurate appraisal. I find Dominic's poetry quite rich in imagery, sometimes brutally so. I think what he means is, his poems are "work horses" not "show ponies" as the old Western adage goes. For example, in the first poem in *Multicultural Symphony* – "Multicultural Harmony":

> As matter and spirit
> animate and inanimate
> visible and invisible
> tangible and intangible
> audible and inaudible
> movable and immovable
> are instruments multitudinous
> of His perfect symphony.

(*Multicultural Symphony*, 15)

We witness a flowing rhythm and gentle cadence. Further on, we see rich, evocative imagery and subtle metaphor invoked:

> Human world is a rose flower
> Each petal adds to its beauty
> But when petals are nipped off
> vanishes its splendour.

(Multicultural Symphony, 15)

Throughout the three books, we often experience this kind of imagery, rhythm, and of course, metaphor.

Dominic draws much of his inspiration from newspaper reports. "Sources for my themes are very often newspaper reports. I love to write more on concrete ideas than abstract ones" (*Multicultural Symphony*, 10). Further on the same page, which reinforces my "work horse" analogy, Dominic says: "I have only one motive behind my compositions—imparting some messages and values to the young minds which are groping in darkness and ignorance."

Newspaper reports may be the trigger to his poems, but it is more the content or subject matter that "itches" Dominic's mind. He sees many of the leaders—political, religious, and intellectual—as a kind of mafia, "...looting and torturing of the innocent masses, itch me almost every day and it gives birth to poems one after the other" (*Multicultural Symphony*, 9). He discusses all the different kinds of mafia in the Preface, including, forest mafia, quarry mafia, sand mafia; and this forces him to react: "through my only medium, poetry."

In the last section of the poem "Dignity of Labour" (*Multicultural Symphony*, 47), after honoring honest, decent, hardworking individuals—such as sweepers, fishermen, tailors and drivers—Dominic then compares them to the parasitic politicians, clergies, and so on, a global situation I might add, not just in India.

> Parasite politicians
> bogus sanyasis and clergies
> white-collar bureaucrats,
> corrupt and inefficient,
> models and heroes.
> and honoured by my society!

For Dominic, no unjust societal action or situation is immune from attack by his penetrating and confronting poetic mind. He is especially outraged by the harm done by the various mafias to animals and females. Numerous poems speak for the animals and nature, who cannot speak for themselves, and also for young girls, who also, because of caste or other social situations, cannot speak for themselves. All three books have poems on these themes; many are quite confronting, and occasionally, emotionally very upsetting.

The poem "Child Labour" (*Multicultural Symphony*, 36) tells the story of a young girl, Dhanalakshmi, sold to a young Advocate and his wife, who live in a luxurious house. They then work her beyond endurance torture her, then inflict an injury so horrible that the girl dies. This poem about the true circumstances published across the nation is heart breaking and "unbelievable" and so disgusting it will make an indelible mark on the reader's mind, and so it should. A few lines from the poem:

*Philosophical Musings for a Meaningful Life*

> Woke her up very early morning
> burning her hand with cigarette ends
> Starved her for sluggishness in work
> Poor lass helpless and crying
> None in the world
> to share her sorrows
> Longed for her parents call
> to take her back home
> Dreamt of a day
> lying on her ma's lap
> caressed by the loving hands.

The poem in "Nature Weeps" (*Write Son, Write*, 71) is no less powerful, but is in one sense more urgent to understand because it affects all of us, regardless of caste, wealth, or position in society. It represents an Eliotesque horrific Wasteland, which could have been avoided, but due to man's arrogance and greed was not; the first two verses:

> Crows and myanahs
> stopped visiting me
> papaya trees bear no fruit.
>
> The sun is angry
> and merciless to man:
> man goes on felling trees.

This poem reminds me of the scenario painted by Rachel Carson in her brilliant, and one hoped, lifestyle-changing book Silent *Spring*—no birds sing, no plants flower, all around the death of nature and of course eventually human beings. It is staggering that Carson clearly and emphatically showed this scenario and we have done nothing to heed the warnings. In Australia we have governments allowing the Great Barrier Reef to be used as a toxic waste dump, mining companies drilling for gas using chemical extraction (CSG), which pollutes the precious underground water table, and fossil fuel corporations holding back the development and deployment of clean energy systems—all for shareholders' greed! These are the sorts of issues Dominic's poems address; he wants the reader to become so outraged that something might be done, even if in small ways, before it is too late. Many of my own poems address these same issues.

A small number of Dominic's poems tell of personal situations, moving away from the visionary prophetic ones for society generally, such as his cats being murdered by his neighbor ("Massacre of Cats", *Write Son, Write*, 46), colleagues dying and the personal anguish this causes ("In Memoriam: George Joson", *Write Son, Write*, 17), and the death of the poet's mother, which is a heart rending poem ("An Elegy on My Ma", *Write Son, Write* 38). This poem is a lovely tribute to the poet's mother and acknowledges his debt to her love and care. In fact this book, *Write Son, Write*, is dedicated to her. The long and beautiful poem to his deceased Ma says it all:

> Ma, that smile on your face
> ripples down
> to a tsunami of
> grief in my mind.
> The glow in your eyes
> darts like lightning
> to my burning heart.

Dominic's cats were poisoned by his pious church-going neighbors. This despicable, unconscionable act has scarred Dominic and his family for life. Anyone who has witnessed an animal die from Strychnine poisoning will share his family's sadness. Dominic just hopes that a necklace of cat's bones are tied around his neighbor's neck to haunt him for this crime, just as happened to the sailor in Coleridge's Ancient Mariner. Here's one verse:

> Heartbreaking carcasses
> welled our eyes
> and tears ran
> like rivers.
> With shaking hands,
> dug a deep grave
> and buried them.

Both books, *Write Son, Write* and *Winged Reason*, have numerous illustrations in cartoon or sketch format. *Multicultural Symphony* has no illustrations and to my mind this works better as a poetry book. I have personally wrestled with the concept of including images in books of poetry and in my opinion they are better off without images. Poems are word pictures and do not really need visual pictures to tell the story; in fact, it possibly detracts from the power of the poems.

Occasional poems reflect Dominic's personal, inner philosophical musings, which balance the sometimes heavy, sometimes angst-ridden poems of all the world's woes. One such poem from *Multicultural Symphony* (p. 55) I really enjoyed is shared in its entirety below.

### Sail of Life

> My morning walk takes me
> to a tea stall
> The lone opened shop
> at the still Gandhi Square
>
> I am astonished
> by the din and bustle
> that comes out
> from all opened stalls
> in the evenings
>
> My boisterous sail will reach
> its harbour one day
> I will be astonished
> by its stillness and darkness

A further poem where Dominic wrestles with a universal conundrum is "A Spider in My Bathroom" (*Multicultural Symphony*, 52).

### A Spider in My Bathroom

> A spider in my bathroom
> To smite or spare?
> Lives on mosquitoes
> who inject me
> The creator has sent

>   it along with mosquitoes
>   Being a poet vowed
>   to love all creations
>   what shall I do?

This is the kind of thing the best poetry does—puts in words that which the non-poet would like to say and also confirms their observations and experiences of life; most of Dominic's poems fulfil this vital and essential function of poetry.

Dominic has published, in addition to his own poetry books, four edited books with critical articles on poets and poetry of established and emerging contemporary Indian poets publishing in English. He is totally committed to his writing and says, "I believe that it is my duty as a writer to promote poetry at all costs" (*Write Son, Write*, 7). Dominic believes in the power of poetry and would like to see it returned to its exalted position in society, as it was in past times. "Poetry is the earliest form of literature and poets were considered seers everywhere" (*Multicultural Symphony*, 7). He asks rhetorically, "And who will save this society? My answer is: writers, particularly poets, who are like prophets" (*Write Son, Write*, 8). This may seem like a fanciful or highly optimistic hope, but I would in turn ask, "Who else will do this?" Surely not politicians, corporate leaders, bureaucrats, the somnambulistic masses, or sports stars!

One of Dominic's most powerful, moving poems in this regard is "Victory To Thee, Mother India" (*Write Son, Write*, 43) where he laments the degradation of the once great and beautiful India. Some lines from the middle section of this long poem follow as:

>   Matha, thy name was echoed
>   in Vindhyas and the Himalayas;
>   birds, and breeze and leaves
>   chanted your name
>   but no birds are there now;
>   neither trees or pure air.
>   Yamuna, Ganga and the oceans
>   woke up then, cheered by your blessings.
>   Bearing now carcass, plastic, garbage
>   and all such filthy human trash
>   thy rivers and oceans face their death.

We learn early on at university that in critical writing it is a very bad practice to engage in criticism (or praise) *ad hominem*. In scientific or academic writing this is of course true. However, I believe in the appraisal of a poet's work, we cannot separate the poet from the poetry. It *may* be possible to do this in the case of a novel, or a work of short fiction, but poetry is very different from these genres. If the poet together with his beliefs and opinions cannot be recognised in his poems then he is indeed a poor and inauthentic poet. In Dominic's second book *Write Son, Write*, the opening poem "Write, My Son, Write" is actually a manifesto of his views and philosophy. This poem is divided into twenty-one parts, which Dominic says, "declares my views on God, Man and Nature."

From this and many other poems, we can see K. V. Dominic "wears his heart on his sleeve"; he has strong opinions about most aspects of life and does not shy away from making them heard. He is a courageous and "existentially authentic" man, who puts his vision in uncompromising terms, in black and white, for the world to read. A verse from his poem *Multicultural Harmony* Part 3 (*Multicultural Symphony*, 17) is one such example:

> Dear my fellow beings
> there's no discrimination
> of male or female in animal world
> But look at the plight of female
> in human world
> Her birth is ill omen
> Millions are butchered
> before they are born
> Parents receive her
> as burden to family
> She is destined to live
> under her brother's shadows
> Has to live on his leftover.

This does not mean of course that the poet is always correct. I find the following statement highly debatable: "The evil influence of visual media and internet dissuades people from serious thinking" (*Multicultural Symphony*, 7). Mindless use or abuse of these new media may encourage this; however, astute use, in my opinion, can actually expand and encourage deep and serious thinking. It facilitates an increased contact with others from different cultures and expands what previously was restrictive parochial thinking. I grew up in the Antipodes and the tyranny of distance was (is?) always a serious disadvantage to scholarship, art, and philosophical thinking. Dominic makes a few other broad generalisations which, as I've just stated, come through in his poems. This will invoke the ire of some readers, no doubt, but this is far more desirable than having a reader bored to distraction or fall asleep mid-poem!

Dominic believes poetry has an important role to play in molding cultured and civilized society; and I could not agree more. But as he also laments, "the tragic irony is that none listens to the poets nowadays." Herein lies our biggest problem as poets, not writing the poems so much as getting them out to the people who need to hear and understand them. There is little point in "preaching to the converted." Poetry for lovers of literature is wonderful, and of course a legitimate reason to write and publish poetry, but I believe the real task before poets in today's world is to find ways, perhaps new methods of presenting their work to the general public. This is where using the Internet, with its social media and instant communication can be very helpful and productive. There is actually an increase in poetry readership due to the Internet; perhaps quality may suffer, if we compare this with the stale, stuffy journals of the academic literature establishment, but the message is being distributed to a far greater audience than previously possible.

Change occurs slowly in all societies because they are basically conservative, so the most we can hope for as activist poets, of which Dominic is surely one, and poets who still have some Dylan Thomas "rage" left is to get our work read so it enters the "dumped down" minds of the global general public and eventually brings about positive change.

K. V. Dominic's poems are important additions to literature and to the growing global movement to bring about positive change and equality for all individuals. The injustices he confronts in his poems are the arrows and thorns that pierce his heart everyday and the gushing blood that runs through his pen to paper. They are the fuel that keeps his "fire in the belly" burning and the world is a much better place because of his labors.

## Works Cited

Dominic, K. V. *Multicultural Symphony*. New Delhi: GNOSIS, 2014. Print.

---. *Winged Reason*. New Delhi: Authorspress, 2010. Print.

---. *Write Son, Write*. New Delhi: GNOSIS, 2011. Print.

# Chapter 10 -
# A Requiem for the Disconsolate:
# K. V. Dominic's Poetry as a Social-Criticism
# by Dr. J. Pamela

Requiem as a literary form is significant for it is the mark of respect and love the living hold for the dead and the dear things lost. The Merriam-Webster Dictionary describes it as "a solemn chant (as a dirge) for the repose of the dead" as well as "something that resembles such a solemn chant." Twentieth century saw the evolution of several new kinds of requiems. While the genre of War requiem has many compositions to its credit, others like environmental poetry, the Holocaust Requiem, requiems on the World War, on particular incidents like earthquakes and other natural disasters were also written. The contemporary practice applies the literary form in discussion to any context that befits its subject matter. Thus the current-day scenario makes it a fit literary vehicle to convey a mature individual's acceptance of life, the temporal nature of human life and the transcending nature of time, which can never be triumphed.

Professor K. V. Dominic, the poet, wonders at the power that human experience exerts on life—desirable or undesirable—in his *Winged Reason* (2010), *Write Son, Write* (2011), and *Multicultural Symphony* (2014), all compilations of his poems. The poet's meanderings into the various aspects of life, the multifarious experiences that inspire change in a very sensitive being, which usually transforms itself into poetic expression, are obvious in the verses. In fact, in "My Teenage Hobby", the poet seems to make a confession to his readers about the source of his poetry. His "Reflections on life / became my pastime" (*Winged Reason*, 48) is a clear demonstration that his poetry unfolds his deliberations on life.

The poet's requiems for the dead and the lost lament not the physical loss, but the honest values—humane, philosophical, or ethical—that have made them worth a mention. More than beauty, the bounty of Nature, and the cheerful aspects of life and love, the poet appears to be wounded by the mortal pain and suffering that suffocates basic human existence. As Aju Mukhopadhyay opportunely states in the blurb to *Write Son, Write*: "Almost all his poems tell us that he never writes a poem to express sheer beauty, passion for possession, spiritual aspiration, or aesthetic pleasure. He is a realist with deep social feelings. Human sufferings make his heart bleed; loss of freedom suffocates him." This social consciousness of K. V. Dominic is hailed as his chief forte by P. C. K. Prem in his foreword to *Write Son, Write* (*Write Son, Write*, 11).

According to K. V. Dominic, "Poetry is the best and easiest medium of imparting messages and values to the people" (Preface, *Multicultural Symphony*, 7). The poet is more than a master of words adept at constructing written magic. He is a social critic who employs his expertise as a poet to impart his message to the reader. His aim—a reformation in society—is an elevated one; his manner—mournful for those lost—is sincere; and his method is the lofty form of poetry, which is simple.

K. V. Dominic is a multifaceted personality. His poems are social criticisms, sometimes scathing, sometimes gentle. A die-hard non-vegetarian for many years, he adapts to Gandhian ideals and changes to a vegetarian. He confidently declares, "Though I am a Christian by birth, I believe in Advaita" (Preface, *Multicultural Symphony*, 8).

The poet, in his simplicity and treatment of subject matter, reflects R. K. Narayan's literary style. The subjects are not of exalted proportions, nor does he write of abstract phenomena that a layman would find difficult to discern. One will find familiar things, normal men and women with their natural imperfections, and social issues that sweep the ordinary man off his routine. The poet's sensitivity to the world around him often expresses itself in the form of a mournful verse. For, though the foibles anger him, he takes a compassionate look at these maladies. As Prem says, the poems' "delicate treatment stirs sensitive hearts, and delicately but brusquely speaks for all of us" (Foreword, *Write Son, Write,* 11). The aforesaid trend, which is the modus operandi of K. V. Dominic, reminds one of an attribute that is typically Narayanesque—the method of portraying the macrocosm through his pictures of the microcosm.

In fact, in his *Multicultural Consciousness in the Novels of R. K. Narayan*, the poet, in his own words, says, "Through the social portrait of a single region, Narayan succeeds in presenting the larger picture of Indian society...." (66). His poems—sometimes of the microcosmic Kerala, the rural, at other times of a small-town fictitious setting—are able to speak for the entire nation. The evils of corruption, lack of love, selfishness, egotism, materialism, exploitation of all kinds, and poverty manifest themselves in different forms in his poems. In spite of the indignation that K. V. Dominic's verses display, one finds in them the predominance of his humanitarianism. His unconditional love for all beings sends forth a message, as Prem states: "if man loves all, he will never hurt or impair even beasts or snakes, for love knows no barriers" (Foreword, *Write Son, Write,* 13). Tragically, this is an impossible feat in the contemporary world and hence the poet's requiems.

Though the poet's goodwill suffers discouragement, his diehard optimism evolves amidst the failure to make "a call to the soul of [a] man to awaken to harsh truths" (Prem, Foreword, *Write Son, Write,* 15). This is actually the agenda of the requiem mode. A prayer to bring peace to a soul and solace to those pained by the loss is accompanied by optimistic thoughts about the living world which still requires those do-gooders to perpetuate all forms of life and sanity.

K. V. Dominic's *Winged Reason* is introduced in the publisher's blurb as a collection of poems "about losses." The poetry reveals the different kinds of losses that human beings undergo during their lifetime. The poet mourns the dead as well as the living dead—those who have lost very precious moments, persons, and values. His requiem transcends the loss and tries to make amends for it whereby others may be spared the pain and suffering. A definite sense of sincere social outlook is evident in all his poems. The poet is deeply hurt by the society and the evils in it. He strives through his requiems to undo the damage that misguided principles and malformed minds do to those around them and the society in which they live.

The title "Winged Reason" itself has a paradox in it. It refers to the poet's flights of fancy. Actually, it is the poet's wanderings into reality, exploiting the vehicle of fantasy. The poems, as the poet himself states in his introduction to *Write Son, Write*, are records of real life incidents that the poet had seen, heard, or read. Rather than favor the beauty of Nature and its elevating powers, the poet acknowledges the loving and the lost, commends the unappealing but compassionate, and appreciates the valuable and concrete. He is convinced of his duty as a poet and declares, "As a poet, I am responsible to my own conscience and I want to convey an emotion or a message often through social criticism" (Preface, *Winged Reason*, 12). The poems in these collections are social criticisms. He critiques the society, the routine, the contemporary scenario, the headlines that may make the day for a few while it may report others' life. Hence, his "conversational style" with his poems, lacking in "imagery and other figures of speech" (*Winged Reason* 12). His audience is those ordinary people whom the poet prefers to reach through his "winged reason" and bring about a social change. The unmistakable influence of many poets—the Romantic Blake, Wordsworth, Shelley, and Keats, the Victorian Browning, Tennyson, and Arnold, and the American Frost and Dickenson—is evident in his writings. More so is the inspiration he derives from the Indian stalwarts in verse like Ezekiel, Jayanta Mahapatra, and Kamala Das (Preface, *Winged Reason*, 15).

"In Memoriam: George Joson" is a poem already titled an elegy by K. V. Dominic. The poet's heart heaves in sorrow for the departed colleague. The untimely death and the listlessness of the dead friend's family move him. The elegiac tone adds to the immeasurable grief of the poet. He philosophizes thus:

> life is uncertain
> for the mighty and the meek
> but the labour
> of the potent and the weak
> grants it certainty.
>
> (*Winged Reason*, 17)

The poem ends with the typical Christian idea of humbling before the Creator's will:

> We are all
> bound by His will
> to be here
> or to be away.
>
> (*Winged Reason*, 18)

It echoes the Biblical "may your will be done . . . ." (Matt. 6.10). The fact that the loss cannot be undone is a clear message. Hence, the poet's call to bow down to the inevitable.

"Long Live E. K. Nayanar" is also titled an elegy written about the Chief Minister of Kerala. The poem reveals that he is the "man of the masses". His popularity is overshadowed by his being "a rare species / compassion and love / and epitome of Socialism" (*Winged Reason*, 19). The poet is moved more by E. K. Nayanar as a true human being than as a powerful person. Even after his death, the poet nutures hope for him. He assures himself and the reader, "You will continue to steer / the ship of our dear nation / to the land of blessings and bounties" (*Winged Reason*, 20).

"A Blissful Voyage" may be called a direct inspiration of S. T. Coleridge. Bacchus is invoked when the poet delivers "Let my mind soar high / on the wings of the Muses" (*Winged Reason* 21). His life/death poem calls for the God of wine to anoint him. The "voyage" is the wish list—the wish to fly to the United States, to fetch the skeletons from Iraq, to meet Gandhi, to become a bullet. The desperate yearning of the poet to do the needful to a fretting society is evident and this is the "semblance of truth sufficient to procure for these shadows of imagination that willing suspension of disbelief for the moment" (*Biographia Literaria*, XIV). Even pathos in the hands of the poet gets a different treatment. He invokes the dead and the defeated. His anger is obvious when he wishes to visit the "inaccessible places." In his wish to "plead all prophets / to inspire and instill humanism / in millions' communal minds" (*Winged Reason*, 21) is proof that his poems are an adoration as well as a yearning.

"A Nightmare" (*Winged Reason*, 22–23) is an example of the nightmare that the disparity between rich and the poor project. The contradiction found between the unhappy rich and the content poor is a thought-provoking one. Rather than seeing the abundance and scarcity of the materialistic wealth, the poem takes a novel view of the thirsting for love in the rich and its abundance in the poor. This unusual perspective of the poet highlights the farce in this.

"Beauty" may well be called an elegy to beauty, for the poem actually focuses on the transcendental nature of physical beauty. While "It fades and decays as a flower does" (*Winged Reason*, 28), the poet reiterates that "Eternal beauty in achievements eternal" (*Winged Reason*, 28).

Though "Cuckoo Singing" appears to be an appreciation of the bird's "Sweetest song in Nature" (*Winged Reason*, 30), the poet alters course to lure the reader back to reality. The poem ends with a:

> Yes, Cuckoo lives
> singing and loving,
> while man exists
> sweating and moaning.
>
> (*Winged Reason*, 30)

The exuberant song of the bird also ends with a philosophical note reminding one of the struggles that man continues to put up against poverty to earn his livelihood.

"Gayatri's Solitude" once again describes the plight of an eighty-two year old octogenarian who is described as "An old lily flower / pale and faded" (*Winged Reason*, 31). The poem is a reminder of the lifestyle of many elders who have been abandoned in old-age homes. The lost bliss of having mothered five children, who are rich in number but poverty-stricken in love, is very obvious in this poem. The final lines "How lucky were her parents / Lived happy, died happy" (*Winged Reason*, 31) shows how times have changed bringing reformation in lifestyle and scarcity in love. The aforesaid lines succinctly sum up the poet's song of sorrow.

While the old Gayatri is abandoned by her children, in "Tsunami Camps", humanity marauded by the tidal waves has been abandoned by hope itself. The relief funds and donations are pirated by the corrupt authorities and what remains is the "Unending wails and unending sobs" of the suffering men and women to which "not even gods listen . . ." (*Winged Reason*, 34).

In "I am Just a Mango Tree", the tree, which has 'fulfilled the Creator's plan', seems to have adapted the Christian ideology of total submission to His will. Yet, when cut, it pains to hear the tree lament to its creator "Did you create him [man] / to disturb this earth's balance" (*Winged Reason*, 41). The eco-consciousness of the poet is evident in the anxious words of the tree.

"International Women's Day" does not laud the day for its uniqueness. Rather, the poet accuses man for the inhuman treatment meted out to the other half of the population. The poet rages:

> She is always the other.
> Patriarchy is his product;
> he dictates the world;
> dictates even God, and corrupts religion.
> He writes scriptures,
> makes sexism predestinate.
>
> (*Winged Reason*, 43)

"What a Birth" can be read in tandem with the previous one. The final lines "Dawn for doom / Dusk to damn / what a birth" (*Winged Reason*, 58) is a woman's bitter memoir of life. The poet is cynical about the irredeemable condition of women and his dirge bemoans it.

The poet praises the laborer in his "Lal Salaam to Labour" by referring to them as "the backbone of the country" (*Winged Reason*, 44). But the society errs in not giving them their due. The poet implores:

> Give them at least their due;
> the more we give, the more we get;
> Put charity in humanity

*Philosophical Musings for a Meaningful Life*　　　　　　　　　　　　　　　　　　　　　　　　89

a spiritual bliss that never dies.

(*Winged Reason*, 45)

The social empathy that emanates from a mind brimming over with humanistic concerns is manifest in these words.

"Laxmi's Plea" actually is the poet's beseeching the society at large to banish the all-pervasive evil, namely dowry. Almost all Indian households are familiar with this vice that involves heavy investing, and one that the poet calls "a stumbling block" to many marital arrangements. Dowry becomes biggest hassle for many Indian brides. It appears satirical given that many of these women are employed. Distressed, with broken dreams, Laxmi resigns to her fate thus: "I have pricked my bubble of dreams; / let none dream for me" (*Winged Reason*, 47).

"Old Age" is one powerful poem that exhibits the truth of life. While youth is merely an adoration of happiness, it is old age that turns a person conscious to the full circle of life with reminiscences, unadulterated by ego, power, or grandeur. With a few lines, he succinctly sums up the completion of the cycle of human life:

> Old age begins to play its colours—
> The monarch of yesterday,
> feels humbled today.
> Imprisoned amidst unripe ripeness;
> utterly helpless.

(*Winged Reason*, 51)

The contemporary practice of being ungrateful and troublesome to old parents is criticized and the final lines point to the irony of human life and act as portents to the younger generation: "Today's torturer / tomorrow's victim; / we live with ironies" (*Winged Reason*, 52).

The poet is witty enough to make the reader smile at the plight of god himself. In "Onam", it is the legendary Maveli who returns to visit Kerala, where "equality prevailed" when he had ruled. Pathetically, the current circumstances do not permit the 'once so powerful ruler' to rejoice and, "Fed up he / he returns in tears" (*Winged Reason*, 54). The revelation that Maveli is also a victim of grief justifies the fact that even gods require a requiem!

The poet is alive to the irony that exists especially between man and the wild. In "Sleepless Nights", his conscious nature makes a mockery of man, who lives in his "safe cell":

> fighting against the man-made heat,
> and the dreary sound of the hot-wave fan.
> The late and heavy supper in stomach,
> and all such unnatural ways of life.

(*Winged Reason*, 56)

On the other hand, the cuckoo lies in his "God-given bed; with gentle breeze caressing him and nocturnal music lulling him to a sound sleep, "free from cares and worries" (*Winged Reason*, 56). The bird wakes the man out of his cell by it's melodious call A similar satiric situation is found in "Human Brain". While animals, with their five senses live a life where "past never haunts, / nor their future" (*Winged Reason*, 59), man, God's creation of distinction, dwells in his past and frets over it. The poet's caustic implication, in short, is that 'Human brain which makes him unique is his bane as well!'

The poet's conscientiousness reacts not only to human suffering but extends to animal life as well. In "Ammini's Lament", he mourns the death of his kittens. More so does he suffer for the wails of the dead kittens' mother, Ammini. He compares her cries to the legendary queen Gandhari's wails.

The poet's fascination for the "Ancient Mariner" is a notable aspect. He avers, "Destined like the 'Ancient Mariner' / I'm desperate for the purging amends" (*Winged Reason*, 63). Like Jesus' apostles—who bore witness to his miracles, his strife, death and resurrection—the poet raises himself off the common man to voice the truth--the evils of society, the quirks of man, the imperfections in Nature, and the sorrow that all these cause. His composition bemoans the love and grace of those dead men, things, and values. His grief is the result of his great love for the society. In fact, in "Ammini's Demise", he pleads, "God, make them humane / and turn them into angels" (*Winged Reason*, 65). Once again it is a reminder of the Ancient Mariner's noble "And I blessed them unaware" (Coleridge, IV. 62), about the repulsive creatures from the sea in his "The Rime of the Ancient Mariner." The Ancient Mariner's love, doing penance and the noble gesture of blessing are being re-enacted in K. V. Dominic's poetry.

Though K. V. Dominic's poetic adventure harps on simplicity, yet, the voracious poet in him often tries a hand at different stylistics. In "Om", he defines the sound 'Om' thus: "It's a celestial music" (*Winged Reason*, 66). He compares 'Om', "representing Vishnu, Shiva, Brahma, and meaning Brahman" (*Winged Reason*, 66), with 'manna', the Christian idea of the heavenly food that fed thousands of Israelites on their way back from Egypt and slavery (*Good News Bible*, Exod. 16: 1-16). This metaphysical pursuit of bringing together two diametrically opposite ideas and finding in them a common focus, which is a socially unifying one, is typically the poet's own.

The educationist and academician in the poet dominate his poetic outpour in "Solar Eclipse" when he challenges the disgruntling forces by his words: "the Sun of Knowledge / can never be eclipsed / by the moon of ignorance" (*Winged Reason*, 67). Yet, society is rife with corruption so that his concluding lines, "Fair is foul / and foul is fair", sing a song of sorrow to the virtuous and the eligible few.

The poet is disheartened about the corruptions in society and crestfallen by the "criminal action done / in the name of God" (*Winged Reason*, 69). In a melodramatic end to his dirge on the corruptions in society, God is cast away in his own name:

> God is dethroned
> in the name of God.
> And human gods are crowned
> in the name of God.
>
> (*Winged Reason*, 70)

Amidst the moral chaos in society, the rural world charms the poet by its innocence and malice-free life. "City Versus Village" may be called an ode to village life. In this verse of adoration, the social critic finds room for nailing the city-dwellers by describing them as "Each one lost / in his own island" (*Winged Reason*, 71).

The Gandhian in him rises up to the chance to pay his respects to a departed Gandhian, the "rarest gem", in "Kaumudi Teacher is No More". 'Kaumudi Teacher', "The beacon which guided many women / was destroyed by the wave of Time" (*Winged Reason*, 74). Once again this is a tragic poem, which reiterates that time reigns and even the best of human beings have to succumb to it.

In his second collection of poems, titled *Write Son, Write* (2011), K. V. Dominic sends a decisive message to his readers. It is his Creator's voice that had bid him to write by 'His' invocative words in "Write, My Son, Write"—the longest poem in the book with twenty-one parts and seventeen pages: "My Son, / I have a mission in your creation" (*Write Son, Write* 21).

The poet's "Elegy on My Ma" is the heart-rending anguish of a son bemoaning the loss of his mother. After the pain, loss by death and the reminders of a past that can never be undone, the poet philosophies thus: "It's better not to fret on morrow; / Surrender unto Him who created you" (*Write Son, Write* 41). His mother's words as they echo through his poems are biblical in tone. The

*Philosophical Musings for a Meaningful Life*

Christian idea of surrendering to God's will completely is very clearly stated. This tone is prevalent all through his poems and lends itself to the solemn construction.

The poet's "Massacre of Cats" is more a prayer for the salvation of those sinners, his neighbors. As a reminder of their heinous crime of poisoning his cats, he wants them to make amends. He says,

> Let my neighbours expiate,
> dig out skeletons
> of my cats;
> tie them to their necks as Coleridge's
> ancient mariner
> did a century back
> since he killed
> the ominous albatross.
>
> (*Write Son, Write*, 46)

It reminds one of Coleridge's "Rime" where the "soft voice" announces "... 'the man hath penance done, / And penance more will do'" (Coleridge, "Rime", V. 117–118).

The poem "Attachment" encourages the reader to draw a parallel with the dramatic monologue. It is not only because of the style but also because the poet questions his own actions, struggling to judge himself amidst turbulent emotions. The loss of a cat makes him question his own feelings thus: "Why is man so over-sentimental? / Why is he too much attached / to earthly and finite things?" (*Write Son, Write*, 52). At the end, he surrenders himself to God. He sincerely solicits, "God, teach me how to detach" (*Write Son, Write*, 52). The poet ventures to overcome by his prayer the human shortcoming of being attached to fellow beings.

Whenever wrath of a just kind descends on him, the poet seems to equip himself with metaphysical arms. He shocks the reader by calling in 'Mahavishnu' for aid. In "Aung San Suu Kyi – Asia's Lady Mandela", he pleads with one of the Hindu Trinity:

> will you descend to Myanmar
> in any perfidious guise you choose;
> as you descended in Kerala
> when Maveli ruled there;
> and envious of his golden rule,
> stamped him to the underworld.
>
> (*Write Son, Write*, 53)

Then he lays a bargain: "Here is your chance to expiate; / dispatch the tyrants and / release the dove from the cage" (*Write Son, Write*, 53). This is a metaphor referring to the South Asian tyrants and the dove is Aung San Suu Kyi. He tries to bring together the legendary tale of Hindu gods and their animosity in a small state in India with the struggle for power in a part of the subcontinent with the political struggle between the armed forces and a lone woman.

K. V. Dominic excels in his witty repartees. In "God is Helpless", God is in a pitiful state that he has to be sympathised with. While the congregation wails to Him to save them from the inclement heat and drought, God, in return, pleads for a favor. Plants and animals had already complained about the irresponsibility of man, and the trouble and destruction that he has caused them. And lastly they had even prayed to God to call back man in order to save their lives. This is actually God's jeremiad which may know no end. (*Write Son, Write*, 63–65)

The Nature-lover that K. V. Dominic is, he persistently sings praises of Nature. But to his horror, the bounty and beauty is evicted by man. The harmonious bond, which is most important between man and Nature, is weakened by man's selfishness and callousness. The poet's dirge to the bounteous nature is "Nature Weeps" (*Write Son, Write*, 71–74).

Another significant aspect of K. V. Dominic's poetry is the accolades he pays to "labour". Being a Gandhian, R. K. Narayan planned the storyline of *The Vendor of Sweets* in such a way that "The Gandhian principles of self-reliance, ahimsa, as well as the dignity of labour are established in Jagan's way of life" (Dominic, *Multicultural Consciousness*, 133). Like R. K. Narayan, the poet hails the laborer. His ode to the hard worker lauds his/her "fight against fate" (*Write Son, Write*, 75) thus:

> Dignity and self-respect--
> she takes as greatest wealth.
> Her resolution reminds me
> of Wordsworth's Leech Gatherer
> and Hemingway's Santiago.
>
> (*Write Son, Write*, 76)

K. V. Dominic's critique of human beings, the animal kingdom, or Nature has an appreciative side too. But a close reading of his poems reveals that he is merciless in reviewing the government and the power structures. They receive a scathing criticism from this socially-conscious poet, whose verses reveal that he is also socially responsible. The title "Rocketing Growth of India" sounds like a compliment. But in contradiction, the poet's scrutinizing eye focuses on the corrupt government in the concluding lines:

> Still Government and leaders
> Beguile innocent millions
> Rocketing growth of our country,
> A wonder to the whole world!
>
> (*Write Son, Write*, 78)

K. V. Dominic's fortitude to challenge the powerful, the bureaucracy, as well as injustice and those who perpetuate atrocities in the name of God is a noteworthy aspect of his poems. His "To My Colleague" is a fine example of his courageous onslaught on one significant contemporary evil namely "religious fanaticism". Having been closely associated with a friend and colleague "TJ", he has composed this requiem aptly after "India's sixty-fourth Independence Day" to mark the brutal attack on "TJ" by religious fanatics. He appeals to India thus:

> India, my independent country!
> Largest democracy in the world!
> . . . . . . . . . . . . . . . . . . . .
> Where is freedom of speech
> and expression?
>
> (*Write Son, Write*, 84)

He also appreciates "TJ" for his "convictions strong and unyielding will" (*Write Son, Write*, 83).

A similar incident is recorded by K. V. Dominic in his "Train Blast": "Another heinous act / of Maoists" (*Write Son, Write*, 85). The poet, who has been inspired by great thinkers, writers, and religious leaders, bemoans the brainwashed terrorists:

> Misquote Marx
> Lenin, Mao:
> Utopian ends;
> Diabolic means.

*Philosophical Musings for a Meaningful Life*                                              93

(*Write Son, Write*, 85)

His conscientious heart wails thus: "How can I ease in / sambhavani Yuge Yuge?" (*Write Son, Write*, 86).

Water, the "elixir of life" that has become scarce, moves the poet to compose this poem, whose title "Water, Water, Everywhere...." echoes the Ancient Mariner's lament when stranded on the ocean. The condition is so miserable that the poet, as if in delirium, beholds apparitions like the old Mariner did in Coleridge's "The Rime": millions of lives exterminated, wrinkled faces, sore and scaly-skinned beings, women like shaved-headed ghosts (*Write Son, Write*, 91–92).

K. V. Dominic's third collection of poems *Multicultural Symphony* (2014) begins with "Multicultural Harmony", where the poet accuses man of bringing in disharmony in a naturally harmonious setting. His lines below refer to the one burning issue in feminist circles namely 'objectification' of women:

> Why is she viewed
> as a consumer product?
> Why do you look at her
> with lascivious eyes?"

(*Multicultural Symphony*, 20)

The poet in his "Siachen Tragedy" once again criticizes the government for its thoughtlessness. Referring to the Siachen Tragedy that occurred in the heights of the Himalayas, killing with its avalanche many soldiers and civilians, he implores to the government, "Isn't it high time the governments / stopped challenging benevolent Nature?" (*Multicultural Symphony*, 24). His argument is that people have tried to control Nature and hence have lost much goodness drawn from it.

The poet is able to glean great philosophical truths through the life and death of his pet kittens, a recurring subject in all three of his poetry collections. In "Cohabitance on the Planets", he is angry that there is no law to punish his neighbor who poisoned his kittens But he believes the truth that in the end, "Empty handed we come / empty handed we go" (*Multicultural Symphony*, 28). He extends the idea by paying his respects to Darwin in "Charles Darwin, Patron Saint of Animals", the poet makes a noble plea to mankind: "Rational man will deem his / relation to the animal world, / respect their claims for coexistence" (*Multicultural Symphony*, 32).

"On Conservation" is a witty retort that a "passive sheet of paper" gives to the poet who prepares to write. The paper that has a soul as vibrant as the poet's makes a solemn request thus: "Kindly write on the need of the day / the necessity of conservation / of plants and animals on earth" (*Multicultural Symphony*, 31).

While the poet insists on the dignity of the laborer and labor, he also takes a newer perspective of it. "Child Labour" (*Multicultural Symphony*, 35–36) is the pathetic tale of the child laborer, a girl of eleven, sold for a small sum of money, who finally succumbs to the corporeal punishment of her masters. In "Dignity of Labour", the poet harshly condemns the Indian habit of aping the westerners. While man aimlessly imitates the western life in dress, food, and other sensory pleasures, western virtues like "industry, perseverance, enterprise, adventure, equality, fraternity, cleanliness, health, love of nature, and environment. (*Multicultural Symphony*, 47) are seldom appreciated. This hypocrisy is condemned by the poet.

K. V. Dominic's wish-list returns once again in his "I Wish I could Fly Back" (*Multicultural Symphony*, 44), with a yearning to "fly back to the past" to the "tsunami" of his mother's love. The pre-Raphaelite quality of linking the devastating tidal waves to the heavenly love of his mother can never go unnoticed. The poem is also a reminder of the truth that "Time waits for none."

The media also comes under the perusal of the socially-conscious poet who scorns the debacle of valueless education in his "Valueless Education." Adolescents being misguided by the media that "inject venoms of violence / communalism and superstitions" is being targeted by the poet. He takes a kindly look at the young and innocent minds who "are bewitched by their illusion" (*Multicultural Symphony*, 57).

"Thodupuzha Municipal Park" illustrates the poet's frustration at how the ecosystem has been tampered with by man whom the poet blames as having dug his own grave as well as other beings'. The ideal park of Thodupuzha is a haven for the local residents who throng from their burning humid houses to cool and refresh their minds and bodies. The poet is also reminded of the joyful times with his children at the park. But now with a heavy heart, he admits "Anxiety of their future welfare has replaced / peace and happiness that haunted in our house" (*Multicultural Symphony*, 71). The poet's method of associating peace and happiness in a house with the quality of being haunted is singular—a metaphysical style that recurs in several poems.

"A Tribute to Sakuntala Devi" is in praise of the "Human Computer", Sakuntala Devi, a child prodigy. K. V. Dominic gives kudos to her and pines for the genius who is no more:

> Marvel to the East and the West
> her loss is literally irreplaceable
> Praise to the Almighty
> for His revelation through the human brain!
> (*Multicultural Symphony*, 76)

The poet is a kind of modern conductor to these requiems he has composed and "sung" in honor of those whose lives are filled with strife, of those whose lives deserve an honor befitting as noble a composition as a requiem. The simplicity of the language that expresses great loss and colossal damage reminds one of the ease with which the unadorned prose of R. K. Narayan facilitates understanding. K. V. Dominic never fails to impress the reader with his conversational mode and direct approach.

God's message to the poet in his "Work is Worship" is actually K. V. Dominic's sincere message to all. He appeals to his readers, "live in Karma, / love all creations, / for I[God] am in everything" (*Multicultural Symphony*, 96). While the reader tries to understand the solemnity of the situation, the poet pays his respects to the departed. His requiems are therapeutic, for they console the losers; they are philosophic, for they impart truths of value; they have a fire in them, one that strives to change the society and which inspires the reader with the poet's will and his poetic prowess.

## Works Cited

Coleridge, Samuel Taylor. *Biographia Literaria*. 1807. Web. 8 July 2014. <http://www.online-literature.com/coleridge/biographia-literaria/14/>.

---. "The Rime of the Ancient Mariner." 1834. Web. 8 July 2014. <http://www.poetryfoundation.org/poem/173253>.

Dominic, K. V. Multicultural Consciousness in the Novels of R. K. Narayan. New Delhi: Authorspress, 2012. Print.

---. *Multicultural Symphony*. New Delhi: GNOSIS, 2014. Print.

---. Preface. *Multicultural Symphony*. New Delhi: GNOSIS, 2014. Print.

---. Preface. *Winged Reason*. New Delhi: Authorspress, 2010. Print.

---. *Winged Reason*. New Delhi: Authorspress, 2010. Print.

---. *Write Son, Write*. New Delhi: GNOSIS, 2011. Print.

*Good News Bible: Today's English Version*. 1966. 4th ed. 1976. New York: Society of St. Paul, 1979. Print.

Prem, P. C. K. Foreword. *Write Son, Write*. By K. V. Dominic. New Delhi: GNOSIS, 2011. Print.

"Requiem." *Merriam-Webster.com*. Merriam-Webster, n.d. Web. 5 July 2014. <http://www.merriam-webster.com/dictionary/requiem>

# Chapter 11 -
# Poetry for a Meaningful Life:
# A Critical Analysis of K. V. Dominic's Poetry
# by Bhaskar Roy Barman

I will try to locate Prof. Dr. K. V. Dominic's philosophical musings in the three poetry collections that I have just now in my hands. All the books are published by Authorspress, New Delhi. They are *Winged Reason* (first collection), published in 2010, *Write Son, Write* (second collection), published in 2011, and *Multicultural Symphony* (third collection), published in 2014.

I will take up the three poetry collections one by one in the order of the years of their publication and pick on a selection of the poems to investigate in order to unveil his philosophical musings, keeping in view the constraint on space. The remaining poems I have left out, I aver, contain a suspicion of his philosophical musing. We cannot bring ourselves to deny the fact that every poem, whoever writes it, is infused with the poet's philosophical thought and his personal idea, because the life human beings live is itself a philosophy.

I shall take up for discussion the first poetry collection *Winged Reason*, which the poet has dedicated to his (late) father, Varghese Kannapilly. Let us, to begin with, hear what the poet himself says apropos of his first poetry collection, *Winged Reason*, in the preface. He tells his readers of how and why he plunged into writing poetry at the age of forty-eight. His sudden desire to write poetry emanated from the question his wife flung at him when he was close on forty-eight years: Why did the poetic muse elude him even at this age?

The question that might sound commonplace sent spurting out the poet's dormant craving into poetic articulation. His poetic craving, though dormant, was drinking imperceptibly in the nectar of Jayanta Mahapatra's poetry. When given the upward thrust by the question of his wife, which was asked, I think casually, his poetic craving erupted into a concrete articulation in his poetry. Of his own poetry, says the poet: "As a poet I am responsible to my own conscience and I want to convey an emotion or a message often through social criticism" (*Winged Reason*, 12). Mr Pronab Kumar Majumder, editor, *Bridge-in-Making*, Kolkata, seconds this assertion in his foreword to the collection by saying: "Prof. K.V. Dominic, a faculty member of the Post Graduate Department of English, Newman College, Thodupuzha, Kerala, India, and the editor of the reputed (sic) bi-annual journal of Postcolonial Literatures, is a sensitive and compassionate man whose sensitiveness and compassion are abundantly manifested in his poems" (*Winged Reason*, 7). Dominic confesses that he gives priority to the content of his poem over its style. This admission explains) the absence of "much imagery and other figures of speech" from his poetry.

In the light of his assertion and admission, we shall proceed to analyze the selection of the poems in this and the other two collections.

This poetry collection, *Winged Reason*, begins with an elegy to his colleague George Joson in the poem "In Memoriam: George Joson". In the poem, the poet philosophizes on death and innocence of a child vis-à-vis death. The child does not know what death is and what it means to the other members of the family left behind.

> The most painful was the sight
> when your youngest kid,
> not knowing what (had) happened,
> kissed your face
> again and again
> and plucked flowers
> from your wreaths;
> tossed them to her sisters weeping and screaming.
>
> *(Winged Reason*, 17)

Note how the poet philosophizes on the innocence of a child when a death has occurred before him/her. When his/her sisters are mourning piteously for their dead father, the youngest child was taking out flowers from the wreaths placed on the dead body and indulge in throwing them at his/her "weeping and screaming" sisters. The death appears to him/her as something to rejoice at, because it was the first time since his/her birth that he/she had experienced such a thing. Only a child can live such innocence.

The next three lines carry a spiritual overtone and a hint of the poet's belief in the immortality of the soul:

> What game He plays!
> When He comes riding His chariot,
> None can say – 'Wait'.
>
> *(Winged Reason*, 17)

"When He comes riding His chariot" sounds Tennysonian. Here, "He" refers to God, the pilot of the chariot ("ship" in the case of Tennyson), comes down to guide the soul of Joson back to his original home, the eternity from which he had come down to visit the world just for a few days as a guest. We are all, as was Joson, guests to stay just for a few days in this world and shall return to our original home, the eternity.

The second poem "Long Live E. K. Nayanar" is another elegy to E. K. Nayanar, a former Chief Minister, who was guided back to his eternal home. The poet showers all his love and encomium on E. K. Nayanar for being "an epitome of socialism".

In the poem "Blissful Voyage", the poet abandons himself to fits of philosophizing on different aspects of social milieu and dreaming of possessing the supernatural power of soaring high "on the wings of the Muses" to visit the places which, he knows, are "inaccessible" and flying out like "mallard" to "the States" to "shake hands with Obama" and thank "my American sisters and brothers". He wishes he had "had the claws of a vulture" so that he could "fetch the skeletons from Iraq" and "build a bone-palace" to imprison Bush in. The poet takes on a soft tone toward the end of the poem in wishing he could fly like an angel to plead with all prophets—

> to inspire and instill humanism
> in millions' communal minds.
>
> *(Winged Reason*, 21)

—and returns to his hostile tone in the concluding lines of the poem, as he wishes he were a bullet to be shot—

> . . . into the chest of that terrorist
> who compels that teenage boy
> to explode and kill that innocent mob.
>
> *(Winged Reason*, 21)

The poem "A Sheep's Wail", when read, is sure to lead the reader to liken it to one of the confessions of Thomas De Quincey. Thomas De Quincey, as we all know, left an autobiographical account in his famous book *Confessions of an English Opium-Eater* about the effect of laudanum, a solution of opium and alcohol, on his life; it was published in 1821. The sheep of this poem addresses the tales of his grievances to "man" which is, let us assume, the poet himself. The "man" of the poem, if you do not mind me saying this, is you or me, too. The sheep exhorts the man, here the poet, to "hark" to the wail of his "enslaved" sheep. Possessed of special powers, brain, and tongue "you conquered us". The sheep does not let slip the opportunity to mock at man's weakness in the face of microbes. Though he boasts of his superiority to inferior animals like sheep, he is "inferior" to the "microbes that kill you." Then the sheep sets out to direct the attention of the man—I mean the poet, you, or me—to the cruelties toward him in the lines:

> The fur God gave me
> mercilessly you shear
> to make you cosy.
>
> The milk for my lamb
> you suck and drain
> and grow fat and cruel.

(*Winged Reason*, 24)

and goes on listing a few other examples of man's cruelties. Then he resorts to philosophizing and spiritualizing on the concept of co-existence.

> . . . you find justification
> and bring false philosophies
> to make you His choicest.
>
> Nothing can be more absurd!
> Aren't we His children?
> How can He forgive you?

(*Winged Reason*, 25)

This poem can easily be linked to another poem entitled "How I became a Vegetarian", which echoes the sheep's philosophizing. In this poem, the poet tells us that he has switched over to being a vegetarian at the promptings of his own mind. His mind has, so to say, taught him on the "relation between man, nature, and God" and that of "human beings and other beings", they being "all children of God". His mind opens his eyes to the illusion:

> that man is the centre of the universe;
> God made other beings
> for his food and assistance.

(*Winged Reason*, 76)

In the poem "Connubial Bliss", the poet unleashes himself into poeticizing on the phenomena of nature surrounding and molding human life, as in the following lines:

> The dancing of the plant;
> the smiling of the flower;
> the chirping of the bird;
> and all merry cries of other beings
> herald Life's march here.
>
> (*Winged Reason*, 29)

Against this background, he speaks of "Connubial bliss" as

> heavenly happiness;
> merging of two souls;
> fulfilment of His plans.
>
> (*Winged Reason*, 29)

The poem "Haves and Have-nots" tells of the poet's compassion for and sympathy with the Have-nots. The poet does not God for their deprivation. Nature is always bounteous and does not discriminate between the rich and the poor, between the high and the low. It is only greedy man who deprives the poor of what they are due from Nature:

> Abundant Nature
> feeds plants and animals.
> Greedy selfish man disrupts
> Mother Nature's feeding;
> uproots millions of trees,
> exterminates thousands of animals.
> His deadly weapons
> pose a great threat
> to life itself.
>
> (*Winged Reason*, 36)

While reading down the poem, the reader gets a clear message to ruminate over. The message is that it is only man, not animals or plants, who divides the earth. The poet suggests to the Have-nots to take refuge in communism and socialism and warns them of the evil effects of capitalism in the following lines with which ends the poem:

> Capitalism rules the day;
> Have-nots numbers swell.
> Shattered and smashed are their dreams
> of health and happiness.
>
> (*Winged Reason*, 37)

The poem "International Women's Day", composed on 8th March, 2009, is a poem wherein the poet points out the anomalies in the celebration of the International Women's Day. The speeches delivered at the celebration do not corroborate the experiences of women and the celebration of the International Women's Day every year has not yet helped noticeably improve the lot of women. The poet cites in this long poem—that runs to two full pages—numerous instances of how women are being tyrannized over by men and societies. The message purports to be re-orientation of the celebration of the international day to the endeavor to alleviate the sufferings of women by awakening them to the causes of their sufferings.

In the poem "Indian Democracy", the poet lashes out at the corruption and fanaticism that has been bred from the misgovernance and the selfishness of the politicians. The poet grieves at the misinterpretation of the true import of democracy in the practice of democracy, as is evident in the following lines:

> Indian democracy;
> the largest on the planet;
> a wonder to the world.
> Parliament elections;
> stage of heinous means.
> Secularism butchered;
> Caste and religion raise their hood;
> regionalism and parochialism
> devour
> nationalism and patriotism.
>
> (*Winged Reason*, 50)

This poetry collection, *Winged Reason*, includes thirty-nine poems. I have dealt with just a few representative poems to leave room for the other two poetry collections to delve into.

Now I shall take up the second poetry collection, *Write Son, Write*, for discussion and my discussion will be, as I have said in the beginning of this article, confined to selection of a few representative poems. The poet has dedicated this second poetry collection to his beloved mother (Late) Rosamma Varghese Kannapally.

As we all know, poetry articulates what the poet thinks—what he feels in a social milieu. So we need to listen, to begin with, to the poet tell us—his readers—about what prompted him into bringing out the second poetry collection in his preface. The poet tells us that second poetry collection (*Write Son, Write*) "is an outcome of my fourteen months" poetic voyage from September 2009 to November 2010. My first anthology, *Winged Reason*, was the outpouring of my five years' itching mind. The long difference in the tenure shows that my mind has been becoming more and more unrestful. Naturally, the more disquiet the world becomes, the more distressed and desperate would be the poet's mind" (*Write Son, Write*, 7).

This disquietude, this desperation reveals itself in all the poems included in this poetry collection. In his foreword to this poetry collection, P. C. K. Prem, an English poet and critic, speaks of the collection, alluding to *Winged Reason*, "as heterogeneity of social complexes": "Here, the poet appears to carry forward and strengthen the argument of social relation he initiated in *Winged Reason*" (*Write Son, Write*, 11).

The first poem in this collection, entitled "Write, My Son, Write", is a very long poem, running to seventeen pages. It is divided into twenty-one parts, touching upon different aspects of social life and how it is sustained. The poem is addressed to "my son" (the poet), exhorting him to write on everything living and non-living that surrounds him. In the first part, God tells the poet of the mission behind his creation; God whispered this mission into his ears. He urges the poet to look "at the tip / of your pen" and go on writing till "I say stop" (*Write Son, Write*, 20). In the second part, God grouses at man's inability to sense "my rhythm", reminding him that plants and animals "dance to my numbers". The third part expatiates upon the "rhythm and harmony / in every molecule / every atom" and in the movement of animals, birds, insects, and so on. The fourth part tells that there is a rhythm in the movement of all the limbs of man's body, but grieves that man does not feel this rhythm in the depth of his mind. The fifth part draws a contrast between man and animals and birds. The remaining parts of the poem describe how man greatly differs from animals, birds, and plants cradled on the lap of Nature in terms of co-existence. I forbear from describing them lest it should jar on the patience of the readers.

In the poem "Victory to Thee, Mother India", the poet showers all his love on Mother India. The poet is all praise and eulogy to Mother India for her having united all races, which were divided on the questions of religion, language, and culture. He mentions her great son, Rabindranath Tagore, who "sang in praise of you". She roused the hearts of Punjab, Sindh, Gujarat, Maratha, Dravida, and Bengal. Now he sees her face has turned "sad and gloomy" because

> . . . thy children heed you not
> but surrender their souls to communal devils
> and because patriotism, nationalism and secularism
> give way to
> terrorism, communalism, and regionalism.
>
> (*Write Son, Write*, 42)

The poem grieves over how the religious, political, and intellectual mafias are tearing her heart and drinking her blood to achieve their heinous and selfish ends. He assures her that she need not shed her tears at the treachery of these mafias. The poet prophesies that as she gave birth to such great men as Tagore, Gandhi, and Nehru, she will also give birth to other great children in the near future—

> who will lift us from this trance
> and tether us back to the global home
> so that she will
> . . . sleep on the lap
> fondled by your Mother World.
>
> (*Write Son, Write*, 43)

The poem "Massacre of Cats" informs us without reserve of an inhuman cruelty committed by the poet's next-door neigbors on "four cats" by poisoning them to death, because they, these four cats, had created nuisance by excreting on their vast compounds.

In the poem "Aung Suu Kyi – Asia's Lady Mandela", the poet alludes to the myth, prevalent in Kerala, of Mahavishnu stamping Maveli to the underground, "envious of his golden rule" and exhorts Mahavishnu to descend to Myanmar to expiate His sin by releasing from prison Suu Kyi, the dove of freedom and epitome of valor who

> showed her people through her life
> liberty is born from the ashes of fear.
>
> (*Write Son, Write*, 53)

The poet has based his poem "For the Glory of God" on *The Malayala Manorama* Sunday Supplement Report of 25th July, 2010. This poem deserves to be remembered and recited at all literary fests to imbibe people with the spirit of helping their fellow beings out of their lurches, no matter which religions they profess. The poem tells of a Muslim woman, named Rusiya Beevi, rescuing a Hindu woman, of the name Chellamma Antharjanam, a vegetarian Brahmin, when she was about to kill herself on a railway track and helped put her back on a firm footing. Resiya Beevi, in the act of rescuing a Hindu woman, epitomizes a communal and religious harmony.

In the poem "God is Helpless", the poet philosophizes, as is his wont, on the greediness of man and the catastrophe that results from it. Man prays God to save him from heat and other natural phenomena hostile to him. God Himself has grown fed up of giving man everything he has needed. He has also given to "non-human beings" the same things.

> I did supply

> whatever you needed;
> I created the earth,
> an oasis for men,
> animals and plants
>
> *(Write Son, Write, 63)*

But man snatched the things He had given to "non-human beings" according to His wishes. God professes Himself helpless. Man himself has brought his wretchedness down on himself by axing the trees that cause rainfall, by denuding forests that block clouds. He himself has defiled the pure and clear sky by emitting toxic gas. Man cannot hold Him responsible for what has befallen him. To him He says:

> You have dug your [own] grave.
> And what am I to do?
>
> *(Write Son, Write, 64)*

The poem "Hunger's Call" spotlights the devastating impact of hunger on humanity in Zimbabwe—a shame on the advocacy of liberalization, globalization, and privatization. Hunger reduces men, woman, and children to eating the flesh of a dead elephant. The few quoted lines convey this feeling.

> Carcass of a wild elephant
> consumed in ninety minutes!
> Not by countless vultures
> but by avid, famished
> men and women and children.
>
> *(Write Son, Write, 66)*

In writing the poem "Musings from an Infant's Face" on 8th May, 2010—the International Women's Day—the poet found himself abandoned to a splurge of visualizing the future of an infant travelling with him on a bus. The appearance of her mother accompanying her "foretold the infant's lot".

The poem "Water, Water, Everywhere", composed on 22nd March 2000—the World Water Day—reminds the reader of how water is taking on gold-value, while warning them of the danger of misusing it.

All other poems in the collection deal in a philosophical vein with how humanity is being ravaged in the world created by God for all human and non-human beings to live in.

Now let us veer to the poet K. V. Dominic's third and last poetry collection, *Multicultural Symphony*. The poet has dedicated this third poetry collection to his bosom friend and chief motivator Sudarshan Kcherry.

As avid readers, we love to listen in the privacy of our separate rooms, and in the silence of the night, when all the members of our families are deep asleep, except ourselves, to the poets we adore speak of their poetry and their poetry collection that enshrines it.

Now let us listen to our beloved poet Prof. Dr. K. V. Dominic say something about this third poetry collection and another something about the motives that govern the composing of the poems contained in this collection, as in the other two collections discussed a while ago.

"*Multicultural Symphony*," writes the poet in the preface, "is my third collection of poems after *Winged Reason*, published in 2010 and *Write Son, Write*, published in 2011. The only specialty of this collection is that the poems were composed after my retirement as Associate Professor of English. There is not much change in my themes or poetic style" (*Multicultural Symphony*, 7).

About the themes of the poems composed for this collection, the poet says that basically "I am a follower of [the] Advaita philosophy. Though I am a Christian by birth, I believe in Adwaita. My consciousness doesn't allow me to see God as a separate entity. I believe that there is a Supreme Power or Energy, which is controlling the universe. We call it God or Creator. That power is the spirit or soul of the universe and its element is present in all its creations including atoms. Thus divinity is there in all bodies, both living and non-living. Based on this reason, I cannot find human beings better than other beings or dearest to the Creator as religion teaches us" (*Multicultural Symphony*, 8).

In the first poem, "Multicultural Harmony", the poet abandons himself to different phases of philosophizing on the principle "Live and let live", which in other words means, "You have the right to live and you must let your fellow beings, human and non-human, enjoy their right to live"... The first four lines attempt to awaken the poet's fellow beings to "the need for / multicultural existence". He very aptly explains about the "multicultural existence which harmonizes unity and diversity as the essence of the universe in the following self-explained lines that epitomize the philosophical message the poet wants to convey in this philosophical poem:

> The entire system
> is a grand concert
> composed by the Solespirit
> since the matter and the spirit, both
> animate and inanimate
> visible and invisible
> tangible and intangible
> audible and inaudible
> are instruments multitudinous
> of His perfect symphony.
>
> (*Multicultural Symphony*, 15)

The second poem, "Siachen Tragedy", written on the tragedy that occurred on 7th April, 2012, which took its toll on one hundred and seventy-four soldiers and eleven civilians, strikes a warning note to the consequences of challenging benevolent Nature.

The poem "Global Warming's Real Culprits" is an interesting poem in this that it tells people of what they feign ignorance about. Man is himself responsible for global warming. The poet says that it is the tendency on the part of America and other developed countries to apportion the blame to the "poverty-stricken third world" for the global warming. "To them firewood and fossil-fuel gas" are "the arch villain of greenhouse gases". The groups of lines under A and B, quoted below, ironize on the proclaimed vociferation of America and other developed countries that they are not to blame for the global warming and the shifting of the blame to the "poverty-stricken third world".

> But thousands die every day
> since smokes don't
> emit from their kitchens
>
> Billions survive each day
> since such noxious gases
> emit out from their fireplaces
>
> (*Multicultural Symphony*, 26)

The poem "Charles Darwin, Patron Saint of Animals" advises us to change the age-old concept bequeathed to us of man being the cream of creation, superior to all other living beings, animals, birds, etc. It was Charles Darwin who eye-opened the fact that human being is not different from or better that any other living being. Typical of the concept fathered by Charles Darwin are the following first few lines:

> Charles Darwin the great scientist
> unravelled history of creation
> linked human beings with other beings
> challenged pseudo religious claims
> Religious fanatics injected
> irrational theories and philosophies
> to establish man's supremacy
> and similarity to the Creator.
>
> (*Multicultural Symphony*, 32)

Let us turn to the poem entitled "Beena's Shattered Dream", written from the poet's own experience of a tragedy that occurred in October 2011. The poem mocks at the fallacy of the democracy practised in India. The poem tells of an unfortunate girl employed in a hospital as a nurse on a meagre salary and compelled to commit suicide when she had sought to come out of the drudgery to find a better job in other hospitals. Democracy looks puppetized against the backdrop of thousands of them. Beenas choosing the path of suicide, stuck in such a situation out of which there is no escape.

The poem "Sail of Life" is one that I like above all other poems in the three poetry collections. The first four lines of the poem symbolize loneliness associated with a tender age. When the poet goes out for a walk to take a cup of tea, he confronts a "lone open shop" with no one inside to welcome him in. Silence prevails around him. "The lone open shop" appears to me to be a tiny bit of social milieu. When the poet who has now sufficiently grown old goes out to take a cup of tea—

> I am astonished
> by the din and bustle
> that comes out
> from all opened stalls
> in the evenings.
>
> (*Multicultural Symphony*, 55)

There is no silence, no peace around him. He finds himself steeped in the social milieu characterized by "din and bustle". Gone is his childhood innocence and tranquillity. But he knows that when his boisterous sail reaches its harbor.

> I will be astonished
> by its stillness and darkness.
>
> (*Multicultural Symphony*, 55)

The poet's philosophy in this poem appears to me that man is born into silence and tranquility and departs again into silence and tranquility.

In the poem "Who Am I", the poet monologizes about his position as an "English poet, short-story writer, critic, editor" vis-à-vis "an illiterate farmer".

The poem "Homage to Swami Vivekananda" is written to commemorate the worldwide celebration of Swami Vivekananda's 150th birth anniversary held on 12th January, 2014.

There are many other poems in this collection as good as those discussed here. Those I have discussed are representative poems of Prof. Dr. K. V. Dominic.

**Works Cited**

Dominic, K. V. *Multicultural Symphony.* New Delhi: GNOSIS, 2014. Print.

---. *Winged Reason.* New Delhi: Authorspress, 2010. Print.

---. *Write Son, Write.* New Delhi: GNOSIS, 2011. Print.

# Chapter 12 -
# K. V. Dominic as a Social Critic: A Study of His Poems by Dr. S. Ayyappa Raja

K. V. Dominic (1956) is an eminent and perceptible poet in the arena of contemporary Indian Poetry in English. He has produced three anthologies of poetry so far namely *Winged Reason, Write Son, Write*, and *Multicultural Symphony*. He closely observes the developments that occurred in the society. He is a lover of mankind and nature. He protests against the evils of the society, which make people suffer to the core. This study aims at an analysis of the poems of K. V. Dominic so as to bring out his treatment of the social issues, such as: poverty, child labor, exploitation of nature, corruption, religious intolerance, casteism, the sad plight of women, protest against war, denunciation of superstitious beliefs, pathetic state of the aged in the society, his love for other living beings, and universal brotherhood. It highlights his concern for the mankind and his love for all the creations of God.

K. V. Dominic, who himself is a reputed critic, writes in the preface of his anthology of poems, *Multicultural Symphony*: "Poetry is the best and easiest medium of imparting messages and values to the people" (*Multicultural Symphony*, 7). In the same section of the book, he gives reason for his writing poetry. He says: "I have only one motive behind my compositions—imparting some messages and values to the young minds, which are groping in darkness and ignorance" (*Multicultural Symphony*, 10). In fact, K. V. Dominic has done what he has said in his preface. In his poems, he highlights the important issues related to the peaceful and prosperous life of common people. He urges them to discard the evils of the society. He considers that economic inequality is a great bane of the Indian society. He laments over the gulf between the rich and poor people in India.

In the poem "Hungry Mouths", he brings the sufferings of the poverty-stricken people to the limelight. They are not even in the position to take a square meal once a day. He advises the children not to waste the food items. There are millions of people struggling to get them. He says:

> Dear, you don't realize
> the price of your leavings;
> it can save
> a child like you
> from his death today.
>
> (*Multicultural Symphony*, 49)

It vividly presents the pathetic state of poor in the world. He urges men not to waste the food items because there are millions of people waiting to get at least something to eat. He makes the child respond:

> Ma, we shall keep
> a portion of our food
> and send it to
> those hungry mouths

*(Multicultural Symphony,* 50)

To alleviate the starvation of the people, everyone should do something for them. It is the responsibility of every individual to wipe out the suffering of poor people. K. V. Dominic vividly portrays this idea in this poem.

He sorrowfully expresses his disappointment on seeing the plight of the poor laborers, who have migrated to other lands for their livelihood and led a life without basic amenities and proper wages, in the poem "Why is Fate So Cruel to the Poor?" In this poem, he brings out the tragic accident that caused the deaths of migrant laborers. They are not even paid their legitimate wages and they get only a meager amount of grains as the reward for their labor. He laments: "Exploitations questioned by none / None to protect the wretched / Not even the One who created them" (*Multicultural Symphony,* 72). The poet feels sorry for those poverty-stricken people and even he does not spare the Creator from his criticism for not helping the poor and needy. It shows his love for humanity and his concern for the poor.

In "Musings on My Shoes", he compares the sad plight of the working-class people with the worn-out shoes. Having used the shoes for some years, he has thrown them away without much botheration. He reminds of the great service that the shoes have done for him by carrying him everywhere. The fate of the used and battered shoes reminds the poet the state of the poor working-class people. They are also exploited by the exploiters and at the end, they are thrown away without much care. He says:

> Same is the plight of proletariat
> They are shoes worn by the rich
> Service being complete
> they are spat out like curry leaves.

*(Multicultural Symphony,* 50)

The rich exploit the labor of the poor. Finally, they are thrown out from the farms or firms by the rich inhumanely. They are even not getting their due salary for their hard labor.

K. V. Dominic vividly presents the sad plight of the poor people in the poem "A Nightmare". Here, he has portrayed how poor girls are struggling even to get proper food at least once a day. He delineates their pathetic plight:

> A lavish wedding feast was served in the town hall,
> rich delicacies heaped on the plates,
> were relished by the pompous guests.
> I could see two ragged girls outside
> struggling with the dogs in the garbage bin.

*(Winged Reason,* 22)

There is a wide gulf between the haves and have-nots. On one side, people enjoy an enormous amount of wealth; on the other side, there are men struggling to eat properly even once a day. This is the sad plight of the poor in the world and the poet highlights the economic inequality in these lines. It amply displays his concern for the poor.

In the poem "Haves and Have-nots", he brings out the fact that rich men do not care for the poor and are not ready to alleviate their suffering. God has created all the beings with balance but man makes imbalance in the order. He divides the society and creates classes under various reasons. He protests against the discrimination:

> What right has the mortal man
> to divide and own this immortal planet?

> What justice is there for the minority
> to starve the majority?
>
> (Winged Reason, 37)

The rich men who constitute minority section of the population of the world control the majority of the poor people in the world by their monetary powers and they exploit them. The poet aptly expresses his displeasure against this ill-treatment meted out to the poor in the world at the hands of the rich men.

K. V. Dominic's social consciousness is revealed when he highlights the social evil of child labor in his poems. Child labor is a great menace and thousands of Indian children are suffering due to this. Poverty has forced the family members to send their sons and daughters to work, which may be hazardous for them. In the poem "Child Labour", the poet portrays the pathetic tale of a girl child named after the goddess of wealth, Dhanalakshmi. She is forced to act as a maid in an advocate's family. The master and his wife are sadists and they torture the tender girl. They commit cruelties against the young girl and the poet portrays the pathetic life of the girl:

> Dhanalakshmi cook-cum-maid
> Her hellish life from dawn to midnight
> Her tender soft palms
> smooth as petals of lilies
> burnt, bruised, bled
> Sadist husband and wife
> drunk and voluptuous
> inflicted wounds on her body
>
> (Multicultural Symphony, 35)

From these lines, the readers could understand the terrible life led by the young girl, who has been forced to serve as a child worker. Poverty of her family and illness of parents have forced her to do the job. The inhumane master couple has brutalized her. She has experienced the hellish life in the home. Unfortunately, one day after a late night work, Dhanalakshmi has become tired and does not wake up and turn up for duty. The cruel wife of the master pours hot water on the sleeping maid. She is hospitalized and she dies there painfully. By the death of Dhanalakshmi, the poet has made an appeal in the poem to the conscience of the readers to stop the evil practice of child labor, which destroys the happy life of tens and thousands of children.

In "Mukesh's Destiny", K. V. Dominic blames the government, which is at a snail's pace in eradicating the evil of child labor. He rebukes the officials of the government for not taking serious steps to curb the menace. He portrays the pathetic state of the child laborer Mukesh, who belongs to the Dalit community. Feeling sorry for the child, he says:

> When his classmates enjoy holidays
> his nimble feet and soft hands
> clash with rough tools and hard earth
> How can government turn face to
> Mukesh and his wretched parents?
>
> (Multicultural Symphony, 60)

It is the duty of the government to protect its citizens. Unfortunately, the rulers are not serious in performing their duty. Hence, it is expected of the socially conscious poet, K. V. Dominic, to highlight the pathetic plight of the child laborers, such as Dhanalakshmi and Mukesh, and it shows his concern for the society.

K. V. Dominic protests against the exploitation of nature in many of his poems. God gives great gifts to man in the form of natural products. Unfortunately, man wastes and uses extravagantly the resources of nature. The poet considers the act of man as a desecration. He condemns the avaricious act of man in the poem "Haves and Have-nots." He says:

> Abundant nature
> feeds plants and animals.
> Greedy selfish man disrupts
> Mother Nature's feeding;
> uproots millions of trees,
> exterminates thousands of animals.
>
> (*Winged Reason*, 36)

Man destroys nature and he does not bother about his future generation. It will be detrimental to the entire mankind if man fails to protect the resources of nature. K. V. Dominic aptly brings out the importance of preservation of nature in the poem.

The eco-consciousness of K. V. Dominic is revealed when he makes the paper speak to him. The poem "On Conservation" presents the dialog between the paper and the poet. The paper asks the poet not to write trash on it. It is the duty of the poet to present truth about life. He should convey important messages to the world, which will be helpful for mankind and all other beings, like flora and fauna. Hence the paper appeals to the poet:

> The less you write the more we live
> the more our plant family lives
> Kindly write on the need of the day
> the necessity of conservation
> of plants and animals on earth.
>
> (*Multicultural Symphony*, 31)

Here, the poet appeals to the readers about the importance of conservation of nature. Nature provides all benefits to man and it is the duty of man to preserve nature. If he fails to protect it then it will be dangerous for his life in future.

K. V. Dominic strongly condemns the exploitation of nature in the form of sand mining on the beaches of Kerala. The poem "Protest against Sand Mafia" speaks about the struggle of a social activist, Jazeera, against the illegal sand mining on the coast of Kerala. K. V. Dominic appreciates the protest of Jazeera and condemns the nexus between the government officials and sand mafia. The writer has made Jazeera to respond:

> "I am doing this for my children
> If we don't stop them now
> there'll be nothing left on the beaches
> Our houses will submerge in the sea."
> For whom is the government?
> Law-breakers and criminals or their victims?
>
> (*Multicultural Symphony*, 82)

The poet expresses his anguish for the belated and ineffective steps taken by the government. Man should realize the importance of natural resources and he should not exploit them. Otherwise, the future generation has to pay a heavy price for his misdeeds and even life on the planet will become extinct. Hence, K. V. Dominic has made a fervent appeal to preserve nature in his poems.

Corruption is a great problem in the country and the poet attacks the politicians who have looted the wealth of the nation. They are responsible for the moral degradation in the social setup. In the poem "Martyrs at the Borders", he laments for the soldiers who sacrifice their lives for the safety of the country. He feels that it is not warranted to spend crores of rupees for the nation's defence. He smells rot about the huge allocation of funds for defence. He says:

> Why then such a huge waste
> for defence unnecessary?
> Why create tension at the borders?
> A means to divert subjects' attention
> and muffle mass' protest against corruption?
>
> (*Multicultural Symphony*, 66)

The politicians create artificial tension between the nations to hide their corrupt deals. K. V. Dominic in unequivocal terms condemns the corrupt deeds of the leaders, and it shows his concern for the welfare of the society.

K. V. Dominic denounces the religious intolerance of certain people. He urges people to discard religious fanaticism and fundamentalism. He laments that in the name of religion, all sorts of evil deeds are carried out by some people. He vehemently condemns them as criminals and antisocial elements. In the poem "In the Name of God" (*Winged Reason*, 69–70), he brings out how in the name of God all types of evils occur in the society. He observes that criminal deeds have outnumbered the philanthropic services done in the name of God. Numerous people are killed. Democracy is devalued and superstitions survive. Sexism prevails and a higher caste exploits the lower ones. All these actions are carried out by the perpetrators in the name of God. Hence he urges man to be careful about the religious fanatics.

The religious mafia cheats the gullible in the name of God and loots their money. He urges the people to beware of such elements. He highlights this notion in his long poem "Write, My Son, Write" (*Write Son, Write*, 21–37). The layman has to be aware about such evil-doers. Such pseudo-religious men are greedy and always eye for the material benefits of themselves. In "To My Colleague", he feels sorry for the religious intolerance of a few men who attacked his colleague Prof. T. J. Joseph. He was attacked by some religious fanatics when he was returning to his home from the church. The poet hails his colleague:

> TJ, you have become an icon;
> an icon of suffering;
> an icon of courage;
> an icon of convictions,
> and icon of forgiveness.
>
> (*Write Son, Write*, 84)

The poet appreciates his fellow faculty member not only for his courage and conviction but also for his forgiveness. It shows his approach to religion, which should be helpful to maintain peace in the society.

K. V. Dominic condemns the caste discrimination in the same way as he has done against the religious fanaticism. He appeals to the conscience of the readers to stop the evil practice of casteism. He contends that there is no superior caste or inferior caste. He has made a plea in the poem "Caste Lunatics". He narrates an incident that took place in Madhya Pradesh. A Dalit man, namely Prakash Jaatav, was brutally beaten for riding a motorcycle. The poet says:

> Prakash Jaatav, aged thirty one
> riding on his motocycle
> attacked by a group of twelve
> beat him and slashed his nose
> The reason for this diabolic act?
> 'The Dalits have no right to ride motorbikes
> in presence of high caste men.'
> My country, the greatest democracy,
> when will it be freed from
> lunatics of caste and religion?
>
> (*Multicultural Symphony*, 37)

Caste is a terrible social evil in India and K. V. Dominic as a socially conscious poet brings out the brutality experienced by the Dalits in the society by his portrayal of the Dalit youth Prakash Jaatav in this poem. It shows his concern for the welfare of people and his desire to eradicate caste-based injutice from the Indian society.

K. V. Dominic opposes the subservient treatment experienced by women. He is for the equality of women in the society. Woman is assigned all household chores, such as cooking, washing, and scrubbing. She does not get enough rest to think of herself. She has to take care of father, mother, brother, husband, and son. In "Multicultural Harmony", K. V. Dominic brings out the sufferings of the woman who does all sort of works in the home. He says:

> She is born with a cry
> goes on crying and crying
> till she reaches
> her destination death.
>
> (*Multicultural Symphony*, 19)

It clearly presents the pathetic plight of women in the Indian society. Their misery begins from their birth and continues up to their death. K. V. Dominic wants to change the position of women in the society. They should be treated in a fair manner and their service should be appreciated by their counterparts.

In the poem "Women's Cricket World Cup 2013", K. V. Dominic urges men folk to appreciate the skills and talents of women. When the match between India and West Indies was played at Brabourne ground, Mumbaim, minimum number of spectators came to see it. The poet questions the poor attendance of the audience. He rebukes men:

> Had it been men's world cup
> galleries full and thousands ticketless outside
> Why such discrimination to women's sports?
> Why such double standards to women's feats?
> Had it been women's beauty contest
> or fashion show with minimum dress
> the stadium would be full
> even if tickets are very high
>
> (*Multicultural Symphony*, 73)

The poet obviously expresses his anger against the attitude of men, who have viewed woman as an object of pleasure and never appreciated her skill and talent. Hence, he vehemently attacks their attitude. It shows his concern for women who are treated badly by men folk in the society.

*Philosophical Musings for a Meaningful Life*                                                                      *113*

In the poem "International Women's Day", K. V. Dominic laments for the sad plight of women, who are treated as an object of pleasure by men folk. Though promises of development are assured on that day, there is no improvement at the ground level. The fate of the woman remains the same. He says:

>All echoes of years of yore!
>Problems remain the same!
>Woman is the game!
>Birth to death,
>an instrument of lust
>and hot-selling sex!
>
>                                   (*Winged Reason*, 42)

Men always see woman as an object of pleasure and nothing more. They exploit women by various means. Unfortunately, they forget that women are responsible for the survival of mankind in the world. Hence, the poet says:

>Venerable is woman,
>for she is your mother;
>she is your sister;
>she is your wife;
>she is your guide;
>she is your teacher;
>she is your nurse;
>and above all,
>she is your angel.
>
>                                   (*Winged Reason*, 43)

K. V. Dominic adeptly brings out the significant role played by women in the society. Without their contribution, the world cannot survive. They are the blessed angels of God. Hence man should treat them properly and there should not be any discrimination on the basis of gender.

K. V. Dominic strongly condemns the warmongers, who have caused death and destruction. He does not like to see loss of life during the time of war. He questions the necessity of placing men in uniform in the world's highest battlefield, Siachen, in the poem "Siachen Tragedy" (*Multicultural Symphony*, 24). He insists that there is no need for enmity between the people of different nations. In the poem "A Blissful Voyage", he strongly attacks the former American president George Bush, who conquered Iraq by killing hundreds of thousands of innocent men, women, and children. The poet says:

>I wish I had the claws of a vulture
>to fetch the skeletons from Iraq
>and build a bone-palace
>to imprison Bush in it. (*Winged Reason*, 21)

It obviously presents his contempt for war. War causes death and destruction. Harmony is important and there should be peace and prosperity in the world. He strongly opposes the warmongers, who always prefer to fight to solve the insignificant issues.

K. V. Dominic strongly denounces the superstitious beliefs of people in his poems. In the poem "Horoscope", he rebukes the believers of the pseudoscience. He says that horoscope is the arch-villain of Hindu marriages. Many men and women suffer due to their faith in horoscope. There is no scientific backing behind this practice. People blindly follow this age-old practice and suffer enormously due to it. He asks the pertinent question about this practice:

> An offspring of pseudoscience astrology
> Man-made by-pass for 'happy' life
> Christians and Muslims never follow
> Are their lives worse than Hindus?
> Do horoscopic matches bring happiness and peace?
> Why then cases of thousands of divorces?
>
> (*Multicultural Symphony*, 25)

The poet urges the people to discard their faith in the pseudoscience. He considers it a superstitious belief. Hence he exhorts them to discard their belief in this practice. It shows his concern for the welfare of the people.

K. V. Dominic expresses his concern for the aged people in the society, who are often deserted and ill-treated by their children. He feels sorry for them. He records their anguish in his poems. In their old age, the elderly people long for love and care but often they do not get them. In the poem "A Nightmare", he portrays a couple that longs for the calls of their children:

> See, that mansion a double-storeyed edifice!
> Luxury rooms, lawn and swimming pool;
> An old man and his wife reside there;
> sitting at the phone with sighs and moans,
> longed for the calls from their sons abroad.
>
> (*Winged Reason*, 23)

Though they have all sorts of material comforts, they are not satisfied in their life due to the absence of their children. They long for their presence and their love and care. Without them, their life is meaningless.

The poet expresses his dismay over the ill-treatment of the aged men. He attacks vehemently the callous children who do not care for their aged ones. He brings out his warning in the poem "Old Age". He says:

> Ageism is contemptible;
> unpardonable too.
> Today's torturer
> tomorrow's victim;
> we live with ironies.
>
> (*Winged Reason*, 52)

He obviously warns the youngsters to take care of the elders. Otherwise, they will be placed in the same manner by their wards in future. It shows his concern for mankind, especially the elders of the society.

K. V. Dominic expresses his desire for universal brotherhood and love for all other beings, such as flora, fauna, He considers that it is the duty of a poet to promote the harmony not only among the human beings but also all other beings. He believes that all are the creations of God. Hence, he urges man to love all and maintain harmony among the objects of the world, both living and non-living. In the poem "Multicultural Harmony", he highlights this notion:

> The entire system
> is a grand concert
> composed by the Sole Spirit
> As matter and spirit
> animate and inanimate
> visible and invisible
> tangible and intangible
> audible and inaudible
> movable and immovable
> are instruments multitudinous
> of His perfect symphony.
>
> (*Multicultural Symphony*, 15)

It vividly presents his vision of unity among all the objects of the world. All are created by God and each object functions within its limits. Only man interferes and spoils the arrangement of God. Man should not interfere into the domains of others, including other beings like flora and fauna. He insists that man should love all the creations of God. It obviously presents his love for mankind and his concern for other beings.

From the analysis of the poems of K. V. Dominic, the readers could understand the social consciousness of the poet. He is very much concerned about the evils of the society which affect millions of people. He contends that as a poet, it is his duty to portray such evils in his poetry to highlight the devastative effects of them to the readers. By his treatment of such issues as poverty, child labour, exploitation of nature, corruption, religious intolerance, casteism, the sad plight of women, protest against war, denunciation of superstitions, pathetic state of the aged, and his love for other beings, K. V. Dominic has carved a niche of his own as a great social critic in the arena of Indian Poetry in English. In fact, this study establishes him as a great lover of humanity and all other God-made creatures of the world.

## Works Cited

Dominic, K. V. *Multicultural Symphony*. GNOSIS, New Delhi. 2014. Print.

---. *Winged Reason*. Authorspress, New Delhi. 2010. Print.

---. *Write Son, Write*. GNOSIS, New Delhi. 2011. Print.

# Chapter 13 -
# Philosophical Voyage of K. V. Dominic
# by Arbind Kumar Choudhary

R. K. Singh, D. C. Chambial, K. V. Raghupati, Mahashweta Chaturvedi, Rita Nath Keshri, Aju Mukhopadhayay, Harish Thakur, P. Raja, Jasvinder Singh, Anil Kumar Sharma, C. L. Khatri, B. K. Dubey, K. V. Dominic, and several others have been glittering in the sky of the creative world with a number of poetry collections to their credits. K. V. Dominic is a poet, a critic, a short story writer and, above all, editor of *International Journal on Multicultural Literature* (IJML), a refereed journal of global repute.

What appeals in Dominic's poetry to the muse-lovers is his candid expression, simple language, mind-blowing thought, and innovative ideas that provoke the imagination of the muse-lovers to its utmost degrees. His dedication to serve the humanity for its prosperity through the poems reserves his berth in the temple of fame across the globe. His minute observation, skilled presentation, provocative painting and appealing realism make him a great poet of Indian-English literature. His poetic prosperity will be proved a milestone in the poetic world of Indian-English poetry:

> Plants and animals never divide
> the earth among themselves;
> What right has the moral man
> to divide and own this immortal planet?
>
> (*Winged Reason*, 36–37)

Like D. C. Chambial, Dominic opines that all living beings, except human beings, can never think of the earthly division. But human beings, though being the wisest creature, try to divide the immortal planet. Ironically the mortal beings divide the immortal planet. Plants and animals grow and blossom for our sake. We, people, grow for our sake only. What a surprising irony it is! All natural things are the sources of our livelihood and pleasure.

> The dancing of the plant;
> the smiling of the flower;
> the chirping of the bird;
> and all merry cries of other beings,
> herald Life's march here.
>
> (*Winged Reason*, 29)

The dancing of the plants, the fragrance of the flowers, and the chirping of the birds provide intense joy to its utmost degrees in our life. Like D. V. Sahani, K.V. Dominic finds the plants, the animals, and other beings more conducive to the human beings. D. V. Sahani sings:

> Make every thing in Nature your friend.
> It won't let you down in your need.
> It will give you the very best in it
> And with raptures of ecstasy

Your being feed.

*(Winged Reason, 53)*

All natural objects are for man's use. The plant gives fruits, the flower gives fragrance, the bird gives melodious song, and the animal gives milk for our livelihood. Man must have friendship with these objects and make the earth a better place to live.

> My dear son, live in Karma,
> love all creations,
> for I am in everything.

*(Write Son, Write, 96)*

God is considered to be the most powerful being of the universe. But God has himself become helpless for his children. Human beings have disobeyed their parent and are madly engaged in annihilation. God instructs us to love one another because he exists everywhere, in all things. To Choudhary, God is a saving grace for those burning in furnace. It is said that God helps only those who help themselves. The plants and the animals complain against the human beings—the worst, crooked creature that cuts the plants and eats the flesh of the animals. In the court of God, human beings have become culprit. The poet writes:

> Petitions come to me
> one after another
> from plants and animals.
> All complain of
> your cruelty and torture:
> they have no food;
> they have no water;
> they have no shelter;
> and not even air.
> They plead to me
> to call your back;
> save their lives,
> and thus save the planet.
> Kindly tell me, children,
> what shall I do?

*(Write Son, Write, 64–65)*

The poet ridicules the modern race here:

> Man, you are the cruelest,
> you are the most ungrateful
> of all God's creations.

*(Winged Reason, 25)*

Man is the prize idiot of the earth. All objects of Nature follow the natural code of conduct. Humans have become the most ungrateful creatures of all God's creations because they destroy jungles, kill the voiceless animals, and eat their flesh, and establish their own jungle Raj by replacing the natural code of conduct. God made the earth and men made the country. God made men and men made caste, religion, and nation. Surprisingly, men, being a minority amidst all living beings, rule over the majority without fear. Men do not follow the universal democratic code of conduct on this earth

> What right has the mortal man
> to divide and own this immortal planet?
> What justice is there for the minority
> to starve the majority?

*(Winged Reason, 37)*

The poet opines his philosophy of beauty in this stanza:

> Bodily beauty is only one among the beauties;
> It fades and decays as a flower does.
> Who thinks of a flower when it is decayed?
> The sun is beautiful but can you enjoy it at noon?
> The objects of nature reveal its radiance and beauty.
> Eternal beauty is in achievements eternal.
> Handsome is he who handsome does.

*(Winged Reason, 28)*

Beauty has remained the source of pleasure from times immemorial. To Keats, "a thing of beauty is a joy forever." To Dominic "Handsome is he who handsome does." To D. V. Sahani:

> Real beauty is not of
> complexion, form or face.
> But of that state of mind
> In which ego does itself efface
> which is verily love
> which come from God's grace
> which make everything beautiful
> and our life on earth blissful.

*(Winged Reason, 53)*

To Dominic, physical beauty is for the time being that blossoms and decays as a flower does. The beauty of the sun reveals its radiance. All things have their own merits and demerits, fragrances, and ill-smelling. Internal beauty is forever. Like Mahashweta Chaturvedi, Dominic paints a terrible picture of the fair sex that has been treated as an instrument of lust and sex rather than as a counterpart. No one tries to peep into women's heart and mind. None takes notice of her desires, moods, mind, and feelings.

> Women is the game!
> Birth to death,
> an instrument of lust
> and hot-selling sex!

*(Winged Reason, 42)*

Like Kamala Das, Dominic has presented a gloomy picture of women community that deserves equal rights and liberty in our male-dominated society.

> Unfortunate crow feeds cuckoo's chicks;
> yet crow is not lauded
> and cuckoo is extolled.
> Crow's counterpart dove;
> icon of love and innocence.
> Why is white attractive

    and black disgusting?

(Write Son, Write, 57)

Ironically, black and white colors have been treated as symbols of bad and good by the scholars. The fair-complexioned bride is preferred to black. The crow, an icon of love and innocence, feeds cuckoo's chicks; yet crow is not lauded. The poet raises a question regarding the superiority of white over black and, lastly, advocates that handsome is that handsome does.

> Intellectual mafia
> assumes omniscient;
> exploits innocent people;
> detracts them
> from their creator;
> makes them pessimists;
> imposes their
> obsolete philosophies.

(Write Son, Write, 37)

Politics is the root cause of all our sufferings. The nexus between the politician, the criminal, and the bureaucrat has made our life hellish in this garden of God. Like Daruwalla, Choudhary, and Chaturvedi, Dominic believes that the dirty political game has made our life worse than curse. All those who are innocent or ignorant are befooled by the politicians in the name of prosperity of race, religion, and region. Choudhary ridicules the political mafia in his *My Songs*:

> A wolf in sheep's clothing
> Sheds crocodile tears for the suffering.
> O Blood sucker of the sufferer!
> Your name is Leader.

(My Songs, 18)

Poverty and unemployment are our enemies. Ignorance is our foe.

> Isn't poverty the greatest enemy?
> Why not fight against it
> and wipe out destitution,
> pointing guns, rifles and missiles
> at the chest of the poor?

(Write Son, Write, 66)

People claim, condemn, and kill each other in the name of injustice and inhumanity. Our worst enemy is our ignorance, not the other beings. Our worst enemies— that are poverty, false beliefs, ego, unemployment etc.— flourish in the breast of the poor. The atomic and other destructive weapons are made in the name of security, humanity, and prosperity at the cost of the advancement of the poor and the exploited. Hence, the poet appeals to God for instruction and guidance.

> God, teach me how to detach;
> and also teach my neighbours
> and millions of my brothers and sisters
> to show love and mercy
> to all non-human beings.

(Write Son, Write, 52)

Aung San Suu Kyi, Asian Nelson Mandela, is the epitome of valor, who embraced a hellish life and solitary confinement for the liberation of the masses from the dark kingdom of the dictator. Her slogan of liberty, by adopting Gandhi's doctrine, bagged the Nobel Prize for Peace and stirred the fire of liberation for humanity, honesty, and harmony.

> Suu Kyi, the epitome of valour,
> showed her people through her life
> liberty is born from the ashes of fear.
> Her twenty years of political life;
> more than fourteen in solitary cells.
>
> (*Write Son, Write* 53)

The Nobel Laureate Suu Kyi molded a generation for peace, prosperity, and pure life. The poet glorifies her sacrifice whole heartedly.

> The sun of knowledge
> can never be eclipsed
> by the moon of ignorance.
>
> (*Winged Reason*, 67)

Knowledge is our best friend while ignorance is our worst enemy. People fall into misfortune for want of knowledge. The light of the sun enlightens the world that can rarely be eclipsed. The moon of ignorance blossoms for want of the sun of knowledge. The poet appeals to get more and more knowledge to quench the kingdom of ignorance. The poet is optimistic that sooner or later the sun of knowledge will replace the moon of ignorance for the restoration of the kingdom of love, peace, and universal brotherhood.

> Om is our breath;
> a tonic to mind and body.
> It's a celestial music
> showering manna on the earth;
> it gives us peace and happiness;
> Om Shanti, Om Shanti, Om Shanti.
>
> (*Winged Reason*, 66)

The poet wishes to fly like an angel to instill humanism in the communal minds and also wishes to replace the vicious circle in favor of the kingdom of wisdom. Like an angel, the poet's ardent desire is to revive the kingdom of wisdom for prosperity, peace, and universal brotherhood. It is also the duty of the poet to make life fragrant for all those who suffer from the cruel hands of tyranny and inhumanity.

> If I could fly like an angel,
> would plead all prophets
> to inspire and instill humanism
> in million's communal minds.
> I would meet Gandhi too
> who is weeping at his shattered dreams.
>
> (*Winged Reason*, 21)

C. L. Khatri's verse "Godsey killed you once / They kill you everyday" (30) finds a great resemblance with these lines because Gandhi's dreams of Ram Rajya have already been the story of the past rather than the present.

K. V. Dominic is the burning voice of Indian English poetry that has been perfuming the poetic scenario over a decade with his melodious song, fragrant feeling, racy style, capital ideas, and philosophical views. Like R. K. Singh, D. C. Chambial, and R. N. Sinha, Dominic is the roaring voice of the creative milieu that has become a twinkling star in the sky of the creative world and has also been promoting the peeping poets for poetic perfection, prosperity, and peace. His forceful voice will remain ever ringing in the womb of time.

## Works Cited

Choudhary, A. K. *My Songs*. Begusarai, Bihar: IAPEN, 2008. Print.

Dominic, K.V. *Winged Reason*. New Delhi: Authorspress, 2010. Print.

---. *Write Son, Write*. New Delhi: GNOSIS, 2011. Print.

Khatri, C. L. *Ripples in the Lake*. Bareily: Prakash Book Depot, 2006. Print.

Sahani, D. V. *Whispering Silence*. Gwalior: Amrit Prakashan, 2005. Print.

# Chapter 14 -
# The Poet of the Marginalized:
# An Analysis of Dr. K. V. Dominic's Poetry
# by Anisha Ghosh Paul

It is impossible for a poet to compose in a vacuum, isolated from his surroundings, like a pearl in an oyster, like Keats's Nightingale pouring forth its soulful music from its embalmed, verdurous forest hideout. Instead, he must live in the real world, not escape from it, experience realities of life, and understand his social responsibility. As Jayanta Mahapatra observes, "Poetry has always been responsible to life. By this, one means that a poet is first of all responsible to his or her own conscience; otherwise he or she cannot be called a poet" (qtd. in *Winged Reason*, 11). Dr. K. V. Dominic is one such poet who is first and foremost responsible to his own conscience and often tries to convey an emotion or a message through social criticism in his poems. Born in 1956, at Kalady in Kerala, Dr. Dominic has served as a professor in the Research and P. G. Department of English, Newman College, Thodupuzha, Kerala, which is also his alma mater, for twenty-five long years. A revered academician, a well-known creative and critical writer and an editor of note, Dominic started composing poems in his late forties, like the great Indian poet Jayanta Mahapatra, who began his poetic endeavors not before the age of forty, and has produced three collections of poems, entitled *Winged Reason* (2010), *Write Son, Write* (2011), and the very recently published *Multicultural Symphony* (2014). Mahapatra is one of the major influences on him and as he explains the reason why the poetic muse eluded him for so long, in the preface to his maiden collection of poems, Dominic refers to Mahapatra:

> As Jayanta Mahapatra wrote, poetry comes out of a "bad heart"—a heart that makes one turn secretly into a leader or a loser, pushing one to choose values, attitudes, and do the not-so-obvious things... I do believe that I matured very late, at the age of forty-eight, to be able to choose values and impart them to my students as well as to readers of my poems. (Preface, *Winged Reason*, 11)

Dominic's poems have a strong philosophical base, as his mind is steeped in the doctrines of Advaita Vedanta philosophy. He draws inspiration from humanitarians and thinkers like Swami Vivekananda, Marx, Darwin, Said, Fanon, Mother Teresa, Adi Sankara, Salim Ali, Steve Irwin, Gandhi, and Nehru, as well as from the tenets of Hinduism, Christianity, and Buddhism. His imagination is nourished by the major English Romantics, like Wordsworth, Blake, Shelley, and Keats—the Victorians, like Tennyson, Browning, and Arnold—American poets, like Frost and Emily Dickinson—and Indian-English poets, like Kamala Das and Nissim Ezekiel along with Jayanta Mahapatra. In an interview to Prof. Elisabetta Marino, Dominic, in an Aristotelian vein, regards poetry as a medium of delightful teaching, a tool for social criticism, as he goes on to explain his poetic creed:

> ... I take poetry and short story as a weapon and reaction to the evils of the society. The function of poetry is to instruct and delight. To me, the aspect of

'instruct'—impart great values and messages—seems more important than 'delight'. Hence I don't care much about rhythm, rhyme, or such decorations which add musicality to the lines. I write in free verse, using very simple vocabulary, with minimum figural language. I have a very clear vision in my compositions: even an uneducated man—one who can just read and write—should be attracted to my poetry and thus the message should enter into his/her mind. Unlike T. S. Eliot and several other modern great poets, I write for the masses and not for just elite and educated.

(Interview with Prof. Elisabetta Marino)

His sensitive and compassionate heart falls upon the thorns of life and bleeds; in the Preface to *Winged Reason,* he clearly names these thorns as cruelty and intolerance toward animals, terrorism and religious intolerance, corruption in politics and public sector, and social inequality. As Dominic himself says: "I am a champion of the marginalized, oppressed and downtrodden. I have composed several poems on the problems of working class, sexism and ageism, child labour, cruelty to animals, casteism, etc" (Interview).

In all three collections of his poems, Dominic voices his proletarian sentiments in poems about the working classes, the daily wagers, and the teeming millions suffering the pangs of poverty. In "Lal Salaam to Labour", Dominic pays tribute to the working-class people who seldom get to enjoy the fruits of their own labors; they farm and we consume the yield, they build houses for us to live in "where they never rest" (*Winged Reason*, 44); build roads for us to drive on; clean our waste and filth; and get discrimination and disgust from us in return. They are even deprived of respect and proper wages. Toward the end of the poem, the poet makes a fervent appeal to the readers to give the laborers at least what they rightfully deserve:

> Lal Salaam to Labour,
> For without them we have no life.
>
> Let us not be unjust
> When we pay them wages,
> For we can't do what they do.

(*Winged Reason*, 45)

The poet does not only sympathize with the working class but also recognizes the greatness of hard work; in his poem "Dignity of Labour" he criticizes his countrymen for aping western trends of fashion but not recognising the ideals of industry, perseverance, equality, health and hygiene followed so earnestly in the West. Instead of honouring an honest farmer, a scavenger, tailor, fisherman, or a barber, our country reveres parasitic politicians, duplicitous god men, or corrupt white-collar bureaucrats. A continuation of this theme can be seen in "Who Am I?" where the poet's superego humbles his id by reminding him of the great service the manual laborer renders to the society:

> An illiterate farmer is greater than you;
> His service is greater than your scribbling;
> Labourers' sweat is dearer than your ink;
> If they strike, your writings will cease,
> and ultimately you yourself will disappear.

(*Multicultural Symphony*, 64)

"Fruits of Labour" treats this theme from a different angle; the poet traces the life and labors of Mr. Mony, the painter, who toiled for the whole day for a meager sum of fifty rupees and did not spare a dime on his own meals, only to give his sons good education; finally fate smiles on him as his sons finish their education, get jobs with good remuneration, but Mr. Mony makes no change to his way of life. The laborer skipping meals to save money for fulfilling the basic needs of his family draws our attention to their pitiable condition in our country.

The theme of social inequality and poverty is treated in several of Dominic's poems, as he writes in "Haves and Have-nots": "Minority always luxuriates / at the cost of / majorities' necessities" (*Winged Reason*, 36). He resorts to the dream convention in "A Nightmare" to delve deeper into the imbalance and inequality in society. In his dream, which gradually turns out into a nightmare because of the horrific sights he witnesses, the poet becomes a hawk hovering around the sky, and from this vantage point witnesses several instances of social inequality:

> A lavish wedding feast was served in the town hall,
> Rich delicacies heaped on the plates,
> Were relished by the pompous guests.
> I could see two ragged girls outside
> Struggling with the dogs in the garbage bin.
>
> (*Winged Reason*, 22)

The poet's heart is pained to see wastage due to plenty and deprivation, overeating and hunger, large mansions with minimum occupancy and overcrowding in one-room huts—all existing side by side in this world. In "Hungry Mouths", through a dialog between mother and son, the poet is trying to drive in his point that before wasting surplus food by overeating or throwing it away carelessly, we should think once about the millions who go to bed with empty stomach every night. He comes up with the view of the haves sharing resources with the have-nots to obliterate social inequality and build a Marxist utopia:

> Leftovers of the
> ten percent Haves
> can sustain
> ninety percent Havenots
> and make this hellish world
> a blissful heaven.
>
> (*Multicultural Symphony*, 49)

Poverty and hunger prompt man to go to such extremes that are unimaginable to a person well-off. Based on a newspaper report about famished people in Zimbabwe eating up a dead elephant, when they had nothing else to eat, Dominic ventures to explore one such extreme in the poem "Hunger's Call":

> Carcass of a wild elephant
> consumed in ninety minutes!
> Not by countless vultures
> but by avid, famished
> men and women and children.
> Even the skeleton was axed
> to support sinking life with soup.
>
> (*Write Son, Write*, 66)

Gender inequality is a big hurdle posed to the progress of any civilized society and Dominic in his poems attempts a critique of the patriarchal bias prevalent in our country. In his poem "International Women's Day", he unveils the sham behind observing any such day, when women in his homeland and the world are subjected to discrimination everyday:

> Problems remain the same!
> Woman is the game!
> An instrument of lust
> And hot-selling sex!
> Her very birth ill omen:
> An unwelcome event
> No guilt in foeticide;
> Foeticide is matricide;
>
> (*Winged Reason*, 42)

She is either killed inside the womb or, if delivered successfully, becomes a victim of sexism from a very young age. She starts making sacrifices as a sister, a daughter, then a wife, and mother. She is denied her rights to education and politics and even to the choice of partner, hardly employed, always financially dependent, exploited and enslaved by husband and in-laws; even religion becomes a tool in the hands of patriarchy to perpetuate her exploitation:

> her individuality
> scantily respected.
> Born to be dictated
> . . . . . . . . . . . . . . . .
> Religions also dishonour her:
> . . . . . . . . . . . . . . . .
> She is always the Other.
> Patriarchy is his product;
> he dictates the world;
> dictates even God,
> and corrupts religion.
>
> (*Winged Reason*, 43)

The poem ends with the poet urging his readers to show more respect and admiration to women whom he calls "angels". In the poem entitled "Women's Cricket World Cup 2013", Dominic lashes against sexism and gender stereotypes as he writes about people's lack of interest in women's sports:

> Had it been men's world cup
> galleries full and thousands ticketless outside
> Why such discrimination to women's sports?
> Why such double standards to women's feats?
>
> (*Multicultural Symphony*, 73)

Games and sports are seen as men's arena, while women are deemed fit for parading their beauty and feminine charm under the male gaze by participating in beauty contests and fashion shows. Thus the poet protests against the objectification of women and insists on encouraging their talent in every field. "Celebration of Girl-child's Birth", based on *The Mathrubhumi* report on 5th June, 2013, The World Environment Day, records Dominic's concern for the girl child. Where instances of female foeticide are so regular all around the country, the poet showers praises on the Piplantri villagers in Rajasthan who have taken to celebrating female birth by planting trees, and collecting a sum of money which, added to the amount spared by the new father, goes to the bank for the child's education and secured future. In "Laxmi's Plea", the poet voices his protest against the social evil of dowry system which compels several girls willing to lead a conjugal life to live alone forever due to their inability to fulfill the groom's demands. The life of a woman becomes even more torturous in the wake of poverty and lack of education, when she is compelled to work and also manage home and children, getting only insults and thrashing from her husband in return, as can be seen in "What a Birth":

> Drunkard husband
> will come at night
> to resume beats and kicks.
>
> Dawn for doom
> Dusk to damn
> What a birth!

(Winged Reason, 58)

The courage and dignity of a woman is celebrated in "Resolution", where a woman undertakes the challenging work of felling thorny branches by standing on a twenty feet high ladder, "when few men risk / such hazardous labour," (*Write Son, Write*, 75).

With the passage of time, man's energies wane away; he becomes weak, senile, emotionally vulnerable, and more and more dependent on his own children for whom he makes so many sacrifices in his youth. But in the present materialistic, acquisitive society, where life has become a struggle for the survival of the fittest, man is forgetting the most precious things in life and racing incessantly against time. He forgets that his parents are getting older and they need him the way he needed them when he was young and helpless, a stage of innocence prior to this rat race. He goes abroad for securing a better lifestyle for himself and his parents whom he leaves behind all alone, waiting the entire day for one phone call from him. This paradox of modern human condition and the helplessness of old age, which is second childhood, is treated with great compassion in poems like "Gayatri's Solitude" and "Old Age". Ageism becomes a curse as an old and decrepit person is of no use to the family; he is seen as a burden by his own children, who forget that youth is not everlasting:

> The dearest children,
> to whom he looked and loved
> turn ungrateful.
> They hate and curse
> And never care.
> Ageism is contemptible;
> unpardonable too.
> Today's torturer
> tomorrow's victim;
> we live with ironies.

("Old Age", Winged Reason, 52)

Poverty itself is a curse which begets several other evils, one of which is child labor. In poem after poem, Dominic highlights the plight of children whose innocence is lost in their bid to earn bread and butter for themselves and their families. These children are excessively overburdened with errands by their employers in exchange for remunerations highly disproportionate to the workload. In poems like "Child Labour" and "Mukesh's Destiny", based on newspaper reports, Dominic voices the cry of such children, who are deprived of their right to education at a tender age and are forced to come to terms with harsh realities of life. "Child Labour" is about the little girl Dhanalaxmi whose parents, under the pressure of poverty, sell her to an affluent advocate for five thousand rupees to work as domestic help. Not only did they make her work round the clock, but also inflicted physical torture:

> Her hellish life from dawn to midnight
> Her tender soft palms
> smooth as petals of lilies
> burnt, bruised, bled
> Sadist husband and wife
> drunk and voluptuous
> inflicted wounds on her body
> . . . . . . . . . . . . . . . . . . .
> burning her hand with cigarette ends
> Starved her for sluggishness in work
> Poor lass helpless and crying
> None in the world
> to share her sorrows
>
> (*Multicultural Symphony*, 35–36)

And when one day she fails to wake up early due to last day's stressful routine, the mistress spills hot water on the little girl's head leading to her death. In "Mukesh's Destiny", the little boy in fifth grade is compelled to work after school hours and on holidays in some nearby estate to support his ailing parents:

> on all holidays and even working days
> When his classmates enjoy holidays
> his nimble feet and soft hands
> clash with rough tools and hard earth
>
> (*Multicultural Symphony*, 60)

Alongside these children, there are others too who are forced to slog and earn for others; off and on, children from different social classes are kidnapped by criminals, who compel them to beg. People take pity on children easily and give them alms, which are appropriated by these criminals. "Anand's Lot" is based on the life and sorrows of a child coming from an affluent family but kidnapped and subjected to a beggar's life by a criminal, who threatens to kill him if he disobeys. Anand remembers his happy past when he used to go to school, how his mother used to shower kisses on him, and how he used to enjoy the company of his friends and sister. The poet, speaking through Anand's own person, draws a dismal picture of his present life:

> I have to sleep in their hut,
> eat dry bread which I hate,
> always wear stinky rags.
> They scold me and beat me
> for not earning as much as they dreamed.
>
> (*Winged Reason*, 26)

Man, under the spell of his pride of being the crown of creation, is slowly turning this world into a living hell. He is reluctant to share space and resources with other non-human forms, which are as dear to the creator as he himself is. He destroys the world of nature, over-uses natural resources indiscriminately, and suffers no pricks of conscience in killing other creatures. In a series of poems

("Ammini's Demise", "Massacre of Cats", "Attachment", "To My Deceased Cats", "Cohabitance on the Planet") dedicated to his cats murdered one after another by his own neighbor, Dominic has showcased the degeneration of man:

> My materialist neighbours
> Go to church every day;
> Read the Bible every day;
> But never read the part
> To love other beings
> As fellow beings.

("Massacre of Cats", *Write Son, Write*, 45–46)

An animal lover himself, Dominic cannot tolerate cruelty against animals and based on his personal loss, he has expounded Swami Vivekanda's views that love and service to animals are tantamount to service to God. "Multicultural Harmony" is a manifesto of Dominic's belief that "this universe is a big concert or symphony, a harmony of diverse notes. All creations play their role in concordance, but man tries to play discordant notes—stands against the rhythmic flow of the system" (Preface to *Multicultural Symphony*, 8). Since the non-human world is not blessed with speech or, in other words, speaks a different language altogether, which is beyond man's comprehension, man goes on exploiting it; but he has no right to do so as the non-human world too is God's creation:

> Man, you are the cruellest,
> you are the most ungrateful
> of all God's creations.
>
> Yet you find justification
> and bring false philosophies
> to make you His choicest.

("A Sheep's Wail", *Winged Reason*, 25)

Poems like "Water, Water, Everywhere", "Nature Weeps", and "God is Helpless" record the poet's ecological concerns and hold up a horrible picture of the future to his readers if man does not stop dominating, exploiting, and destroying the natural world. "Nature Weeps" presents grim pictures of havoc wreaked by man on the natural world: tigers roaming about the city since man has killed all its natural prey; lily flowers turning reddish as they are washed in acid rain; cuckoos have no trees to sit on; and rainbows don't appear in the sky; the sky turns pale and colourless due to pollution; and cloudy smoke hides the sun from showering its rays on lotus buds. The best things in the world are free, like water—our life spring, but over use and pollution will lead to fast depletion of this natural reserve in near future. In "Water, Water Everywhere", the poet delineates an apocalyptic future world without water:

>  Desalinated water,
>  the elixir of life.
>  In place of shower,
>  sponging with mineral oil.
>  Disposable dress;
>  heaps of garbage everywhere.
>  . . . . . . . . . . . .
>  Water stolen
>  at gun point;
>  armed forces guarded
>  water reservoirs of nations.
>
> *(Write Son, Write, 92)*

In his poems, Dominic champions the cause of the marginalised and oppressed, not only by sympathizing with their lot but also by presenting inspirational stories of their success by fighting against all odds. In poems like "A Desperate Attempt" and "Tears of a World Champion", we find people overcoming their physical and financial limitations and striving to achieve their goals. He does not only give to airy nothings a local habitation and a name through his poems, but writes about what happens around him, about real people, real problems and real emotions; that is why many of his poems are inspired from true incidents reported in newspapers. His approach is definitely postcolonial as he tries to bring the peripheral into the center and obliterate the hiatus between centre and margin.

## Works Cited

Dominic, K. V. *Multicultural Symphony.* New Delhi: GNOSIS, 2014. Print.

---. *Winged Reason.* New Delhi: Authorpress, 2010. Print.

---. *Write Son, Write.* New Delhi: GNOSIS, 2011. Print.

"Interview with Prof. K. V. Dominic by Prof. Elisabetto Marino." Web. 2 May 2014. http://www.profkvdominic.com/?page_id=1160.

# Chapter 15 -
# K. V. Dominic's Poetry:
# Rebellion and Reticence on Winged Reason
# by Joe Palathunkal

"Poetry is rebellion," wrote Pablo Neruda, the Nobel Prize winning Chilean poet. In fact every true poem contains in it the streaks and streams of rebellion, a shriek of revolt. In some poems, the rebellion is very obvious; but in some others, it is camouflaged by various hues and shades. I would place K. V. Dominic's poetry in the second category. His poems in the *Winged Reason* and *Write Son, Write* bear eloquent witness to this. And for this very reason, in his poetry rebellion and reticence go hand in hand. When I read his poems, I get the impression that though he wants to cry out loud, something makes him hold back, and so he prefers to sob in silence; but the silence carries with it an eloquence, which is awakening and enlightening on many vexed issues related to human life as he has observed in his socio-political situation. He has heard the call of the situational imperatives and has responded with his mind and heart which reflect the strands of emotions and thoughts one comes across in his poetry.

## *Sympathy and Empathy*

Almost all the poems in *Winged Reason* reflect sympathy and empathy through and through starting with the first one "In Memoriam: George Joson." It is the arrow of grief that pierced his soul due to the sudden death of Joson that catapulted Professor K. V. Dominic to the stage of poetry, a compulsion which he could not resist like Valmiki, the ancient poet of India, from whom poetry flowed out as anguish when he witnessed a hunter's arrow bringing down a bird-couple. That anguish at the fatal accident that snatched away Joson's life made Dominic too to ask a question from the agony of his soul: "Why did you leave us so soon, dear Joson?" The poet is moved by Joson's innocent baby kissing him again and again where one can see the sympathy and empathy moving out of his heart but it was smothered by the line "What a game He plays!", perhaps an allusion to the Hindu theology of "Leela", a concept that makes even the most tragic happenings as mere godly flirting. Good enough to console oneself in a tragic situation but it takes away the poignancy from the poem. This Leela concept is reinforced in the last lines he quotes alluding to a great poet:

> We are all puppets in His hands,
> dancing to the tunes He plays.
> The best is to resign
> to what He ordains
> in time and out of time.

(*Winged Reason*, 18)

However, sympathy and empathy for the family is very much evident in the poem "In Memoriam". Even in a poem like "Long Live E. K. Nayanar", the poet has not forgotten to bring in sympathy and empathy to depict a Communist political leader to whom conventionally people may not link these qualities because of the very image of Communism in world history. Yet Dominic feels: "You were a true Communist / a comrade to the core of your being / a rare species / compassion and love / an epitome of socialism." (*Winged Reason*, 19) By calling Nayanar "a rare species", the poet might have been hinting at what I indicated about Communism just now. But for the poet, compassion is a leitmotif in most of his poems established by this rare poem also. What one could notice in his poems is the nature of his sympathy, a feeling with the victim or the underdog, which we call empathy in modern psychological terms.

The poet gets into the shoes of the underprivileged and the victimized to feel with them as one of them reverberating the dominant spirit of Asia, what the great scholar Michet calls "the Bible of kindness" in his famous work "The Bible of Humanity", published in 1864:

> Let me look towards Asia and the profound East for a little while. There lies my great poem, as vast as the Indian Ocean, blessed, gilded with the sun, the book of divine harmony wherein there is no dissonance. A serene peace reigns there, and in the mist of conflict an infinite sweetness, a boundless fraternity, which spreads over all living things, an ocean of love, of pity, of clemency. I have found the object of my search; The Bible of Kindness.

The poet of the *Winged Reason* is also a great votary of that 'boundless fraternity' and so he does not forget to include in it a sheep's wail, a cat's demise, a cuckoo's singing, and a mango tree. The sheep has a serious complaint against man and so she wants God to shut out man from heaven for all the inhuman practices he heaps on sheep: "The fur God gave me, / mercilessly you shear / to make you cosy. / The milk for my lamb / you suck and drain / and grow fat and cruel" (*Winged Reason*, 24).

In "Ammini's Lament" and "Ammini's Demise", the poet's empathy is very evident as his heart throbs with the sorrow of a cat and finally with its death: "Ammini's heart-breaking wails, / her unnatural reverberating cry, / piercing through my heart / ... / Ammini's incessant cry, / like Gandhari's wails, / echoes my premises." (*Winged Reason*, 62) But when Ammini was poisoned to death by a perverted man, the rebel in the poet comes to the fore to tell a terrible truth:

> Thousands of fiends
> inhabit this planet
> turning the earth
> to a big slaughter house,
> as if man alone has
> the right to live here.
>
> (*Winged Reason*, 65)

We know that this presumed right has not turned the earth as an abattoir for just animals but even for plants and humans as well. Man has turned this blue planet into a perfect slaughterhouse so that now even humans cannot live here in an environment full of poison and pollution. Patron of Environment Saint Francis of Assisi has rightly said that if we are cruel to animals, we will be cruel to human beings too. This is quite evident in "Gayatri's Solitude", "Tsunami Camps", "Haves and Have-nots", "Laxmi's Plea", and "Old Age". "Tsunami Camps" and "Haves and Have-nots" speak out very loudly the poet's rebellion and empathy in an obvious manner: "How dreadful the life in Tsunami camps / People burnt in man-made hells / ... / Unending wails and unending sobs, / not even gods listen to their cries." (*Winged Reason*, 33–34)

But in "Haves and Have-nots" the poet's empathy and rebellion are much more pronounced:

# Philosophical Musings for a Meaningful Life

> When millions die of hunger,
> thousands compete for delicacies.
> Minority always luxuriates
> at the cost of
> majorities' necessities.
> . . . . . . . . . . . . . . .
> Capitalism rules the day;
> Have-nots numbers swell.
> Shattered and smashed
> are their dreams
> of health and happiness.
>
> (*Winged Reason*, 36–37)

In these lines, one can easily notice the fluttering and flapping of the poet's wings of reason reminding one of what Ivor Armstrong Richards said: "Poetry is a perfectly reasonable means of overcoming chaos." Since human behavior depends on the nature of individual and the nature of situation, Dominic's poetry helps us to overcome chaos by bringing a harmony between the nature of individual and the nature of situation because his poetry is a perspicacious response to human condition or situation. Look at "Laxmi's Tea", perhaps the most moving poem in *Winged Reason* for those who know the gamut of socio-cultural situation of India, where woman is the most despised with a sociometry which is awfully misogynist; yet, that schizophrenically deifies and glorifies woman. She is the goddess who is burned alive on the funeral pyre of the husband (sati) or in the rising flames of dowry-greed. See these lines:

> She is a lamp to any house
> A lamp destined to burn out
> under a hot pot.
> Plenty of proposals;
> appeared with tea
> before many young men.
> None complained my looks.
> 'What's the dowry?'
> A stumbling block to all proposals.
> Father died when I was ten;
> Mother bed-ridden with cancer;
> A thatched house in five cents;
> . . . . . . . . . . . . . . . . . . .
> I have pricked my bubble of dreams;
> let none dream for me.
> Leave me alone;
> leave me single.
>
> (*Winged Reason*, 46–47)

Through this poem, the poet tells us the inner turmoil and anxiety of a single Indian woman, perhaps an allusion to what we call Abstract Expressionism in painting, which shows turmoil through colors and lines because of a disturbing situation or an impending threat. This is quite evident in the paintings of Michael Goldberg, and in *Winged Reason*, the poet has done it through words and verse. Laxmi is the archetype of the negation of individuality, a typical reflection of Indian worldview. If we can see sympathy and empathy in "Laxmi's Tears" in relation to Indian womanhood, the rebel in the poet very clearly comes out in "International Women's Day": "Problems remain the same! / Woman is the game! / Birth to death, / an instrument of lust / and hot selling sex! / Her very birth ill omen: / an unwelcome event. / No guilt in foeticide; / foeticide is matricide; / no life without mother. / Sexism in childhood; / priority to her brother; / her food, his leftover. / Chained in kitchen, / she rarely goes out. / No toys, no plays; / always envies him /... / her individuality / scantily respected. / Born to be dictated; / tyranny everywhere;" (*Winged Reason*, 42–43) But the poet's rebellion comes to us as several brain-racking questions.

## Rebellion as Questions

Who is woman for you in Indian society? This is the unasked question I could find in most of Dominic's poems related to women, a sharp critique of the society in which he lives and moves. This question comes from a rebel who does not pose as an obvious rebel like the poets of Latin America or other countries, where the people went through barbaric oppressions and political suppressions. But as a sensitive poet, who deals with the theme 'woman' in relation to India, he asked this pertinent question because of the situational imperatives he confronts in his daily life. When we consider the conventional and dominant Indian ethos, woman appears to be a mere commodity to be used and abused by an all-powerful and perverted patriarchy. To cover up this patriarchal putrefaction, we will find some beautiful philosophical and religious notions that glorify and 'godify' (deify) woman. This deification is the cover-up for all the inhumanities heaped on Indian woman, and the numerous temples built all over the western and northern India in honor of the mother goddess is the hard proof for this deification. But the sex ratio in these parts of India has hit the rock bottom—800 females for every 1000 males. So an alarmed Narendra Modi Government has introduced a new scheme in the union budget—beti bachao, beti parhao' (save the girl, educate the girl). What a paradox—worship and rubbish!

In most of the 19 poems relating to women, the poet depicts a distraught woman or a girl who has a disturbing question to ask: "Ma, why didn't God create me a little more beautiful?" ("Beauty", *Winged Reason*, 28) This is a congenital question with which every Indian woman is born, and it is compounded by the mad adoration Indians have developed for the physical beauty and white color, and you will understand this social psychology better if you can read "The Continent of Circe" by Nirad C. Chaudhuri. The children of Circe, a euphemism for Indians, like fair-skinned beauties, not the dark ones from the original stock of the subcontinent. The first ones who created this color-complex were the fair-skinned Aryans, who invaded the Gangetic plains. The white Europeans continued it. All the matrimonial advertisements loudly proclaim this and this has created a complex in an Indian girl with a gnawing grief for her life. The poet consoles her, saying the inner beauty is more important than the physical one: "Look at and think of / Shakespeare, Shaw, Gandhi, Lincoln, / Mother Teresa, Navaratilova, Venus, Serena / . . . / My dear lass, be like the sun, / brightening the dark world with your inner beauty." (*Winged Reason*, 28) Besides these consoling words, the poet has a sharp question to ask:

> When will the Black be
> kindred to the White?
> When will the Black and the White
> dwell in the same house
> and dine from the same plate?
> When will we behold God's creation
> with impartial eyes
> and find His beauty in all forms?"
>
> ("Crow, the Black Beauty", *Write Son, Write*, 57–58)

These lines remind me of the famous speech "I have a Dream" by Martin Luther King, Jr. For the poet, the wrong concept of beauty is a vexing problem and equally complex is the individuality implied in this concept of beauty. Since an Indian woman is male-dependent through and through, marriage with a man entails physical beauty, and here is the crux of the problem. But the poet wants to show woman independent of man and yet having personality of her own. "Helen and Her World" and "Sister Mercy" tell us that woman can have a personality of her own, independent of man, and yet contribute a lot to the onward march of humanity. Helen is the "Light fighting against darkness, / Eternally! Hopefully! Surely! / Helen is comfortable in life." (*Winged Reason*, 39) If Helen can do it alone as a woman, there is another one among the tribal people or adivasis of Madhya Pradesh working against all the odds to show the world that the first Article of the Universal Declaration of Human Rights is not a mere decoration: "All human beings are born free and equal in dignity and rights."

> Sister Mercy, alias Daya Bai
> a life worth her name
> ...............
> Devoted life for the tribal;
> A lone fighter for their right;
> fought against slavery;
> ...............
> Even in her late sixties
> this brave woman from Kerala
> shines like the sun;
> illumines thousands in Bykal,
> A village in Madhya Pradesh."

(*Write Son, Write*, 79–80)

K. V. Dominic's other poems of rebellion are: "A Blissful Voyage", "A Nightmare", "A Sheep's Wail", "Haves and Have-nots", "International Women's Day", "Lal Salaam to Labour", "What a Birth!", "Indian Democracy", "In the Name of God", (*Winged Reason*); "Write, My Son, Write", "Aung San Suu Kyi", "Bravo Katie Sportz!", "God is Helpless", "IAF Vayu Shakti", and "To My Colleague" (*Write Son, Write*). These poems are the best examples of the poet's spirit of rebellion; but among these, the best one is "Write, My Son, Write" which comes across to me as if the poet has put all his rebellion in the volcano of an impatient truth that encompasses everything that must be revolted against. In this long didactic poem, he has not spared anyone. including his own breed—the intellectuals.

In "A Blissful Voyage", the rebel in the poet wants to have "the claws of a vulture / to fetch the skeletons from Iraq / and build a bone-palace / to imprison Bush in it." (*Winged Reason*, 21) He goes even further: "I wish I were a bullet / and shoot into the chest of that terrorist / who compels that teenage boy / to explode and kill that innocent mob." (*Winged Reason*, 21). This is an angry outburst from a genuine mind and that is what makes it a beautiful poetry, coupled with the language of imagery the poet has employed very judiciously.

In "A Nightmare", the poet could not bear the scene where a fat plumb boy is beaten to eat while "a bony child was crying for a crumb." (*Winged Reason*, 22) The same spirit is echoed in the "Haves and Have-nots": "When millions die of hunger, / thousands compete for delicacies / Minority always luxuriates / at the cost of / majorities' necessities." (*Winged Reason*, 36) He does not spare either Communism or Capitalism. That is why in "Lal Salaam to Labour", the rebel poet laments: "They sow the seed; / reap the corn; / and we eat and sleep." (*Winged Reason*, 44) But in "Write, My Son, Write", the rebel comes out in full force doing justice to God, who asked him to "Write till / I say stop." (*Write Son, Write*, 21) This poem appears to be a commendable realization of what Dr. Samuel Johnson said: "Poetry is the art of uniting pleasure with truth, by calling imagination to the help of Reason." So the poet rightly asks: "Don't you feel / the symphony / of the universe?" (*Write Son, Write*, 22) But the questions in the poem are the arrows of rebellion: "Who gave you right / to kill my creations? / . . . / Why don't you / learn from Nature?" (*Write Son, Write*, 29–30) He is angry with the three which mislead the innocent folk: religious mafia, political mafia, and intellectual mafia.

In "Aung San Suu Kyi" and "Katie Sportz", the poet presents before us two rebels whose life itself is a message in rebellion. While the first one fought for democracy against the military suppression of freedom, the second one showed through an adventurous voyage that a woman can do what men think she cannot. "Suu Kyi, the epitome of valour, / showed her people through her life / liberty is born from the ashes of fear." (*Write Son, Write*, 53) When it comes to Katie, the poet says, "You are the icon of women's valour, / a scud missile darting through patriarchy." (*Write Son, Write*, 55)

In "Hunger's Call", the poet asks "Isn't poverty the greatest enemy?" (*Write Son, Write*, 66) And the answer is in the next poem "IAF Vayu Shakti 2010": "The dropping of each missile, / an explosion in my heart." (*Write Son, Write*, 68) Military spending while millions starve makes the rebel in the poet ask: "Who are major victims of war? / Civilians as innocent lambs; / ignorant of the bogus rift / between border nations." (*Write Son, Write*, 68) But in the poem "To My Colleague", a poem written on a barbaric act imposed on Professor T. J. Joseph of Newman College, Thodupuzha, Kerala, on July 4, 2010 (TJ's hand was chopped off by religious fanatics over a question paper row), the poet asks:

> India, my independent country!
> Largest democracy in the world!
> Largest secular State!
> Equality, fraternity, liberty,
> Liberty to do anything?
> Where is freedom of speech
> and expression?"

(*Write Son, Write*, 84)

These lines are the rebellious note of the poet that goes against the forces which curtail the freedom to think and express, which has become a major threat all over the world with the unabated rise of religious and cultural fundamentalism of every brand. But in all these rebellious waves created by the poet, one can also see a certain silence and reticence walking hand in hand.

## Worldview and Reticence

The poet's worldview is very clear from his several poems where he sees all the creatures and plants as interconnected and intra-connected, where one cannot alienate from the other. It is an all-encompassing worldview and he does not give or human beings any hallowed place in creation. In such a weltanschauung, reticence will be a corollary of rebellion because you cannot really rebel against the other as the other is part of you. Aham Brahmasmi and Tatvamasi emerge from such a worldview. We may call this Hindu worldview, or Asian worldview, where there is no "other" to rebel against. All the so-called rebel poets of Asia were merely rebel at a spiritual level or a rarefied realm. This explains why there were no revolutions or radical changes in India or even in Asia (China being an exception). Kabirdas could be called the greatest rebel poet of India, but in his case also, the rebellion stops with the spiritual realm. Dominic as an Indian has naturally imbibed this worldview and it reflects throughout his poetry.

Another reason for the reticence is the poet's view of man or human being. Unlike in the Jewish-Christian worldview, the poet does not give any special place for man as the image of God or the crown of creation, but he is merely "one" among "many"; he is not the "Manav tum sab se sundartam" (Man you are the most beautiful) of the Hindi poet Sumitranandan Pant or the Jewish philosopher Abraham J. Heschel's "Man is a peculiar being trying to understand his uniqueness" ("Who Is Man?", Stanford University Press, California, 1978). All the rebellions and revolts throughout history took place to restore human being's image which was the image of God but was disfigured by inhuman structures. So poets from Jewish-Christian worldview hollered out like prophet Amos of the Jewish history. I consider Amos as the greatest rebel poet in world history for his undiluted, direct utterance against injustice: "Hear this word, you cows of Bashan,... / who oppress the poor, who crush the needy... / behold, the days are coming upon you, / when they shall take you away with hooks" (Amos, 4).

Though Dominic has not said anything that harsh, yet I could see a spirit of rebellion in his poetry even when he was expressing sympathy and empathy in a given situation within his worldview. For him, man is the villain who predates on every living being. Though reticence is very much evident in almost all of his poems, he has not forgotten to speak through the rebel in him in a simple language that is intelligible for all. There is no ostentatious exhibitionism nor any shadow of conceit, but everything comes across as coming from a genuine mind with a touch of heart. Through simple themes, he has woven a tapestry of insights, images, and messages for all who care for good poems. All his poems are daunting and haunting questions to man, his favorite antagonist, who appears to be on a ravaging spree, devastating God's vineyard like a raving lunatic, and so the poet's sheep has rightly told him: "Man, you are cruelest, / you are the most ungrateful / of all God's creations." (*Winged Reason*, 25) That is why K. V. Dominic made God ask this penetrating question of man: "Who gave you right / to kill my creations?" (*Write Son, Write*, 29) I am sure his poems will compel man to search for an answer for God and His creation.

## Works Cited

Dominic, K. V. *Winged Reason*. Authorspress, New Delhi. 2010. Print.

---. *Write Son, Write*. GNOSIS, New Delhi. 2011. Print.

Heschel, A.J. "Who Is Man?", Stanford University Press, California, 1978

# Chapter 16 -
# Critical Analysis of K. V. Dominic as a Philosophical Poet by Patricia Prime

In looking at the progress of a poet, the elements most often examined are style and content, vocabulary, subject matter, and ease, or difficulty of understanding. Technique and subject matter must match, in mutual support, to produce the message the poet is trying to convey. We listen and look and read in order to weigh up the worth of the poet's exercise and our response to it—whether it "means" anything, whether it "touches" us, whether it is "worth it", if we recognize a tightening within our minds and hearts.

With the poet, Professor K. V. Dominic, his compulsion to write poetry has been pursued, consciously and rigorously. The images necessary to illustrate, to convey his ideas and thoughts when reading his work, have been meticulously researched. I am reminded of these thoughts when reading Dominic's work. He writes free verse, often with short lines and varied structure. His poems tend to be snapshots or notes along his journey through life, catching impressionistically at passing perceptions and thoughts.

Professor Dominic's first collection of poetry, *Winged Reason* (2010), contains 39 poems where the themes are those of social issues surrounding poverty, cruelty, old age, unemployment, and female foeticide. Dominic's writing emerges as an open space that takes readers back to the distress, poverty, and sickness of the slums. In "A Nightmare", the poet dreams he is a hawk above the city. Then, as he awakens to the sound of siren, he is brought to tears by the poverty of the city:

> Tears streaming down my cheeks,
> I could see nothing more,
> nor did I wish for it.
> The siren sounded as usual
> to disturb my nightmare!

(*Winged Reason*, 22)

The poet's focus on women is notable in this collection. He writes on the dignity of labor, service, maternity, the evils of dowry, and in "Gayatri's Solitude", he writes about the death of a woman at the age of 82, who was widowed and left to bring up five children, all of whom left to live in the United States:

> Dawn to dusk,
> sitting in an armchair,
> looking at the far West,
> longing for her children's calls,
> she remains lonely.
> How lucky were her parents!
> Lived happy, died happy!

(*Winged Reason*, 31)

In experimental spirit, "Kaumudi Teacher is No More" is another of Dominic's fine elegies to those people he revers in this volume. This poem is dedicated to a woman who gave her life to the services of others:

> Kaumudi pledges to wear no ornament;
> she led a humble life,
> taught Hindi in Malabar schools,
> closely followed Gandhi's footsteps,
> taught national language
> till her death at ninety-two.
>
> (*Winged Reason*, 74)

In this collection, readers engage with Dominic's poetry in a sensuous fashion; the senses, especially audition, smell, and touch are the medium through which readers enter a space of freedom and rebirth with which Dominic aims to transcend the cultural, economic, and intellectual boundaries of modern life.

*Write Son, Write* (2011) is Dominic's second volume of poetry. The book is dedicated to the poet's mother and includes a fine elegy to her: "An Elegy on My Ma". This is the conclusion of the poem, in which the son listens to his mother's words of wisdom and is now able to forge his way into the uncertain future:

> What would be our fate, Ma,
> when we become old as you?
> Who will care for us
> as we cared for you
> one after other?
> "It's better not to
> fret on morrow;
> Surrender unto Him
> who created you."
> Ma, we will go ahead
> boosted by your divine words.
>
> (*Write Son, Write*, 41)

Feminine imagery appears to suggest that Dominic's reconceptualization of the world inevitably requires the strength and resilience of women. Dominic's voice connects with a contemporary tradition of poets that seek to find the answers for a new modernity, rebuilding the bridges with nature and humanity that the stresses of modern life have buried under the rubble of its particular vision of rationalization.

The poem "Coconut Palm", for instance, exemplifies the short line, shortage-of-syntax mode. It fulfils one requirement of a poem—keeping the mind actively entertained in trying to make sense of it. In part, this is a matter of trying to determine the construct, the image and the meaning:

> Standing erect on lean tall foot
> and growing up to a hundred feet
> bearing tons of leaves and fruits.
> A marvel of all architects.
> No human hand can build
> such a parallel pillar.
> Kudos to the Architect of architects!

*(Write Son, Write, 56)*

In free verse, the run-on (or not) is particularly significant. The interplay between lineation and the syntax or flow of the sentence modulates the intonation. A lineation that disrupts or modulates the syntactic structures is potentially more expansive.

Dominic is a more sophisticated writer than the common run of free-verse poets. Even in a relatively simple descriptive poem like "Crow, the Black Beauty", the movement makes for interesting reading: "Crow, the commonest bird in the world, / cleaner of kitchen garbage / has seldom been sung / in praise by the poets" (*Write Son, Write*, 37). The subtle nuances of Dominic's poetry evoke a distinctive, telling tone that marshals the reflective elements of a coherent spectacle.

*Multicultural Symphony* (2014) is the third collection of poetry in Dominic's oeuvre. It was here that I found the opening lengthy poem "Multicultural Harmony" in six parts in which the poet addresses his readers:

> My dear fellow beings
> when will you learn
> the need for
> multicultural existence?

*(Multicultural Symphony, 15)*

Dominic becomes more alive to us as he reveals himself and gives a glimpse of the cerebral process that informs his impulse to write. Much of this book is about people reflecting on, affected by, their situation, chosen or fortuitous. The writer here shows something of his own situation and freedom of mind, and the effect that humanity has on our planet, as we see in the following poem "Global Warming's Real Culprits":

> America and other developed countries
> stamp poverty-stricken third world
> and developing countries as
> main culprits of global warming!

*(Multicultural Symphony, 26)*

The language is simple, until we begin to question it, but Dominic can manipulate words as well as anyone. The power of his writing comes to the fore in this volume; in poem after poem he thrusts forward themes and ideas with an economy of words that pushes our minds to comprehend: the images however remain to recur in our memories, as I feel these lines from the following poem show "Multicultural Kerala":

> My native State Kerala
> blessed with equable climate
> and alluring landscape
> crowned by the Sahyas
> she lies on the lap of Arabian Sea

*(Multicultural Symphony, 29)*

Like many other poems in this collection, this one demands to be re-read and thought about, as the poet follows the beauty of his country with the fact that "Education makes one cultured and civilised / teaches one noble values and principles" but "Alas high rate of literacy / doesn't yield fruit to my fellowmen" (*Multicultural Symphony*, 29). The writer strikes home immediately, in a manner that seems effortless. It is this ability to adapt the writing to the subject that is a central part of

Dominic's craftsmanship. The seemingly artless lines, indirectly resembling fragments of thought or conversation, build up to a whole that moves us by the directness of its communicative flow.

Formal preoccupations are also very apparent in Dominic's poetry. It could be said that this is poetry that gets to the "nitty, gritty" of life, that is, poetry of careful observation and painstaking thought. But that would be to understate its cumulative power; Dominic does not shy away from difficult subjects, and his craft is flexible and adaptable enough to encompass a variety of topics ranging from global warming, conservation, child labor, poverty and environmental issues. Poems about Charles Darwin, the Mullaperiyar Dam, hunger, lottery ticket sellers, and martyrs, among many other themes, are all grist to his mill. A remarkable poem "Thodupuzha Municipal Park," about the poet sitting in a park, with his senses feasting on beauty, ends with these words:

> Gone are those happy days with little kids
> They have grown up and flown away from us
> Anxiety of their future welfare has replaced
> peace and happiness that haunted in our house.
>
> (*Multicultural Symphony*, 71)

And yet, underlying this meditation is a sense of anxiety at change, an environmental awareness that is never dogmatic or strident, but is nevertheless persistently adumbrated. This comes to a head in the questioning poem "Where Shall I Flee from this Fretful Land?"

> Once God's own country with equable climate
> Rainy season for six months
> and mild summer for the rest of the year
> Blessed with brooks, rivers, lakes and greeneries
> Now people crazy for material pleasure and luxuries
> tumbled nature's balance and bounties
> resulting scanty rain and intolerable heat
> So where shall I flee from this fretful land?
>
> (*Multicultural Symphony*, 78)

There is a sense here of everything coming full circle, from the poet questioning his fellow beings in the opening poem of the collection, to questioning himself in this; but these poems describe a tragic situation and a growing problem: how does one extricate oneself from the problems of modern life?

Nevertheless, despite the anxieties darkening the edges of these poems, Dominic's is ultimately a celebrant's voice. In the final poem of this collection "Protest against Sand Mafia", we see the protest of one woman against the police and government when the sand mafia loot thousands of tonnes of sand from the beaches: the poet asks, "Will her protest go unnoticed?" and her answer is

> "I am doing this for my children
> If we don't stop them now
> There'll be nothing left on the beaches
> Our houses will submerge in the sea."
>
> (*Multicultural Symphony*, 82)

Such moments of affirmation, therefore, are far from facile; rather, this work implies that they are hard-won through experience instead of simply claimed, and this finely-judged collection makes Dominic's witness to them eminently believable.

The poet performs in private and the only time he can perform in public is when a collection of poetry is published—and then he has to wait in trepidation for its criticism.

Perhaps Dominic the poet is less likely to play to the mood or expectations of his readers, but there is a sense in which he does have to know what people think when they read his poems. All the time, through these three volumes, he is honing his ideas and vocabulary in terms of what has gone before, what can be said again, and what baggage readers carry. People become habituated to the way poetry reads and looks on the page; and if the poet wants them to address the subjects of the poems, to seek change in society, then somehow he has to encourage them with new ideas, satisfactory rhythms and excellence.

Here is a poet who has much to tell us, whose writing is clear and worth the effort to read. These books fulfill expectations and lead us to hope that Dominic will not keep us waiting too long for his next book of poems. Indeed, as we can see in the progress of these books, big issues have inspired new poems throughout Dominic's oeuvre: from poverty, unemployment, and other social issues to themes of family, love and loss, and on to ways of understanding and change.

The books reveal Dominic's curiosity about the things people do and say, so unravelling his ideas and narrative is not necessarily straightforward. There are ways for people to understand his work. The first is simply to look at it, read it, and ask oneself what it's about and, second, to let it sit for a while and then go back to it with fresh eyes and understanding.

## Works Cited

Dominic, K. V. *Multicultural Symphony.* New Delhi: GNOSIS, 2014. Print.

---. *Winged Reason*. New Delhi: Authorspress, 2010. Print.

---. *Write Son, Write*. New Delhi: GNOSIS, 2011. Print.

# Chapter 17 -
# The Relation between God, Man and Nature in K. V. Dominic's Poems
# by Mahboobeh Khaleghi

> The relation between
> Man and Nature and God;
> human beings and other beings,
> all children of God;
> Man has no right
> to torture any other being.

("How I became a Vegetarian", *Winged Reason*, 76)

Dr. K. V. Dominic—reputed poet, short story writer, critic, and editor—has authored three collections of poems: *Winged Reason* (2010), *Write Son, Write* (2011), and *Multicultural Symphony* (2014). His sensitiveness, compassion and affection are manifested in his poems. The poet depicted his point of view and philosophy of life through his poems with his straightforward style, great critical sensibility, sincere and simple expression, and truthful presentation. For him, the content is more important than the style. He agrees that his poems "lack much imagery and other figure of speech" (*Winged Reason*, 12).

In his poems, Dominic deals with a wide range of topics embracing multiculturalism, environmental problems, interconnectivity of God-Man-Nature, terrorist attacks, anti-social leaders, exploitation, corruption, politics, religion, poverty and unemployment, child labor and dignity of labor, the deep-rooted system of caste, the marginalized, the old, communalism, the contrast of city and village, happiness and sorrow, human cruelty, female foeticide, maternity, beauty, death, superstitions, etc. Through his poems, he fights with inequality, injustice, and inhumanity.

*Winged Reason*, Dominic's first collection of free verse, consists of thirty-nine poems with different subjects. In his preface to this book, he noted that "The major theme of my poetry is the external relationship between Man, Nature and God" (*Winged Reason*, 14). The survival of nature and humanity are interdependent. He believes that the earth is the home for all creatures of God. The poet tries to highlight the interconnectivity among the plants, animals, and humans. He also reminds us of our responsibilities toward nature and environment. This collection of poems is dedicated to Dominic's beloved father, late Varghese Kannappilly.

In his second anthology of thirty-one poems, *Write Son, Write*, Dominic talks about various subjects and themes. In this collection, the poet emerges, as in *Winged Reason*, the champion of peace and mercy to animals and plants. Dominic declares in his preface that "The opening poem 'Write, My Son, Write' is indeed the manifesto of my views and philosophy. Divided into twenty-one parts, it declares my views on God, Man and Nature" (*Write Son, Write*, 9). He reveals his concern for the loss of human values among human beings who do not hesitate to show their violence toward other creatures and exploit and mislead them for selfish motives. Dominic dedicated this book to his beloved mother, late Rosamma Varghese Kannappilly.

In his third poetic collection, *Multicultural Symphony*, Dominic exhibits topics such as nature, global warming, environment, multicultural beauty, social problems, violence, poverty, the deep-rooted system of caste, sexism, patriarchy, torture of elephants, belief in horoscope, and the needs for conservation of nature, value-based education and other themes. "There is not much change in [his] themes or the poetic style" of these forty-seven poems as he mentioned in the preface to this book (*Multicultural Symphony*, 7). This book is dedicated to Dominic's bosom friend and chief motivator, Sudarshan Kcherry.

In this paper, I have selected these poems for discussion: "How I Became a Vegetarian", "I am Just a Mango Tree", "Haves and Have-nots", "Nature's Bounties", "Cuckoo Singing", "A Sheep's Wail", "Sleepless Nights", "Ammini's Lament", and "Ammini's Demise" from the first collection, *Winged Reason*; "Flowers' Greetings", "Coconut Palm", "Work is Worship", "Attachment", "Write, My Son, Write", "God is Helpless", "A Cow on the Lane", "Wolfgang, the Messiah of Nature", and "Massacre of Cats" from the second anthology of poems, *Write Son, Write*; and "Multicultural Harmony" and "Ananthu and the Wretched Kite" from *Multicultural Symphony*.

"I am Just a Mango Tree" is a good example of "external affinity" between Man, Nature, and God. The poet personifies the tree when it says:

> I am Just a Mango Tree;
> still an accomplished life;
> I've fulfilled my Creator's plan.
> Standing like a Himalayan Umbrella,
> I shelter my student-friends
> waiting for the buses.
>
> (*Winged Reason*, 40)

The Mango tree reminds man of its usefulness for him. It shelters every creature in sun and rain. The tree makes fruits for them. Birds use its branches as their beds and they sleep on its lap when night comes. The tree is filled with joyousness and loveliness. "My God, how happy I feel-- / The fruit of service!" ("I am Just a Mango Tree", 41) The Mango tree gives its wood, leaves, and sweet mangos, and it gets nothing but man's cruelty in return. Its pleasure leads to sorrow due to human beings' cruelty and gracelessness.

The poem expresses the poet's sympathy for plants and trees that are uprooted by man for his own benefit. "Nature is caring, divine, and loving whereas man is violent, cruel, selfish, and egoistic" as P. C. K. Prem declares in the foreword to *Write Son, Write* (12). No one is permitted to destroy nature. Plants' and animals' life is as precious as man's life.

> "Dear, why should they cut this tree,
> a cool shelter to countless?"
> "They plan to build a waiting shed here."
> God, what do I hear? Is it true?
> 'True, my daughter, I am helpless.'
> . . . . . . . . . . . . . . . . . . . . . . . . .
> Haven't I [the tree] the right to live?
> God, why is your Man so selfish and cruel?
> Did you create him,
> to disturb this earth's balance?
> This planet would be a paradise

*Philosophical Musings for a Meaningful Life*                                                                              147

> If You kindly withdraw him.
>
> ("I am Just a Mango Tree", *Winged Reason*, 41)

God regrets and feels ashamed of man's creation for his acts of destruction and expresses His bitter feelings with pain and remorse:

> 'My child, I created him
> in My own image
> but he's gone astray;
> My agony is endless.
> That's the fate
> of the Father everywhere.
> I shouldn't have created this human species;
> But how can a father kill his sons?'
>
> ("I am Just a Mango Tree", *Winged Reason*, 41)

But God forgives man because He created man in His own image and human being is the manifestation of God's perfection. Man, like other mortal creations of God, is not allowed to ruin the earth. The sole owner of the whole universe is its Creator. In the poem "Haves and Have-nots", the poet expresses man's unequal and irrational treatment toward plants and animals.

> Plants and animals never divide
> the earth among themselves;
> what right has the mortal man
> to divide and own this immortal planet?
>
> (*Winged Reason*, 36–37)

The poet skilfully adds beauty to his haiku series "Nature's Bounties" with the personification of the nature of Almighty. He presents a heaven of natural beauty.

> The sun kisses
> The eye opens
> Lotus blooms
>
> Fragrance of the rose
> Intoxication to the fly
> Dancing round the plant
>
> Jasmine's hand
> Caressing touch on my neck
> Utter dilemma
>
> (*Winged Reason*, 49\

In this poem, the poet describes the celebration of God's nature. The cuckoo sings. Lotus blooms by the sunlight. The fly dances around the plants, intoxicated by the sweet smell of the roses. The touch of jasmines purifies body and soul. Crows and mynahs feast on yellow mellow papaya. Lightning and thunder are followed by summer rain that tastes like honey to the lips and enchants a child to dance. The snow-covered mountains and the "multi-coloured sky" are natural beautiful paintings of God.

"Flowers' Greetings" describe the beauty of nature. It is another poem that demonstrates the poet's love for nature when he feels he can understand the language of the flowers and communicate with them. On his way to the university, the roses smile at him and greet him with "Good Morning". And he smiles back.

> I noticed the petals
> waving at me
> "Bon Voyage!"
> The lilies then
> wished me,
> "Good Health!"
>
> (*Write Son, Write*, 59)

"Coconut Palm" is a short poem that presents the rapid growth of the tree whose every part is used for human welfare.

> Tall and majestic coconut palm
> shot like a rocket to the sky
> with a brilliant view of
> sparkling leaves and alluring nuts.
> Best friend of human beings;
> foot to tips not any inch useless.
>
> (*Write Son, Write*, 56)

This very tall tree bears "tons of leaves and fruits. / A marvel to all architects." And God who created the majestic tree is "the Architect of architects!" ("Coconut Palm", 56)

Nature teaches man the philosophy of life. The correct use of nature can even be a source of pleasure, peace, enlightenment, fulfilment, solace, and salvation.

Cuckoo's voice is the sweetest song in nature. It is heard even sweeter than any music composed by human being. Cuckoo's song is a "waking call for dreaming day".

> What do the sounds mean?
> "Wake up mate,
> let's start love" or
> "Wake up man and
> sweat for your bread"?
> Yes, cuckoo lives
> singing and loving,
> while man exists
> sweating and moaning
>
> ("Cuckoo Singing", *Winged Reason*, 30)

The songs of birds, the dance of plants, and the fragrance of flowers provide joy in man's life. Nature is fundamentally generous. All other creations of God are at the service of man if human beings contemplate properly and values God's gifts. Man should have friendship with everything in nature:

> My dear son, live in Karma,
> love all creations,
> for I am in everything.
>
> ("Work is Worship", *Write Son, Write*, 96)

The poet asks God to teach man to love non-human:

> and also teach my neighbours

> and millions of my brothers and sisters
> to show love and mercy
> to all non-human beings
>
> ("Attachment", *Write Son, Write*, 52).

In the poem "A Sheep's Wail", the sheep tells that man, as the most intelligent creation, has certain "special powers" that the sheep doesn't have. Man uses fur, milk, and flesh of the sheep. The sheep is there for man's benefit. But man is the most ungrateful of God's creations since he creates disharmony and imbalance in life. The sheep addresses man:

> Man, you are the cruellest,
> you are the most ungrateful
> of all God's creations.
>
> (*Winged Reason*, 25)

Man does not deserve to live in Heaven; it's the sheep and other animals that serve man, God's "choicest" being while man, social animal, exploits them for her gains.

> we will reach there [heaven] first
> and pray to God to shut you out.
>
> (*Winged Reason*, 25)

The harmony of nature and disharmony of man have been juxtaposed in the following lines:

> Accipitrine birds like kites, hawks, eagles,
> God created them carnivores
> Prey on birds, insects, animals for survival
> Whereas we human beings
> butcher animal world
> not for existence but for taste
> . . . . . . . . . . . . . . . . .
> When will we begin to love
> kites, eagles, bats, owls
> as we long for parrots, cuckoos,
> skylarks and nightingales?
> When will we stop the massacre
> of animals, birds and fish
> and learn to respect
> other beings and their right to live?
>
> ("Ananthu and the Wretched Kite", *Multicultural Symphony*, 51)

Human rebels even on God's will when He doubts at His creation.

> I breathed in him
> celestial values:
> happiness, beauty,
> peace, love, mercy;
> but he fosters
> hate and violence;
> kills his kith and kin;
> shows no mercy
> to animals and plants.

("Write, My Son, Write", *Write Son, Write*, 28)

Even man can learn virtues from plants, birds, and animals. He can learn from nature to live in harmony as the poet explains in "Write, My Son, Write":

> Why don't you
> learn from Nature?
> Animals and birds
> present you models.
> Models of pure love,
> happiness, hard work,
> suffering, kindness,
> patience, sharing,
> fellowship, gratitude.

(*Write Son, Write*, 30)

What God has created is useful. Before Him, all are equal. God loves all. Even thunder is not His wrath:

> You can't enjoy
> the beauty
> of lightning
> and thunder;
> your people think
> thunder is my
> sword of punishment.
>
> . . . . . . . . . . . . . . .
>
> [God] never hates;
> will never punish;
> only showers love
> and looks after
> His creation.

("Write, My Son, Write", *Write Son, Write*, 31)

God has created plants, animals, and nature for man's company but human being just destroys them as it is revealed in the following lines:

> You species
> can't live alone.
> . . . . . . . . . .
> I created
> for your company;
> neither can they
> exist without you.
> You speak to them
> in strange tongue,
> and they reply
> in divine speech;
> unintelligible,
> you scourge and

*Philosophical Musings for a Meaningful Life* 151

even kill them.

("Write, My Son, Write", *Write Son, Write*, 26)

Man creates imbalance between God's creations and for that God is angry with him. In the court of God, the plants and the animals complain against the human beings thus:

> Petitions come to me
> one after another
> from plants and animals.
> All complain of
> your cruelty and torture:
> they have no food;
> they have no water;
> they have no shelter;
> and not even air.
> They plead to me
> to call you back:
> save their lives,
> and thus save the planet.
> Kindly tell me, children,
> what shall I do?

("God is Helpless", *Write Son, Write*, 64-65)

The poem "Sleepless Nights" compares cuckoo's natural life with human artificial environment. The bird enjoys living in the heart of nature with gentle breeze and sleeping with no tension and full of peace:

> The cuckoo lies on the God-given bed;
> the gentle breeze always caresses him;
> the nocturnal music lulls him throughout,
> and his sleep is sound
> free from cares and worries

(*Winged Reason*, 56)

In contrast, man wakes up by the cuckoo's song every early morning; but nowadays,) man lies on his bed restless for hours, is unable to sleep well at nights because of "hot-wave fan" and late and heavy dinner. He is deprived of "God's own gift", in his "concrete house" and has lost his peace, waiting for the cuckoo's call to get rid of his prison and take refuge in the "morning beauty":

> I lie in my concrete house,
> fighting against the man-made heat,
> and the dreary sound of the hot-wave fan.
> The late and heavy supper in stomach,
> and all such unnatural ways of life
> take away that God's own gift.

("Sleepless Nights", *Winged Reason*, 56)

"A Cow on the Lane" depicts the animal's right on the lane. A smile comes on the reader's lips while reading this poetry. The man has only fifteen minutes and has to drive five more miles to reach the station to catch the train. The man honks continuously to make a cow clear the road:

> The cow retorted smiling:

> "Don't disturb my slumber."
> . . . . . . . . . . . . . . . . . . . .
> "Dear cow, kindly clear the road,"
> I pleaded her with folded hands.
> "This world is not your grandpa's.
> It's so vast and wide.
> Can't you take another route?"
>
> (*Write Son, Write*, 47)

The man admits that "What she said is right." (48) He chooses another way and reaches the station on time. Therefore, if human also shows flexibility sometimes, all creations can live in harmony. They will coexist in a warm and peaceful environment.

The interaction between Nature, God, and Man has been shown in the poem "Wolfgang, the Messiah of Nature" obviously. The poet talks about the sacrifice of Wolfgang, Nature's Christ, who departed from Berlin to Kerala "at the tender age of twenty" in order to connect Nature, God, and Man. For more than forty years, he taught people how to live in harmony with nature.

> He has realised the truth,
> the truth of eternal relations:
> between God, Man and Nature.
> Wolfgang is Nature's Christ;
> born to redeem Nature;
> his life is a sacrifice;
> atonement for human cruelty;
> expiation for felling and killing
>
> (*Write Son, Write*, 94)

Wolfgang's arrival was a blessing for snakes, amphibians, butterflies, and plants. "He has created a heaven; / a haven for his fellow creatures" (*Write Son, Write*, 93). Wolfgang dedicated his life for the animals, birds, and trees on this planet where people are destructive and cruel to other creations of God. Man doesn't have wisdom and mercy to show his love toward nature and also toward other human beings.

Besides human species, all other forms of life including animals, birds, plants, trees, and insects have the right to live with peace and kindness in God's land. Man is criminal and merciless toward other creations although all live for his benefit and comfort:

> be humble as all other beings
> This planet is a home
> to all objects living and non living
> Kindly learn your position
> You were born
> as the youngest ones
> All objects have
> the right to exist here
> You may live here
> Let other things also live
> Since you are selfish and greedy
> you take more than
> what is due to you
> Other beings struggle for necessities

> whereas you are after
> comforts and luxuries
>
> ("Multicultural Harmony", *Multicultural Symphony*, 20)

They complain to God regarding the inhuman nature and unlimited greed of man thus:

> Inhumane to animals,
> they do believe,
> all creations are for men,
> since they are born
> in God's own image.
>
> ("Ammini's Lament", *Winged Reason*, 62)

The poet prays to God to make the devils human.

> Thousands of fiends
> inhabit this planet,
> turning the earth
> to a big slaughter house,
> as if man alone has
> the right to live here.
> God, make them humane
> and turn them into angels.
>
> ("Ammini's Demise", *Winged Reason*, 65)

Through his poems, Dominic motivates humans to realize the value of God's gifts. Man should preserve nature instead of destroying it. The poet asks God to show human beings the way to peacefully exist with all other creations in the universe thus:

> God, open the eyes
> of all human beings
> and show them
> the flow of the universe
> and make them all
> as participatory beings.
>
> ("Massacre of Cats", *Write Son, Write*, 46)

## Works Cited

Dominic, K. V. *Multicultural Symphony* (A Collection of Poems). New Delhi: GNOSIS, 2014. Print.

---. *Winged Reason* (Poems). Delhi: Authorspress, 2010. Print.

---. *Write Son, Write* (A Collection of Poems). New Delhi: GNOSIS, 2011. Print.

# Chapter 18 -
# K. V. Dominic, the Messenger of
# Humanity, Peace and Harmony in the Universe
# by Sangeeta Mahesh

K. V. Dominic, a great poet of social awareness has published three collections of poems so far—*Winged Reason, Write Son, Write,* and *Multicultural Symphony.* Through his poems in all these collections he, as a true poet, sings the songs of humanity, peace, and harmony in the universe. He is the poet of social reforms. As a poet, he understands his responsibility as he writes in the preface of *Winged Reason,* his first collection of poems: "As a poet, I am responsible to my own conscience and I want to convey an emotion or a message often through social criticism. I have a commitment to my students as a professor; to the reader, scholars and writers as an editor; and to all human and non-human beings as a poet" (*Winged Reason,* 12).

His poems are full of feelings and emotions and directly touch the heart, compelling the reader to think and act. As far as style is concerned, he uses simple conversational style without any vanity and affectation. As his poetry is meant for the common people, he has covered myriad problems of the common people like poverty, Illiteracy, ignorance, superstitions, corruption, terrorism, inequality on the basis of caste and money, gender biases etc. These are "the arrows and thorns that pierce my heart every day and the gushing blood runs through my pen to paper" (Preface, *Winged Reason,* 12). He presents the harsh realistic picture of the society that can easily move the emotions of the readers. He dreams of a humanistic, peaceful, and harmonious society and requests his fellow human beings to cooperate in this mission.

*Winged Reason* is a collection of 39 poems, published by Authorspress, New Delhi, in 2010. He has touched almost all the subjects related to the universe and its inhabitants. The book opens with an elegy "In Memoriam: George Joson", written about a colleague who died in a car accident on May 14th, 2004. The poet has a very sympathetic heart. He feels unbearable pain by the demise of his friend:

> The most painful was the sight
> when your youngest kid
> not knowing what has happened,
> kissed your face
> again and again
> and plucked flowers from your wreath;
> tossed them to her sisters weeping and screaming.

(*Winged Reason,* 17)

The second poem is also an elegy titled "Long Live E. K. Nayanar", written on the death of E. K. Nayanar, thrice Chief Minister of Kerala, a State in India (delete). Nayanar was the man of the masses, who passed away on May 15th, 2004. He was truly a patriot and his "heart bled at the sight of the tears of the poor." The poet is in a trance and bids Lal Salaam to his dearest CM in the elegy:

> Our dearest CM is no more.
> A vast surging
> sea of humanity
> followed wailing and weeping
> you on your last journey.
>
> (*Winged Reason*, 19)

The poet dreams of a humanistic society free from communalism, and for that, he wants to "soar high / on the wings of the Muses / and visit the places / inaccessible." ("A Blissful Voyage", *Winged Reason*, 21).

He is afraid of the increasing terrorism, particularly of training teenagers for terrorist activities by misguiding them in the name of the religion. His emotions burst out:

> I wish I were a bullet
> and shoot in to the chest of that terrorist
> who compels that teenage boy
> to explore and kill that innocent mob.
>
> ("A Blissful Voyage", *Winged Reason*, 21)

Tears scream down his cheeks when he sees inequality in society. On the one side, he sees "A lavish wedding feast", and on the other side "two ragged girls outside, struggling with the dogs in the garbage bin" ("A Nightmare", *Winged Reason*, 22). In his poem "A Nightmare", he takes the form of a hawk and hovers in the sky:

> I could view the cry of an obese boy
> whose mother was beating him to eat more.
> A cry of a different note was heard from the next door,
> where a bony child was crying for a crumb.
>
> ("A Nightmare", *Winged Reason*, 22)

In the poem "Anand's Lot", he raises the problem of child trafficking. He gives the realistic, pathetic description of how the innocent children are kidnapped and then tortured forced into begging (*Winged Reason*, 26). In another poem, "Beauty", he teaches the lesson that one should not be concerned about physical beauty. It is the internal beauty or the great deed of a man that makes him beautiful. He writes in the poem "Beauty":

> Bodily beauty is only one among the beauties
> It fades and decays as flower does.
> . . . . . . . . . . . . . . . . . . . . .
> Eternal beauty is in achievement eternal.
> Handsome is he who handsome does.
>
> (*Winged Reason*, 28)

In the poem "Cuckoo Singing", cuckoo's song is the wakeup call for him. He hears the note: "Wake up man and / Sweat for your bread" (*Winged Reason*, 30).

In the modern time, aged persons are facing the problem of loneliness as their children are very busy and mostly working abroad. The poet's emotions for aged persons are described in the poem "Gayatri's Solitude":

## Philosophical Musings for a Meaningful Life                                                157

>   An old lily flower
>   pale and faded.
>   Dawn to dusk,
>   sitting in an armchair
>   looking at the far West,
>   longing for her children's calls,
>
>                                                           (*Winged Reason*, 31)

Dominic emphasizes maintaining harmony not only among human beings but with nature also. Today, in the name of development, man is exploiting natural resources resulting in many natural disasters. In the poem "I am Just a Mango Tree", he personifies a tree and makes him speak:

>   Don't I have feelings and pains
>   though I endure in silence?
>   Haven't I the right to live?
>   God, why is your Man so selfish and cruel?
>   Did you create him
>   to disturb this earth's balance?
>
>                                                           (*Winged Reason*, 41)

He is concerned about the condition of woman in society and wishes that woman should be "venerable". He criticizes the evil tradition of dowry in the poem "Laxmi's Plea" (*Winged Reason*, 46–47). In many of his poems, he motivates the readers to face the challenges of life with positive attitude. In the poem "Vrinda", he gives the example of the girl with one leg, "dancing like a peacock" in a TV programme:

>   Thousands of miles ahead
>   to tread with one leg.
>   She turned her challenge
>   to strength and success.
>   A loud message for the world!
>
>                                                           (*Winged Reason*, 57)

The poet, like a painter of realism, presents a very pathetic picture of a poor Indian woman in the poem "What a Birth!" (*Winged Reason*, 58) He satirizes the political scenario of India in the poem "Indian Democracy": "Thus Democracy Reigns / Drinking Tears of Thousands!" (*Winged Reason*, 80) The poet believes that not only human beings but all the creatures in this universe are God's creation. Human beings should not show their supremacy by torturing or killing other beings for their pleasure. He is shaken and shattered completely on the murder of Ammini, his dear pet cat:

>   Thousands of fiends
>   inhabit this planet,
>   turning the earth
>   to a big slaughter house,
>   as if man alone has
>   the right to live here.
>   God, make them humane
>   and turn them into angels.
>
>                                              ("Ammini's Demise", *Winged Reason*, 65)

We see the note of spirituality in his poem "Om":

> Om is our breath;
> a tonic to mind and body.
> It's a celestial music
> showering manna on the earth;
> it gives us peace and happiness;
> Om Shanti, Om Shanti, Om Shanti.
>
> (*Winged Reason*, 66)

Dr. K. V. Dominic's second collection of poems is *Write Son, Write,* published by *GNOSIS*, New Delhi, in 2011. The poems in this collection also deal with the theme of humanism, peace, and harmony. In many poems, the poet condemns man for running after materialism, forgetting the values, family, and social relations. Man today is neither in harmony with himself nor with his fellow beings and nature. The book starts with the title poem "Write, My Son, Write", which is divided into twenty-one parts and describes the philosophy of the poet. The poet writes in his preface, ". . . It declares my views on God, Man and nature" (*Write Son, Write*, 9). This poem is written in the conversational style, a talk from God to man in which the Supreme power tells about the purpose of man's life and the ways to live a life that is for the welfare of the universe. The poet hears the divine voice, "I have a mission / in your creation, / . . . / Write my son write. / Write till / I say stop" (*Write Son, Write*, 21). In parts two, three, and four, he asks to feel and understand the symphony, rhythm, and harmony, "in every molecule / every atom; / every movement;" (*Write Son, Write*, 22). In parts five, six, and seven, he tells that all creatures on this earth—whether animals, birds, insects, or human—have equal importance and they are dependent on each other for their existence. Further, he says that God created man by filling his brain "with seeds of knowledge" and infusing in him "celestial values: / happiness, beauty / peace, love, mercy;" (*Write Son, Write*, 28), but man is not using these gifts; rather he is fostering hate and violence. He says that man has no right to kill the other species of nature. He should be humble to every creature, whether a mosquito or a snake. In part seventeen of the poem, he criticizes the religious mafia:

> Religious mafia
> created thousands of gods.
> Creator, creation, creature--
> simple enough
> to learn the relation.
> Myriads of religions,
> gods, saints, prophets;
> religious mafia needs
> them to exploit
> innocent laymen.
> Heaven and hell
> they created
> to frighten the masses.
>
> (*Write Son, Write*, 33)

He further writes about these religious mafias:

> They never preach
> Karma is the best prayer;
> work is worship;
> service to the poor;
> service to the needy;

> service to the tortured;
> service to animals
> and plants and trees
> are services to me.
>
> (Write Son, Write, 34)

In part nineteen of the poem, he attacks the political mafias:

> The political mafia
> exploits masses;
> dictates, strangles
> and make them slaves;
> imprisons, kills
> those who question
> their authority.
>
> (Write Son, Write, 36)

In part twenty of the poem, he curses the intellectual mafias by comparing them with religious mafias. In part twenty-one, the poem ends with the alarming note:

> Enough, my son,
> enough;
> nothing more
> to tell your species.
> If they heed
> they will be saved;
>
> (Write Son, Write, 37)

The next poem, "An Elegy on My Ma", was written in the memory of his mother after her death. In this poem, he remembers the love and care provided by his mother, and feels, "Truly mother's love / is the purest love" (*Write Son, Write*, 39). After the death of his mother, he is deeply moved, but in the end of the poem, he tries to console himself:

> "It's better not to
> fret on morrow;
> Surrender unto Him
> who created you."
> Ma, we will go ahead
> boosted by your divine words.
>
> (Write Son, Write, 41)

Another poem that comes out of his tears is "Massacre of Cats" that was written after the death of his four favorite cats, which were poisoned to death by his cruel neighbor (*Write Son, Write*, 44–45).

The poet hates racism or the color discrimination. His views are well expressed in the poem, "Crow, the Black Beauty":

> When will "crow-crow" be
> pleasing as "koo-koo"?
> When will the Black be
> kindred to the White?
> When will the Black and the White

> dwell in the same house
> and dine from the same plate?
> When will we behold God's creation
> with impartial eyes
> and find His beauty in all forms?
>
> (*Write Son, Write*, 57–58)

In the poem "For the Glory of God" (*Write Son, Write*, 61–62), the poet highlights the example of humanity and benevolence. Resiya, though of a different religion, helps Chellamma, an old lady of seventy-five, who is rejected by her relatives and society. The poet believes that service to humanity is service to God. In the poem "God is Helpless" (*Write Son, Write*, 63–65) the poet wants to tell that only man is responsible for any kind of natural devastation as he is continuously exploiting nature. God is helpless and he cannot do anything for man in this condition. In the poem "Hunger's Call", the poet gives a very horrible description of poverty:

> A startling news with
> photos from Zimbabwe!
> Carcass of a wild elephant
> consumed in ninety minutes!
> Not by countless vultures
> but by avid, famished
> men and women and children.
> Even the skeleton was axed
> to support sinking life with soup.
>
> (*Write Son, Write*, 66)

The poet is the worshipper of peace and dislikes any demonstration of power or force by any country. In the poem "IAF Vayu Shakti" (*Write Son, Write*, 67–68), the poet raises voice against spending billions on arms that could instead be spent "to feed millions' hungry mouths". In the poem "Rocketing Growth of India" (*Write Son, Write*, 77–78), he makes a satire on the development of our country by talking about the poverty, illiteracy, and superstitions prevalent in our country. We very often hear of incidents of stampede and chaos at such places where) free meals are distributed. One such incident is quoted by the poet in this poem. The poem "Train Blast" (*Write Son, Write*, 85–86) describes the terrorist activities that cause thousands of deaths. The poet composed the poem "Water, Water, Everywhere..." on World Water Day. In this poem, he tells about the importance of water:

> Water, the source of life;
> Omnipresent and abundant
> like its parent oxygen.
> Free and 'insignificant'
> for millions;
> going to be more precious
> than gold and diamond.
>
> (*Write Son, Write*, 91)

He also highlights the problem of global warming and its consequences. In the poem "Work is Worship" (*Write Son, Write*, 95–96) the poet tells that the best way to please God is to work. In the last poem "Lines Composed from Thodupuzha River's Bridge" (*Write Son, Write*, 99) the poet enjoys nature's beauty in the morning.

*Philosophical Musings for a Meaningful Life*

*Multicultural Symphony* is his third collection of poems, recently published (in 2014), by GNOSIS, in New Delhi. It includes 47 verses on various topics. In this collection also, he imparts moral values to people. He writes in the preface of this book, "Poetry is the best and easiest medium of imparting messages and values to the people. In this busy cyber-age, which is fast deteriorating in eternal human values, poetry has a great role in moulding cultured and civilized society…" (*Multicultural Symphony*, 7). The book opens with the poem "Multicultural Harmony" that consists of six parts. In the first part of the poem, the poet praises the beauty of diversity:

> Multiplicity and diversity
> essence of universe
> From atom to the heavens
> multiculturalism reigns
> This unity in diversity
> makes beauty of universe.
>
> (*Multicultural Symphony*, 15)

The poet hates any kind of discrimination on the basis of caste, color, religion, gender, or nationality. At one place, in the same poem, he describes the plight of female in human world, while there is no such discrimination in the animal world. He writes in part three of the poem:

> in human world
> Her birth is ill omen
> Millions are butchered
> before they are born
> Parents receive her
> as burden to family
>
> (*Multicultural Symphony*, 18)

He advocates vegetarian food as human beings have no right to kill the poor animals. He advises man not to fight in the name of culture:

> Is there any culture
> which is not hybrid?
> Is there any language
> which is not mixed?
> How many millions have been killed
> in the name of culture?
> Look into the pages of history
> Most of the wars have been waged
> for the supremacy of culture
>
> (*Multicultural Symphony*, 22)

The poet gives the message of harmony in the beautiful concluding lines of the poem "Multicultural Harmony":

> Dear my fellow beings
> break away all fences and walls
> Fences of your petty minds
> Compound walls of your houses
> Walls of your religions and castes
> Boundaries of your native States
> And ultimately borders of your nations
> Let there be no India, Pakistan or China
> America, Africa, Europe or Australia
> But only one nation THE WORLD
> where every being lives in perfect harmony
> as one entity in multicultural world
>
> *(Multicultural Symphony, 23)*

The second poem "Siachen Tragedy" (*Multicultural Symphony*, 24), reminds the heartbreaking tragedy in which a hundred and twenty soldiers were buried under snow and died. In the poem "Horoscope" (*Multicultural Symphony*, 25), the poet criticizes the matching of horoscopes at the time of marriages and calls it ignorance and superstition:

> Peace and happiness are fruits of Karma
> Horoscope is the product of religious mafia
> A means to exploit laity's ignorance
> Millions are trapped in this vicious circle
> No sign of redemption in near future
>
> *(Multicultural Symphony, 25)*

The poet raises environmental issues in many poems of this collection. He warnsman against global warming. In the poem "Cohabitance on the Planet" (*Multicultural Symphony*, 27–28), the poet gives the message that all the creatures on this earth have equal right to live and so man should not consider himself the best, and live in harmony with other human beings. In the poem "Multicultural Kerala" (*Multicultural Symphony*, 29–30), the poet hurls satire at those people who, even becoming literate, remain superstitious:

> Alas high rate of literacy
> doesn't yield fruit to my fellowmen
> They are puppets in the hands of
> religious and political mafias
> Become preys to superstitions,
> offshoots of religious blind faith
> Millions are spent for
> senseless rituals and ceremonies
>
> *(Multicultural Symphony, 30)*

He satirizes the development of our country, India:

> Sixty percent of my countrymen
> defecate in open place
> Six hundred and twenty six million!
> My country is number one in the world!
>
> ("India, Number One", *Multicultural Symphony*, 34)

*Philosophical Musings for a Meaningful Life* 163

The poet's ecological concern is visible in the poem "On Conservation" (*Multicultural Symphony*, 31) when he makes an appeal to save paper. "Though I am a passive sheet of paper/I have a soul as vibrant as yours" (*Multicultural Symphony*, 31). In the poem "Child Labour" (*Multicultural Symphony*, 35–36), the poet portrays the very shameful condition of India, where parents are bound to sell even their own children out of poverty and hunger. These children are treated very inhumanly by their masters, sometimes resulting in their painful death.

In the poem "Caste Lunatics" (*Multicultural Symphony*, 37), he describes the incident that took place in Madhya Pradesh, where a Dalit fellow was beaten mercilessly because he was riding a motorcycle. The poet's emotions burst out: "My country, the greatest democracy, / when will it be freed from / lunatics of caste and religion?" (*Multicultural Symphony*, 37). "Beena's Shattered Dreams" (*Multicultural Symphony*, 40–41) portrays the pathetic picture of inhuman working conditions at workplaces that compel the youths to commit suicide. The poet wants to fly on time's shoulders and be a kid again to enjoy his childhood and the love of his parents in the poem "I Wish I Could Fly Back" (*Multicultural Symphony*, 44). In the poem "Dignity of Labour" (*Multicultural Symphony*, 47), he condemns the imitation of the West only in the outward ways of living and not following their qualities:

> My countrymen fail to imitate
> noble qualities:
> industry, perseverance,
> enterprise, adventure,
> equality, fraternity,
> cleanliness, health
> love of nature
> and environment
>
> (*Multicultural Symphony*, 48)

The poet has a tender and compassionate heart. He is deeply moved by the death of the two teenagers, who, while trying to learn swimming to serve their motherland, drowned in the river. In this poem, "Drowned Dreams", he asks: "Bharat Matha, / why didn't you hold them from sinking / who were willing to guard you from enemies?" (*Multicultural Symphony*, 48) Dr. K. V. Dominic is a teacher. He always imparts moral values and creates social awareness through his poems. Through the poem "Hungry Mouths", the poet imparts the message not to waste food:

> Dear, you don't realize
> the price of your leavings;
> it can save
> a child like you
> from his death today.
>
> (*Multicultural Symphony*, 50)

In the same poem, he further says:

> whenever you
> sit before food
> lend your ears
> to the hungry cries
> of millions of kids
>
> (*Multicultural Symphony*, 50)

In the poem "Sail of Life", the poet becomes philosophical:

> My boisterous sail will reach
> its harbour one day
> I will be astonished
> by its stillness and darkness
>
> *(Multicultural Symphony,* 56)

His love for animals is visible in the poem "Multilingual Black Drongo":

> How sweet and musical
> are the sounds of animal world
> when compared to the toxic sounds
> vomited by the human species
> defiling air chaste and pure!
>
> *(Multicultural Symphony,* 60)

The poet is a worshipper of peace and dislikes war between nations. In the poem "Martyrs at the Borders", he portrays the plight of the soldiers:

> thousands of soldiers patrol day and night
> deprived of warmth of love
> from their spouses and children
> How their families long to meet them
> counting down months and days!
> How these guardian angels
> thirst for communion with their families!
> How much of a country's revenue
> allotted for its defence every year!
> Total money spent on defence
> can wipe out poverty from the planet for ever
>
> *(Multicultural Symphony,* 67)

The poet is grieved by the ills of human life and his emotions are reflected in many poems like "Tears of World Champion" (*Multicultural Symphony,* 68–69), "Thodupuzha Municipal Park" (*Multicultural Symphony,* 70–71), "Why is Fate so Cruel to the Poor?" (*Multicultural Symphony,* 72) etc. In the poem "Where shall I flee from this Fretful Land", he writes:

> Now people crazy for material pleasures and luxuries
> tumbled nature's balance and bounties
> resulting scanty rain and intolerable heat
> So where shall I flee from this fretful land?
>
> *(Multicultural Symphony,* 79)

He has written many poems like "A Tribute to Shakuntala Devi" (*Multicultural Symphony,* 76) and "Homage to Swami Vivekananda" (*Multicultural Symphony,* 79) etc. as a tribute to the great persons of the history, who have achieved greatness by their qualities of head and heart. Dr. K. V. Dominic is the poet of social consciousness. In the last poem of this collection, "Protest against Sand Mafia", the poet quotes the strike of "Thirty-one-year-old Jaheera / with her three little kids" against sand mafia, who are responsible for many natural calamities by the side of rivers:

> New Delhi's Jantar Mantar
> Haven of Satyagraha strikers

> Thirty-one-year-old Jazeera
> with her three little kids
> The youngest boy only two
> Tented on the footpath
> Staying on a cot under plastic sheet
> Neither torrid heat of summer
> nor freezing cold of winter
> can defeat her will power
>
> (*Multicultural Symphony*, 83)

Thus we can say that Dr. K.V. Dominic is the poet of humanity, peace, and harmony. He has a tender heart that bleeds not only for the sufferings of mankind but also for animals, birds, fish, and even insects. He is the painter of realistic imbalanced society, full of pain and sufferings, and the dreamer of idealistic society, where all creatures in this universe live in harmony and enjoy the bounties of nature. He believes that human survival is possible only when man learns to care for nature and all its inhabitants. The poet does not write merely for aesthetic pleasure, but in his poems, he always conveys some message to the society. He believes that poetry comes out of the wail of the poet's heart. P. C. K. Prem writes about him in his foreword to the book *Write Son Write*:

> There are very few poets who have shown so much anxiety and anguish for the poor and the exploited. Dominic is a poet of the masses, it is evident, but he is not a philosopher. He wants social status with prestige to the poor and the miserable, and thus he is a poet of the downtrodden. And so, these beautiful lyrics reveal that Dominic is an artist of social panorama. (*Write Son Write*, 16–17)

## Works Cited

Dominic, K. V. *Multicultural Symphony*. GNOSIS, New Delhi. 2014. Print.

---. *Winged Reason*. Authorspress, New Delhi. 2010. Print.

---. *Write Son, Write*. GNOSIS, New Delhi. 2011. Print.

# Chapter 19 -
# Philosophical Musings for a Meaningful Life: An Analysis of K. V. Dominic's Poetry by Dr. Radhamany Sarma

This paper is a modest attempt in tracing, by way of vital analysis, some of the issues which are inherent in society, both as salutary and laudable, and at the same time, some elements both cankerous and detrimental for the growth of the society. Prof. K. V. Dominic, with his cosmopolitan outlook, and extensively pervasive insightful eye, observes the society and records his legitimate cogitations in his poetry. This paper highlights some of the select issues, such as: human rights and human dignity-related concerns around the world, the grandeur of Nature, environment, war and peace, child labor, social criticism, cruelty to animals, religious fanaticism, etc. K. V. Dominic, needless to say, is a multifarious personality. The Indian-English poet, critic, short story writer, and editor, who's been widely published and anthologized, has authored nineteen books to his credit, inclusive of three collections of his poems: *Winged Reason* (2010), his maiden book of poems; next, *Write Son, Write* (2011); and the third being *Multicultural Symphony* (2014). These three books are extensively quoted and cited, to establish the line of argument cited in the title of the paper. Dominic, a retired professor of English, is a pragmatic soul, seeking solution for all the ailments of society. There is no pitfall or human shortcoming which escapes his prudent notice.

## Human Rights and Human Dignity

His is a soul with unflinching loyalty; his is a voice for the Call of Conscience, also commiseration for the downtrodden and afflicted. In his first volume of poems, *Winged Reason*, Dominic emphatically speaks his voice in his poem, a noteworthy write "Lal Salaam to Labour" how we have scant respect for them, for those doing hard labor—be it a mason, or weaver, farmer, or road-builder; it is not their work that counts; it is their sweat, their hard labor that we need to pay for, pay heed to . Awareness should creep in that we must pay them more than they deserve. Worshipfully they deserve our attention and genuine acclaim.

> Lal Salaam to Labour,
> the backbone of the Country!
> They sow the seed!
> reap the corn;
> and we eat and sleep.
> . . . . . . . . . . . .
> They build houses
> where they never rest,
> and we live and snore.
> . . . . . . . . . . . . .
> They tar the road;
> melt in the furnace;

>     and we ride and drive.
>     . . . . . . . . . . . . . . . .
>     Lal Salaam to Labour,
>     for without them we have no life.
>
>     Let us not be unjust
>     when we pay them wages,
>     for we can't do what they do.

(Winged Reason, 45)

Placing ourselves in their desperate position, toiling and moiling, where would we be? That is the vexed, exhausted, unanswered question foraying most of the thinkers and reformers, and writers as well.

Yet, in another simple but honest, plain poem, "Dignity of Labour", he bemoans the loss of values and how Indians, our own countrymen, ape the western color and dress and style, but irredeemably fail to imitate noble qualities:

>     industry, perseverance,
>     enterprise, adventure,
>     equality, fraternity,
>     cleanliness, health
>     love of nature
>     and environment

(Multicultural Symphony, 47)

The writer also is saddened to record and admit that a class called "underdogs"—those sweepers, scavengers, barbers, and drivers—is seldom recognized for their service to humanity. Is it not a blatant denial of human dignity, the due recognition of their service? This emphatic, avowed craving for human rights, stemming from the kernel of the poet's heart, is seen throughout his writing corpus.

In another significantly composed poem running to six parts, titled "Multicultural Harmony", he insists on equal human rights to live on this planet. In part four, he affirms or asserts in his own way:

>     This planet is a home
>     to all objects living and non living
>     Kindly learn your position
>     You were born
>     as the youngest ones
>     All objects have
>     the right to exit here
>     You may live here
>     Let other things also live

(Multicultural Symphony, 20)

Yet, man continues to delve and divide and apportions land and kind among his kith and kin.

## Nature's Grandeur

For Dominic, jasmine and rose, summer and lightening, thunder and the song of cuckoo delight and worshipfully mystify his poetic aura. The ordinary day today events, the poet transforms into delectable images of bounty and action by his insightful observation and vivid touches of poetic hues and vibrancy. Right through the ages, literature abounds in myriad examples of this apotheosis of

# Philosophical Musings for a Meaningful Life

nature. Dominic, here, with a dexterous stroke of modernity, paints "Nature's Bounties"; they are a beautifully carved series of Haiku:

> The song of Cuckoo
> Night's Dirge
> Day's trumpet
>
> The birth of morn
> Temples and mosques chanting hymns
> Heaven on Earth
> . . . . . . . . . . . . . .
> Fragrance of the rose
> Intoxication to the fly
> Dancing round the plant
>
> Jasmine's hand
> Caressing touch on my neck
> Utter dilemma
>
> (*Winged Reason*, 49 )

The poet is thrilled by the aroma of the rose; morn's chant runs a note of vibrancy in him. Coleridge, in his poem titled "The Rose", deftly paints a similar adoration for roses. If intoxication could affect a fly, what would be the amazing thrill of an entity lost in love?

> As late each flower that sweetest blows
> I plucked the Garden's pride!
> Within the petals of a Rose
> A sleeping Love I spied.
>
> Around his brows a beamy wreath
> Of many a lucent hue;
> All purple glowed his cheek, beneath,
> Inebriate with dew.
>
> ("The Rose")

With the same pride and privilege, a mango tree speaks with the well-observant eye of a yielding Samaritan, its selfless sacrifices and service-oriented motives in Dominic's poem titled "I am Just a Mango Tree" in a first-person conversational tone, taking the readers into intimacy. In a sweet gesture of goodwill, affection, and endearment, the mango tree entwines the looks of passersby. The tree also philosophizes man's folly and brutal selfishness in perpetuating deforestation, and concludes in the final line: "God repents, His own Creation." In humble tone, the mango tree starts thus:

> I am Just a Mango Tree;
> Still an accomplished life;
> I've fulfilled my creator's plan.
> Standing like a Himalayan umbrella,
> I shelter my student-friends
> Waiting for the buses.
> . . . . . . . . . . . . . . . .
> My branches are the beds for birds;

cuckoos, crows,and mynahs come;
when my fruits are ripe, a feast to them.

(*Winged Reason*, 40)

The tree is a shelter, manna, and a cathartic agent. In the concluding lines, the poet puts in the words of God that man is a cruel, destructive weapon. Yet, in another extraordinary poem, "Coconut Palm", he extols the bounty, beauty, and its status as "Architect":

> Tall and majestic coconut palm
> Shot like a rocket to the sky
> with a brilliant view of
> sparkling leaves and alluring nuts.
> Best friend of human beings;
> . . . . . . . . . . . . . . . . .
> and growing up to hundred feet
> bearing tons of leaves and fruits.
>
> A marvel to all architects.
> No human hand can build
> Such a parallel pillar.
> Kudos to the architect of architects.

(*Write Son, Write*, 56)

His threadbare description stemming out of observation excels our imagination.

## Environment

Dominic is keen in the preservation of animals and birds, and his affection toward animals is explicitly dealt with elsewhere. Like any other deep-thinking individual, he takes up the issue of preservation of animals and plants. It is a profoundly felt cry, a deep-rooted issue, a plea for the readers. When science is taking its upper hand, deforestation is crumbling nature's toil and Gift, urbanization seeks the shambles of greenery, it is the incumbent duty of every individual to give heed to conservation. In his poem titled "On Conservation", he opines thus:

> Hey poet, kindly heed to my plea
> before you thrust your pen
> into my bleeding heart
> . . . . . . . . . . . . . .
> I have a soul as vibrant as yours
> . . . . . . . . . . . . . . . .
> Kindly write on the need of the day
> the necessity of conservation
> of plants and animals on earth.

(*Multicultural Symphony*, 31)

This urge for conservation takes the root of indelible care attuned by admiration for the birds and plants in his poem "Bulbul's Nest":

> My Jasmine's plant
> with myriad's of hands
> embraced the slender pole
> Entangled like a

*Philosophical Musings for a Meaningful Life* 171

> lass's dishevelled hair
> Sprinkled with flowers
> Sparkling like stars
> Allured a pair of
> red whiskered bulbuls
> . . . . . . . . . . . .
> We tried our best
> not to frighten
> our divine guests
>
> (*Multicultural Symphony*, 38)

This is the utmost form of our conservation with care which fosters our environment.

## War and Peace:

Even from the days of *The Ramayana* and *The Mahabharata*, in western epics and biblical themes, war has been a perpetual theme of universal notation; why, ever since the Creation of God, war has been a painful theme of a grim threat and matter of irreparable loss and ruin, heavy destruction of blood and breath. It is a global issue. Writers, poets, seers, sages, and dramatists have time and again, in various modes, meticulously, meaningfully, tirelessly impacted upon the ruthless realities of war by illustrating episodes and anecdotes in the minds of people. Literature abounds in myriad examples in recordation. Dominic also mirrors such a painful reality by recalling an incident in his moving poetry "IAF Vayu Shakti 2010":

> Indian Air Force
> demonstrates Fire power
> at the desert of Pokhran:
> "*Vayu Shakti 2010.*"
> . . . . . . . . . . . . . . . .
> Major share of nation's budget
> Much more than spent on food,
> amassing arms, ammunitions, missiles.
> Billions have been spent
> by my country and my neighbouring countries,
> and all developed countries
> to kill their fellowmen abroad:
> upright men and women and children.
> Who are major victims of war?
>
> Civilians as innocent as lambs;
> Ignorant of the bogus rift
> Between border nations.
> Even the warriors who die;
> Die martyrs for their motherland;
> Have no rancour for their opponents;
> They are all puppets
> In the hands of vile rulers.
>
> (*Write Son, Write*, 67–68)

Dominic thoughtfully cites that martyrdom occurs in the sacrifice, bloodshed of war.

## Peace in OM:

In a way, War field is the antidote of war, for Ashoka, the great warrior, after the Kalinga War, took a vow not to touch the weapons and armaments anymore. That was the viable method of peace for him. Writer Dominic seeks solace and peace in the Divine, celestial utterance of Peace. His poem "Om" marvellously unravels many meanings of the sacred word "Om" and the essential component of peace derived thereon:

> Om, the birth-cry of this world;
> The very first sound echoing everywhere;
> the rhythm of all creations;
> from atom to stars
> Om goes on ringing.
> ................
> Om, the holiest mantra of mantras;
> Key to all problems of the world;
> Om is our breath;
> a tonic to mind and body.
> It's a celestial music
> Showering manna on the earth;
> It gives us peace and happiness;
> Om Shanti, Om Shanti, Om Shanti.
>
> (*Winged Reason*, 66)

Om is not only a Mantra of peace, but also universal peace and serenity.

## Water, Water, Everywhere

Water is one of the sacred, essential components, five elements without which we, humans can hardly survive, as it is well-accepted dogma. From time immemorial, ever since Creation, either drought or excessive floods are the ruling factors, dominating us. Right from the Himalayas down to the Ganges, water is the source of myth and flow, a holy and cathartic agent. In his poem, titled "Water, Water, Everywhere..." (composed on 22 March, 2000—the World Water Day) the poet, with a seer's mind, anticipates that water is:

> going to be more precious
> than gold and diamond.
> .............
> Desalinated water,
> the elixir of life.
> In place of shower,
> sponging with mineral oil.
> Disposable dress;
> heaps of garbage everywhere.
>
> Water rationed;
> per day quota
> half a glass.
> Kidney failure,
> major cause of mortality.

*Philosophical Musings for a Meaningful Life* 173

> Water stolen
> at gun point;
> armed forces guarded,
> water reservoir of nations.

(*Write Son, Write*, 92)

He concludes the poem with quotes by Coleridge, which have gone into English Literature adage, like "Water, water, everywhere / not a drop to drink." The scarcity, the dire need, the urge even for a single drop, as narrated and experienced by writers and people all over the world, is so saddening. Why, in our own lifetime, we have come across episodes where sages have propitiated the Rain Gods?

## Multicultural Kerala

Every poet or writer has his/her own liking or adoration for the locale, the native place in which the writer is fortunate to have been born. Even the noted Indian poet and contemporary writer Sarangi also has an abiding, worshipful fascination for his birthplace. Poet Dominic shares the same delectable experience in his poem "Multicultural Kerala". At the same time, he focuses on some of the pitfalls, leading them on to "indolent" people, a sad situation hampering the growth of the society. In the following lines, he brings out the salient features of the venerable state in which he is rooted, and his culture is shaped.

> Multicultural Kerala
> blessed with equable climate
> and alluring landscape
> crowned by the Sayhas
> she lies on the lap of Arabian sea
> Multitudes of brooks and rivers
> flow through her veins
> Thousands of species of flora and fauna
> Six months long rainy season
> followed by summer bearable
> Autumn and winter fear to enter
> Tourists call it God's own country
> . . . . . . . . . . . . . . . . . . .
> Alas high rate of literacy
> doesn't yield fruit to my fellowmen
> They are puppets in the hands of
> religious and political mafias

(*Multicultural Symphony*, 29)

The committed writer feels sad about the educated people doing menial jobs abroad. At the same time, there is an influx of people from other states of India, say Northerners, and serve the "indolent Keralites" via construction and plantation etc., This way, Dominic feels: "My state has thus become / cent percent dependent and multicultural" (*Multicultural Symphony*, 30). This is a clear example showing how the poet is concerned for the people, for his soil. The patriotic fervor is ingrained in his blood.

In another poem, he extols the beauty of the park, the comfort it affords during summer, and also regrets how man has despoiled its trilling nuances of bounty and birds' chirping, heavenly abode for those seeking rest or asylum in the park. His patriotic fervor combined with the exuberance of the park is seen in the following poem, titled "Thodupuzha Municipal Park":

> Municipal park at Thodupuzha
> beckons me my evenings
> A haven for the townsmen
> fleeing from their burning houses,
> Afternoon heat of thirty eight degrees
> Sweating throughout due to humidity
>
> Though not vast, an ideal park
> Full of trees and river adjacent
> Symphony of the chirpings from above
> Rustling of gentle leaves
> Mixed sounds of flowing vehicles

(*Multicultural Symphony*, 70)

Here also the locale, his favorite and salutary place of public service gaining significance, engages our attention.

Next, poets in almost all ages are drawn toward the sanctity of the flow of the rivers, tall cliffs, and mountains, where sages did penance; where, and in whom, Vedic miracles are deemed to have taken place. Dominic envisages rivers as embodiments of cosmic realities. In his poem, titled "Lines Composed from Thodupuzha River's Bridge", he recalls a beautiful, pleasant, enlivening, almost religious memory:

> Looking down from your girdle bridge
> my eyes and mind bathe in thy morning beauty.
> Invigorating cool water gushing through your vein
> overflows my mind with eternal realities.
> The waters I gaze now also flow beyond my eyes.
> Rivers and oceans are embodiements of cosmic reality.

(*Write Son, Write*, 99)

Thus he sees rivers as emblems of perpetuation of taking us into a realm of regions beyond regions, into cosmic reality a fable.

## Child Labor

After so many years of hard-gained independence, India still lives in a state of abject poverty, squalor, acute unemployment, corruption and above all exploitation of women, and child labor—a matter of grim apathy and concern beyond solution; for equally, there is also a growing population and the evil of illiteracy. Dominic in a moving tale, rehearses the plight of a young lass of eleven being sold by her toiling parents to an advocate's house. The victim's name is Dhanalakshmi, who was tortured, ill-treated, and her hands burnt. Dominic describes in his poem "Child Labour" the painful agony of this exploited innocent lass thus:

> Dhanalakshmi cook-cum-maid
> Her Hellish life from dawn to midnight
> Her tender soft palms
> smooth as petals of lilies,
> burnt, bruised, bled

> Sadist husband and wife
> drunk and voluptuous
> inflicted wounds on her body
> . . . . . . . . . . . . . . . . .
> When children of her age
> strolled gaily to their schools
> tears ran like brooks
> Tired of overnight's late labour
> couldn't fall in for duty at dawn
> The monster mistress poured
> hot water on her sleeping head
>
> (*Multicultural Symphony*, 35–36)

Although she left this world of cruelty, her memory lives; her example of child labor should serve as an eye-opener to all of us. Dominic observes that the tragedy took place in February 2011. Throughout the year, the newspapers flashed on such gruesome incidents. We have to pray to God that this horrendous situation should improve.

## Social Criticism:

It is not the admiration of the flora and fauna that always matters; for the poet, society in which he lives, matters more. He sounds like, "I am part of the society, hence my concern for the uncared for, downtrodden, afflicted, and hungry ones, my primary duty." The poet in Dominic sees the pitfalls of society through the critic's eyes. He views issue such as sabotage, hunger, poverty, and Tsunami Camps. In a way, bombs hurled at meetings, trains, and places of religious worship are all not merely horrendous evils but sins against all makind. In his poem "Train Blast", he wails at the disasters of grim tragedy and hurls a series of concerns and queries.

> Train blasted;
> A hundred and fifty died;
> Another heinous act of
> of Maoists.
>
> Are their hearts
> made of stone?
> Have their tears
> dried in the furnace
> of spite?
> Have they plugged
> their ears
> with their
> victim's bones?
>
> (*Write Son, Write*, 85–86)

The poet sadly recollects a grandma's wail asking why Krishna cannot punish those terrorists as he punished Asuras? Such cogitations are meant to reach God's ears; will they reach those terrorists? This is a great concern of the hour.

In another moving poem, he depicts the hunger of a child, the mother unable to feed the child for she has to take an exam, but cannot concentrate, though questions are easy; she must get employment to feed her family. The poet speaks through her heart, sadly, in his poem "Cry of My Child":

> God, can't bear that
> heart rending cry,
> like an arrow
> piercing through my heart.
>
> Oh! My child is still crying;
> Sister-in-law is helpless.
> Should I quit and feed my child?
> God, don't you hear my cry?
>
> (*Winged Reason*, 73)

There is pain, pathos, hunger, and helplessness depicted in this ponderable write. Angst and anger are pictured well here. Elsewhere he also caringly infuses advice to his son in the form of a conversation between mother and son, while the latter being fed, about food not to be wasted. He writes about the millions of hungry mouths yearning for food, such being the case, wastage is a colossal sin to be abhorred. In "Hungry Mouths", he yearns:

> Leftovers of the
> ten percent Haves
> can sustain
> ninety percent have-nots
> and make this hellish world
> a blissful heaven.
>
> (*Multicultural Symphony*, 49)

She emphasizes the precious "leavings" can be a source of savings and life-savings for myriads in the famished world.

To have an immediate picture of tsunami camps and the victims therein helplessly suffocated, the poet thoughtfully questions, how the money collected for relief fund was not spent appropriately, and wails at the failure of the people at the helm of affairs. In the poem "Tsunami Camps", he mirrors the agony, life, and starvation in cells amidst insanitary conditions:

> How dreadful the life in tsunami camps!
> People burnt in man-made hells;
> God crazy seeing their sufferings.
> Camps built of GI sheet
> melt inmates trapped in the cells.
> A furnace inside, a furnace outside;
> Mind and body burn with agony.
>
> (*Winged Reason*, 33)

The human in the poet swells with anger at the inhumane behavior of the worst, hard, diabolical devils in the society in which we live.

## Cruelty to Animals

Dominic feels like most of the many kind people around us that the voiceless animals deserve our attention and special care more than us—the privileged with a gift to profoundly voice our grievances. He bemoans that the earth has been turned into a slaughterhouse by ruthless fiends on

*Philosophical Musings for a Meaningful Life* 177

this earth. He recalls the sad end of his pet cat, poisoned to death. Every minute detail dovetailed in the description of the pet cat reveals his affection for the voiceless. In the poem "Ammini's Demise", he portrays his feelings thus:

> My Ammini cat's demise
> steals my sleep.
> day in, and day out,
> her snow-white figure,
> her emerald eyes,
> black bushy tail,
> her genteel demeanour,
> her sleep on my lap,
> throng my heart,
> and hangs me down.
> Let me add to Keats':
> A thing of beauty
> is a joy forever;
> and its loss
> sorrow for ever;
> Poisoned to death
> Ammini's struggle
> for breath and water;
>
> (*Winged Reason*, 64)

A loss, a death due to cruelty inflicted on a voiceless pet, invites all the more pain and irretrievable sorrow.

## Rhythm and Harmony in Creation

Dominic highlights a universalized philosophy that there is a universal rhythm governing the entire system, be it a plant or body, animals or birds, cells or gods or creations. Yet, man, without realizing this grand concept of rhythm governing all of us, derives cheap thrill and pleasure in being constantly at loggerheads with his own self, as well as in destroying the environment. In a lengthy poem comprising twenty-one parts, entitled "Write, My Son Write", the observant poet dexterously analyzes, the rhythm or pervasive harmony prevailing everywhere around us:

> There is rhythm
> and harmony
> in every molecule;
> Rhythm is there
> in your breath;
> your heartbeats;
> your eyewinks;
>
> Write, my son,
> write.
> Your species
> cant live alone.
> I risked a test
> in man's brain,

(*Write Son, Write*, 21–27)

The poet ardently brings forth the idea that man, not knowing his limitations, undertakes ventures into Nature's arena, thinking them his own feats but actually not so, just bypassing Nature's symphony of rhythm.

## Religious Fanaticism

Religion ever since Creation, in some form or the other, plays a very predominant role in the univers; mankind has been going through many shifts and sacred serendipities of religious fervor with a stiff tegument of no flexibility in most incidents. On the other side, there have been atrocities committed in the name of religion, mostly in the name of God, Dominic opines. The well-meaning critic in the poet lists a number of *isms* and terrorists' activities perpetrated in the name of God. In a way, it is fanaticism in many faces. In the poem "In the Name of God", he ardently enumerates many *isms* that hamper the growth of the society and they are the cankering evils and extreme form of fanaticism.

> Nepotism is supported
> in the name of God.
> Superstitions survive
> in the name of God.
> Communalism poisons
> in the name of God.
> Communism is strangled
> in the name of God.

(*Winged Reason*, 69)

The concerned poet feels that man's fanatic principles extend far beyond his reasoning oeuvre that God is dethroned. On the contrary, man deifies man in the name of God. Godhead is dethroned in the name of fanaticism.

## Multicultural Symphony:

Symphony or harmony is the only panacea for all the deadly evils that persist in the world. Now, the poet feels that if man's evil desire persists for questioning of God's creation, disintegration and destruction, the only remedy by the seer poet with a message of profundity is multicultural symphony. Be it color, race, species, or nationality, it is all man-made law or mean, vulnerable attitude to label an animal as an Indian or American cow. It is blatant denial of multicultural instinct or negation of multicultural beauty that exists in woods, forests, or birds, or even among humans. Similarly the poet sees divinity in all human beings as the poet explains in his preface (which is the best source of his motives and messages and criticism of his own writing oeuvre):

> "Now coming to my themes in this book. Basically I am a follower of Advaita philosophy. Though I am a Christian by birth, I believe in Advaita. My common sense doesn't allow me to see God as a separate entity. I believe that there is a supreme Power or Energy which is controlling this universe. We call it God or the Creator" (Preface to *Multicultural Symphony*, 8). T

hroughout his works, this reiteration or craving for symphony we see that binds the downtrodden and marginalized that enhances the quest for betterment of the society.

## Technique

Throughout his poetic journey, one can observe that Dominic uses much of prose. His is a prose poetry form presented in his written works. His ulterior motive is to reach the mass, to extend his poetic messages to his reading public. His concern is amelioration of society, a verve of amalgamation of much of the uncared for, the downtrodden into the matrix of comfort and care. To quote his own words:

> Let me make a criticism of my poems, as Seamus Heaney, the Nobel Laureate, has always been doing to his poems. As a poet, I am responsible to my own conscience and I want to convey an emotion or message often through social criticism. I have a commitment to my students as a professor; to the reader, scholars and writers as an editor; and to all human and non-human beings as a poet. Hence I give priority to the content of a poem than to its style. That is why my poems lack much imagery and other figures of speech. I am of the opinion that poetry should be digestible as short stories and novels are as appealing to the laymen. I adopt a conventional style in poetry, which again attracts the ordinary readers. Here, I am influenced much by the Victorian poet, Browning. (Preface to *Winged Reason*, 12)

## Conclusion

In the philosophical entourage, we see hawks and eagles soaring high, viewing the world of collusion and conspiracy, and we view those aerial birds with an agnostic eye, partially in the sense of slighting their existence and beauty and bounteous duty in their own way; we overlook their part in this soil. The poet, with a large-hearted vision, wonders at the crow, the commonest bird, and ascribes the label as the cleaner of garbage, and he questions as to why it is dethroned, while the cuckoo is enthroned. Be it a bird or man, for him, society matters much. Each has an ideological purpose. While establishing connectivity with literature and society, it is worthwhile to quote F. R. Leavis' take in his essay "Literature and Society", a must for every student of English Literature. Tracing the development of literature down the ages, with tradition ingrained into it, F. R. Leavis observes thus:

> It originated in the great changes in civilisations that make the second part of the seventeenth century look so unlike the first, and its early phase may be studied in the works of John Dryden. The conventions, standards and idioms of its confident maturity offer themselves for contemplation in The Tatler and Spectator . . . . The relevant point to be made about it for the present purpose is that it laid a heavy stress on the social. The characteristic movements and dictions of the eighteenth century, in verse as well as in prose, convey a suggestion of social deportment and good manners, an age in which such a tradition gets itself established is clearly an age in which the writer feels himself at one with the society.
>
> (F. R. Leavis, in *Scrutiny*, December 1943, pp. 2–11)

Such oneness Dominic establishes with the society, by projecting the primary, the necessities, pitfalls to be ameliorated and redeemed. Here we see the duty of the writer and critic merging into one. He goes down in literature as a writer with special concern for his fellow beings, for humanity afflicted and marginalized.

## Works Cited

Coleridge, S. T. "The Rose." Web. 11 Jul. 2014. http://www.poetry-archive.com/ c/the_rose.html.

Dominic, K. V. *Multicultural Symphony*. GNOSIS, New Delhi. 2014. Print.

---. *Winged Reason*. Authorspress, New Delhi. 2010. Print.

---. *Write Son, Write*. GNOSIS, New Delhi. 2011. Print.

# Chapter 20 -
# The Landscape of Kerala in K. V. Dominic's Poetry
# by Anisha Ghosh Paul

A poet's mind is shaped by the world he inhabits—his birth place, its culture and traditions, and the realities surrounding his life since birth to the time of maturation of his poetic sensibility. They are the greatest influences in shaping his art and become an indispensible part of his poetic journey. In Wordsworth's poetry, we see the English countryside coming to life, and the landscape of Odisha becomes the major influence in Jayanta Mahapatra's poetry. In an interview with the Hyderabad-based poet Sridala Swami, Mahapatra thus answers when asked about the impact of Odisha, its landscape, and language in his poetry:

> It's difficult to say expressly how place, language, and landscape affect my poetry. I have lived here in Cuttack all my life, and this is the land of my ancestors. Isn't it but natural that these should come into my poems? Can I forget "hunger" when my own grandfather almost died of starvation in the terrible famine that struck Odisha (Orissa) in 1866? Can I forget the starving millions who live in the remote hinterland and subsist on dried mango seeds and tubers they collect from the jungles? It is the place that has shaped me: its traditions, myths, and more importantly, its history. These make the arms of my poetry. ("Jayanta Mahapatra: Interview")

What Odisha means to Mahapatra is equivalent to what Kerala means to Dr. K. V. Dominic. Born in 1956 in Kalady, a holy place in Kerala, where Adi Shankara, the propounder of the doctrine of Advaita Vedanta, was born, Dominic has spent all his life till present in Kerala. A renowned poet and short story writer, a critic, and an established editor of many international refereed journals, as well as an author of more than twenty titles, Dominic has served for twenty-five years of his professional life in the P. G. and Research Department of English of Newman College, Thodupuzha, which is also his alma mater. Kerala is his Lake country and his Malgudi, his Yoknopatawpha county and his Odisha.

Unlike his friend Stephen Gill, the Indo-Canadian poet, whose poetic energies were spurred on by the extreme experiences of communal violence and discrimination that he witnessed in New Delhi during his youth, Dominic's life had been "smooth and comfortable without much itching of the mind or arrows stuck into it" (*Winged Reason*, 11), which may be a probable reason for his late maturation as a poet. In the Preface to *Winged Reason*, Dominic writes:

> Compared to Stephen Gill's younger days in New Delhi, I have been living in this part of the country where there has been no communal riot or terrorist attack, and I must have been positioned in the midst of plenty. Kerala, my State, is known outside as God's own land. There is equable climate; greenery and natural beauty distinguish it from other states and tourists flood in from all parts of the world here. Literacy is cent percent here and a majority of teenagers receive education in schools and

colleges. People have a tendency to imitate the West, but unlike the Western people, the major concern of the people is religion. (*Winged Reason*, 12)

The landscape of Kerala, its beauty and bounty, the multicultural atmosphere as well as various social realities and problems that prevail in the state become the subject of several poems in all three volumes: *Winged Reason* (2010), *Write Son, Write* (2011), and *Multicultural Symphony* (2014). In his poem "Multicultural Kerala", Dominic sings of the scenic beauty and congenial climatic conditions of his state:

> Thousands of species of flora and fauna
> Six months long rainy season
> followed by summer bearable
> Autumn and winter fear to enter
> Tourists call it God's own country
>
> (*Multicultural Symphony*, 29)

Though literacy rate is cent percent, the Keralites are in the shackles of blind faith and superstitions propagated by the "religious mafia" and the ploys of the "political mafia". Being highly educated, people are always on the lookout for white-collar jobs, making the agrarian communities vanish from the fertile soil of Kerala, turning the arable lands into "deserted wastelands" (*Multicultural Symphony*, 29), thus making the state dependent for food on other states. Dominic criticizes the indolence of Keralites, which has led to a huge influx of laborers from outside making it a multicultural state:

> Thousands flood to this heaven
> and serve the indolent Keralites
> Construction, agricultural, plantation
> commercial, domestic and
> such daily wage labours
> go through their rocky hands
> My State has thus become
> cent percent dependent and multicultural! (
>
> *Multicultural Symphony*, 30)

In "Wagamon", Dominic's musings on the natural world remind us of Wordsworth's pantheism, as he too feels God's presence in every aspect of nature. The poet describes the virgin beauty of the green valleys of Wagamon: the steep street, high precipices, deep caves, and series of cataracts reveal to him the unseen presence of God, who—like an artist—reveals himself through this beautiful picture:

> Miles long canvas
> Black and high;
> Green patches
> Here and there:
>
> God with His brush! (*Write Son, Write*, 88)

The beauty of nature triggers off his philosophical musings as the "eternal curtains" of the cataracts remind him of the curtain of life. The tall pine trees become a symbol of man's communion with God as the poet envisions them to be ladders that help the angels to descend from the ethereal heights to carry humans' prayers back to the Almighty.

"Thodupuzha Municipal Park" and "Lines Composed from Thodupuzha River's Bridge" take us to the poet's present hometown. The park symbolizes a sort of spiritual rejuvenation and bodily refreshment in the scorching summer's heat. The sight of mirthful children playing around, accompanied by their parents, stirs the poet's philosophical mind and takes him back to his carefree childhood days, just as the river Wye reminds Wordsworth of the "dizzy raptures" (*Fifteen Poets*, 237) of his childhood in "Tintern Abbey":

> Those little kids' merry pendulum swings
> pull me back to childhood days
> How much I longed for a swing
> made of ropes and coconut leaf!
>
> (*Multicultural symphony*, 70)

The poet's mind also travels back to the times when he and his wife used to visit the park with their children, and laments the passing away of those happy days:

> Gone are those happy days with little kids
> They have grown up and flown away from us
> Anxiety of their future welfare has replaced
> peace and happiness that haunted in our house
>
> (*Multicultural Symphony*, 70)

In the second poem, the poet, standing on the bridge, addresses the river flowing underneath. The constant flow of the river makes him realize that just as one cannot touch the same water twice, so is the unidirectional flow of life—one cannot relive the moment past: "Every second passed in our lives / is irredeemably lost forever" (*Write Son, Write*, 99). But the moments past are always recorded in eternity; the river's journey through its course to the ocean is analogous to human being's temporary sojourn on earth and ultimate merger into the greater soul or "*paramatma*". Dominic's pantheistic views are reflected in the final lines of the poem: "The Creator thus reveals to His creations / His perpetual relation and incessant love. / Rivers and oceans are embodiments of cosmic reality." (*Write Son, Write*, 99). In "Sail of Life", the poet's regular morning walks take him to a place called Gandhi Square, normally crowded and noisy in the evenings, but calm and quiet in the early morning hours. The contrast makes him realize the ultimate truth that human life, so full of action, is destined to be quietened one day, when the ship of life reaches its harbor, the abode of the Almighty.

Dominic's poems are peopled by some remarkable personalities from the soil of Kerala and "Long Live E. K. Nayanar" is one such poem. It is an elegy sung on the death of the socialist leader and ex-Chief Minister of Kerala, loved and revered all over the state. In the preface to *Winged Reason*, Dominic writes: "Nayanar was the most lovable CM Kerala had ever borne. He was highly humorous, simple and as innocent as a lamb. Being a socialist, I have great love and respect for him" (14). A believer in the ideals of Communism, Dominic pays homage to the deceased CM in following words:

> You were a true Communist;
> a comrade to the core of your being,
> a rare species,
> compassion and love
> an epitome of Socialism.
>
> (*Winged Reason*, 19)

In "Kaumudi Teacher is No More", Dominic pays tribute to this strong single woman, who, following the ideals of Mahatma Gandhi from a very young age, donated all ornaments for raising funds for the *Harijans* at Vadakara. She spent all her life following the ideals of Gandhi, and teaching Hindi, the national language in Malabar. "Sister Mercy" celebrates another strong woman from Kerala, who dedicated her life to public service; she fought for the tribal people, fought against slavery and flesh-trade, was hunted and tortured by the police, and took a law degree for self-pleading; and even in her late sixties, she is inspiring people in some village in Madhya Pradesh. Sister Mercy's life exemplifies the path of Karma and proves that: "serving God in human form / is more rewarding than / serving Him in abstract terms" (*Write Son, Write*, 80).

In the poem "Onam", readers are acquainted with Keralite customs, rituals, and legends. Onam, a ten-day celebration is the biggest and most lavishly celebrated festival in Kerala, like Durga Puja in West Bengal. The poet describes how the celebrations start with a harvest festival, called *Atham*, first day, and how people decorate their homes with *pookalams*, a floral art, with people donning new dresses and participating in Onam sports like snake boat races, and songs. There is happiness and gaiety all around, but the festival has a deeper significance. The poet also traces the legend of the ideal King Maveli, who was stamped on and thrown to the netherworld by Vishnu in the incarnation of a Vaman (a midget); Vishnu also granted Maveli a boon that he may visit his subjects every year, and the day of this supposed visit is celebrated as Onam. Maveli ruled his kingdom on egalitarian principals:

> Equality prevailed in society;
> No lies, no crimes, no deceit,
> And no cheat;
> No poverty, no child death.
> All were happy;
> Heaven cannot be different!

(*Winged Reason*, 54)

Sadly, this utopia of the Maveli legend is extinct in the present society; the poet's critical eye sees this legend as a tool for social criticism as he comments in the last two lines of the poem that seeing the degeneration of his people, Maveli returns every year in tears.

This dystopian view is further seen in the poem "Where Shall I Flee from this Fretful Land", in which the shock and trauma due to the sordid realities experienced by the poet's sensitive soul make him plead for an escape from the Kerala he has grown up in and loved more than any other place on earth. The poet is grieved by the moral and spiritual degeneration of his people, their intolerance and indolence, their materialistic aspirations and exploitative habits that have disturbed the balance of the natural world, and corruption prevalent in the political world. Earlier, Kerala was a land of multicultural harmony where: "Hindus, Muslims, Christians lived as brothers and sisters / respected each other and their religious views / Now hell of intolerance and religious fundamentalism" (*Multicultural Symphony*, 78).

The theme of communal violence is carried forward in the poem "To My Colleague", which is occasioned by a real-life tragedy involving Prof. T. J. Joseph of Newman College, Thodupuzha, the poet's friend and colleague. On 4th of July, 2010, while he was returning home after Sunday mass, religious fanatics chopped off one arm of Prof. Joseph. Like a true Christian, Prof. Joseph forgave the assailants and became a symbol of pain and suffering, of courage and conviction, of mercy and forgiveness. This instance of religious fundamentalism is counterbalanced by another true incident of communal harmony that moved Dominic to compose the poem "For the Glory of God". Based on a report published in *The Malayala Manorama Sunday Supplement* on 25th July, 2010, the poet depicts how a Muslim lady Resiya Beevi takes in Chellamma Antharjanam, a seventy-five-year-old destitute Brahmin lady and supports her, "Risking taunts from kith and kin" (*Write Son, Write*, 61). Respecting Chellamma's wishes to die in her own home, Resiya buys a plot and builds a small house for her availing government's funds, and bears all her expenses of food and clothing for more than a decade as she believes "service unto her, service to Allah" (*Write Son, Write*, 61). Toward the end of the poem, Dominic alludes to the tragedy with Prof. Joseph highlighting the contraries in human nature:

> Resiya's life is an ideal Muslim's life;
> all will agree that God is pleased.
> Resiya's own State witnessed another act:
> religious extremists hacked off a
> a professor's right palm
> and cut his legs to slaughter him.
> And they did this to please their God!
>
> (*Write Son, Write*, 62)

The social reformer in Dominic speaks out in poems like "Mullaperiyar Dam" and "Agitation Through Farming". In the first poem, Dominic takes up the issue over the precarious condition of the Mullaperiyar Dam that has been a bone of contention between Kerala and the adjacent state for quite a long time. The dam is a hundred and six years old, made of *surkhi* and lime, and leaking at several parts; if broken, the adjacent five districts of Kerala will be ruined. But the people on the other side are objecting to the construction of a new dam, fearing a breach of the water-sharing treaty by the government of Kerala. The masses are being affected by the power games of the political mafia that is totally ignorant to their plight:

> People on both sides lived as one family
> Alas! Anti-social forces injected
> regional, racial venom in masses;
> . . . . . . . . . . . . . . . . . . . . . . . . .
> Borders are closed, police patrol,
> Inter-State buses and trucks stop run;
> . . . . . . . . . . . . . . . . . . . . . . . . .
> Rulers of State and central governments
> living in midst of pomp and luxury
> heed not to the wails and moans of the masses.
>
> (*Muticultural Symphony*, 42–43)

The second poem is about the agitation of an Adivasi group in Arippa in Kollam, Kerala, for putting unused government lands to agricultural use that can be a source of living for the poor tribes: "They have spread a strong message / Unassessed government lands lying idle / could be used for feeding hungry mouths" (*Muticultural Symphony*, 80)

Being a socially conscious poet, Dominic in the Aristotelean vein sees poetry as a medium of delightful teaching: "I take poetry and short story as a weapon and reaction to the evils of the society. The function of poetry is to instruct and delight. To me, the aspect of 'instruct'—impart great values and messages—seems more important than 'delight'" ("Interview with Prof. K. V. Dominic"). He does not believe in the "art for art's sake" theory and uses poetry as his weapon to fight against social evils and thus, newspaper reports become the greatest source of his poetic musings. Poems like "ACTS—Saviors on the Road", "Beach Beauticians", "An Ideal Festival", "Valueless Education", and several others, including those mentioned above, are the poet's reactions to several day-to-day incidents taking place in his state that are reported in the newspapers.

Kerala thus becomes his muse, the greatest inspiration of his poetic endeavors. Dominic's paper presented in the SAARC Literary Festival in Agra (include date, at least the year of the event) is devoted to his ecological concerns over the devastation of the natural world going on in Kerala. He sums up man's exploitation of the natural world and the callousness of those in power in the final words of this paper:

> Modern man's crazy race after material comforts and luxuries has destroyed forests, wet fields, ponds, lakes, and rivers which stored water for the sustenance of human beings and others beings and as a result, this God's own land is facing severe drought in summer which lasts to even eight months. Lack of sufficient rain causes shortage of drinking water in addition to power crisis. Thus this God's own country is turning into Devils' own hell now. ("Kerala: God's Own Country Turning into Devil's Own Hell")

Dominic never romanticizes Kerala nor aggrandizes his fellowmen, but gives us a rather realistic portrayal of his home state and, as a responsible citizen, criticizes what deserves censure and applauds what deserves ovation. Dominic's success in delineating the landscape of Kerala in his poetry lies in his ability to see in every local spot, individual, and incident a higher philosophical significance and thus investing the particular with a greater universal truth.

## Works Cited

Dominic, K. V. "Kerala: God's Own Country Turning into Devil's Own Hell." Web. 25 July 2014. <http://www.boloji.com/index.cfm?md=Content&sd=Articles&ArticleID=14257>.

---. *Multicultural Symphony.* New Delhi: GNOSIS, 2014. Print.

---. *Winged Reason.* New Delhi: Authorpress, 2010. Print.

---. *Write Son, Write.* New Delhi: GNOSIS, 2011. Print.

"Interview with Prof. K. V. Dominic by Prof. Elisabetto Marino." Web. 2 May 2014. <http://www.profkvdominic.com/?page_id=1160>.

"Jayanta Mahapatra: Interview by Sridala Swami." Web. 24 July 2014. <http://www.livemint.com/Leisure/Tejg57qNEfUBT7jGQV0UbI/Jayanta-Mahapatra--Something-in-me-refuses-to-die.html>.

Wordsworth, William. "Lines Composed A Few Miles Above Tintern Abbey." *Fifteen Poets.* Ed. OUP. New Delhi: OUP, 1960. Reprint 2006. Print.

# Chapter 21 -
# Eco-Critical Perspectives in the Poetry of K. V. Dominic
# by Dr. S. Barathi

Eco-critical theory investigates the relationship between human activities and the natural world, particularly in terms of the influence of each upon the other. It stresses sensual and spiritual experience with the outer world for individual and cultural changes. The primary function of art is to heal the stress. This is an effort to unite human beings and nature, in which the distinction between subjectivity and objectivity blurs. This paper examines the poetry of K. V. Dominic in eco-critical consciousness.

Indian poetry in English is rich due to its multicultural background, tradition, myth, legends, landscape, flora, fauna, climates, etc. According to Dominic, nature is not just a symbol of destruction, but it also fuses with perpetual harmony. He views nature at two levels. On the one hand, nature is shown as caring and divine. On the other hand, man is selfish, cruel, and full of ego. The poet sings of the splendid nature in "I am Just a Mango Tree" (*Winged Reason*, 40–41). The poem, on the other hand, also shows the materialistic attitude of man. The poet is more concerned with the protection of our globe. "On Conservation" is a poem where the poet talks about the importance of preserving the flora and fauna. He writes: "Though I am a passive sheet of paper / I have a soul as vibrant as yours" (*Multicultural Symphony*, 31); it shows his utmost care to preserve our earth and at the same time, he wants to expose the hypocrisy of humans who never value their ecosystem.

In an age of modernization and materialism, very few writers have turned toward environment for motivation. K. V. Dominic is among those rare writers who were inspired by the ecosystem. He brings in nature to his poems not as a deliberate act, but a subconscious one. His poems have the manifestations of this consciousness. Though nature is not a subject in many of his poems, it forms a background to his poetry. It also depicts a world of "inhumanism" in which nature is neither sentimentalized nor subjectified, and he also creates poetry that is grounded in the poet's personal experience and seeks to reconcile the supposedly irreconcilable modern division between humans and the natural world. His work culminates the consideration of human and non-human relations. His poetry suggests the interdependence of man and nature in the modern industrial age.

"A Sheep's Wail" (*Winged Reason*, 24–25) is melancholic in tone on the attitude of the human beings, who are indifferent to the suffering animals. According to him, God has created from the lowest to the highest organisms to live in perfect harmony. But in contrast, to the dismay of the poet, we the human beings create diversity in the name of race, religion, gender, and culture. We fail to understand the ways of God, our creator and protector.

"Nature Weeps" (*Write Son, Write*, 71–74) is a poem filled with melancholy and shows the poet's care for his environment. The ironical ending of the poem shows the poet's kindness toward even the lower forms of life. The poet himself writes in the preface to his first anthology: "The death of my favourite twin cats haunts me every day and pricks my heart to bleed to new pastures of social criticism" (*Winged Reason*, 12). He expresses his great hatred toward the cruel treatment of animals.

The poet's message to humanity is to be compassionate and sympathetic toward all creations. He also dreams of a world to "cross all the borders to find harmony".

"Attachment" (*Write Son, Write*, 51–52) is a poem on his lost kitten named Poppy. He compares his love for the little creature to that of his wife and children. According to him, all forms of life are equal. In his anthology *Write Son, Write*, the poet explores nature and environment; reflects on contemporary issues based on newspaper reports, etc. His poems show his greatest concern for nature and his poetry reflects his thoughts on pollution, deforestation, and so on.

"Nature's Bounties" (*Winged Reason*, 49–50) praises God's beautiful creation, big and small. The poet is at his best in the elegies on the death of his friend, a political leader, a teacher and his beloved cats that have appeared in his anthology *Winged Reason*. These poems highlight his human nature. The poet is much pained by the massacre in Iraq. As a sensitive man, he wishes to imprison Bush in the palace made of bones from those who died in Iraqi war. The poet hopes to plead to the prophets to "inspire and instil humanism" in the minds of people. Aju Mukhopadhyay observes on the features of the poetry of K. V. Dominic that, "Sufferings of any kind inflicted either by fate or man on man or animal make his heart bleed; loss of freedom suffocates him. With an empathic heart he often sustains wounds at others' sufferings" (*Write Son, Write* Cove Page).

Dominic draws his themes from everyday happenings of life as in "Saichen Tragedy" (*Multicultural Symphony*, 24) or "Mullaperiyar Dam" (*Multicultural Symphony*, 42–43), which are based on newspaper reports. Current issues pertaining to our environment becomes a subject matter for his poetry. "I Am Just a Mango Tree" (*Winged Reason*, 40–41) shows his concern for our globe's flora. The poet is distressed to find humans destroying nature's child, the trees. As a human, he is much perturbed by the selfish nature of humans. Pranab Kumar Majumder has a similar view on this poem and he calls the poet "a sympathetic and compassionate poet who is pained at humans' wanton felling of trees and destroying of nature's body" (*Winged Reason*, 8).

The poet was born in Kerala, God's own land with abundant natural beauty, and it is quite natural that nature inspires him a lot. He himself quotes in the preface to his maiden anthology that, "I find the eternal affinity between Man, Nature and God" (*Winged Reason*, 14). "Nature's Bounties" (*Winged Reason*, 49–50) is a Haiku and it contains a marvelous description of nature, wherein the poet writes, "The Sun kisses / The eye opens / Lotus blooms" (*Winged Reason*, 49). Again in the same poem, the poet writes, "yellow mellow papaya / Longing violent kisses / Feasting crows and mynahs" (*Winged Reason*, 49) is a best example for his style. The poet uses simple and effective images having a great pictorial quality. At times, the poet's play with words becomes poetry. P. C. K Prem, a renowned poet and critic comments on Dominic's poetry that "The poet avers that his areas of concern are man, nature and God and truthfully this encompasses life in entirety with no derivations" (109).

"Harvest Feast" is a poem about harvest day and it reveals the interdependence of man and nature. In yet another poem "Onam" (*Winged Reason*, 53–54), we can find the interaction of nature, culture, and tradition. "Cuckoo Singing" (*Winged Reason*, 30) and "Sleepless Nights" (*Winged Reason*, 56) also contain description of nature. Nature is scattered throughout the anthology *Write Son, Write*. The title sequence "Write, My Son, Write" (*Write Son, Write*, 21–37) is in twenty-one parts and it expounds on the theory of nature that all creatures are interrelated and dependent on one another. The poem is filled with zoomorphic aroma, explaining the characteristics of animals large and small. The poet observes perfect harmony in all creatures from plants to animals, big and small. Though animals appear everywhere in his poems, they are not about animals, but instead it talks about the animalistic nature in man. In Part Eleven, the poet questions man: "Why don't you / learn from Nature?" (*Write Son, Write*, 30) His poetry creates a memorable impression in the mind of the readers. His vision extends beyond its focus upon man and society. He uses nature to explain the concept of man's place in the society. His poem has rural scenes and the landscape produces a tremendous impact on the mind of the readers. Man learns from his failures and he is willing to accept the pain and gain profit out of it. The poet, a true environmentalist, is distressed to see the condition of our globe with heaps of garbage all around and the non-availability of potable water in many areas.

This view is expressed in "Water, Water, Everywhere" (*Write Son, Write*, 91–92) which disturbs the mind of readers. In yet another poem, "Thodupuzha Municipal Park" (*Multicultural Symphony* 70–71), the poet drives home the point that human's intervention with nature is only derogatory. The poet writes, "Afternoon heat of thirty eight degree / Sweating throughout due to humidity / Why to blame sun or gods / Man has dug his grave" (*Multicultural Symphony*, 70) shows that man has become more or less a negative force intervening with the natural cycle. Man's connectedness with environment is manifold and literature, especially, can compress nature into a mere social or cultural agenda. At the same time, it can also provide an alternative solution for a symbiotic human–nature association, thus facilitating green consciousness. K. V. Dominic's poems too concern with environmental hazards, deforestation, exploitation of natural resources and the latest environmental issues in India, like the Mullaperiyar Dam issue and the proposed Aranmula airport in Kerala, which pose a threat to the environment. His poetry centres on the environmental problems in India, particularly in Kerala.

According to John F. Lynen,

> "Man can never find a home in nature, nor can he live outside of it. But he can assert the reality of his spirit and thus can exist independently of the physical world in the act of looking squarely at the facts of nature" (146).

This concept is reflected in "Wolfgang, the Messiah of Nature" (*Write Son, Write*, 93–94). The poet focuses not only on nature but also upon man and society. This is clear in the following lines: "He has realised the truth, / the truth of eternal relations: / between God, Man and Nature" (*Write Son Write*, 94). According to him, man cannot thrive without nature and as humans, we all must learn to compromise with nature. Dominic's poetry creates an impression that man and nature are one. For the poet, Wolfgang is Nature's Christ who has come to unite nature, man, and God. Arbind Kumar Choudhary, reputed poet and critic, remarks on Dominic's poetry: "The poet appeals to God to instruct how to attach and detach with the neighbours and other beings... The poet appeals for the restoration of divine code of conduct and also for Ram Rajya where fauna is ever free and easy" (121).

Born in the land of Adi Shankara, the great saint of advaita philosophy, it is quite natural that the poet too shows a deep interest in Hindu philosophical thoughts. His third and latest anthology *Multicultural Symphony*, contains such musings of the poet. According to him, God the Lord, whatever you name him—Jehovah, Allah, or Shiva—is equal to him. He is a secular poet showing mercy toward the lower forms. Throughout his poems, the poet looks at men as ego-centric and wants them to become eco-centric. The poet is a tireless experimentalist and his critical poems that venture on nature stand as epitomes for his care toward nature.

## Works Cited

Choudhary, Arbind Kumar. "Poetic Pigments of K. V. Dominic: A Critical Study of *Write Son Write*." International Journal on Multicultural Literature 3.2 (July 2013): 119-126. Print.

Dominic, K. V. *Multicultural Symphony*. GNOSIS, New Delhi. 2014. Print.

---. *Winged Reason*. Authorspress, New Delhi. 2010. Print.

---. *Write Son, Write*. GNOSIS, New Delhi. 2011. Print.

Lynen, F. John. *The Pastoral Art of Robert Frost*. New Haven: Yale University Press, 1960. 142-146. Print.

Prem, P. C. K. "K. V. Dominic's *Winged Reason*: Poems of Man's Earthly Life and Painful Realities." *Labyrinth* 2.2 (April 2011): 104-110. Print.

# Chapter 22 -
# Ecological Issues Reflected in the Selected Poems of K. V. Dominic
# by Rincy Mol Sebastian

Environmental studies or eco-criticism has stepped up new areas of multidisciplinary inquest and is the soul of recent trends in literary studies. The environmental issues seem to go hand in hand with literature. Literary studies, especially poems, have a new attention in contemporary discussion of environmental issues.

Environmental disturbances hang over our heads to remind us of the ecological disaster. Concern for the environmental future is moved to mainstream consciousness through the issues of global warming, deforestation, nuclear issues, pollution, ozone depletion, toxins, waste, exploitation of natural resources, etc. And these problems primarily appear as scientific problems and involve only climatologists, or glaciologists, rather than poets or critics. But the environmental and ecological studies have opened up in literary scenario. "While literature can reduce nature to a specific ideological or humanistic agenda, it can also represent an alternative kind of human nature relationship, facilitating green consciousness and place bonding" (Speek, 162).

Dr. K. V. Dominic is always fascinated by the work of nature. His poems spread the environmental consciousness regarding the relationship between God, Man, and Nature. P. C. K. Prem, reputed poet, novelist and critic, estimates Dominic's poetry thus: "The poet avers that his areas of concern are man, nature and God and truthfully this encompasses life in entirety with no derivations" (109).

Some of his poetic works have a special space to address the major environmental problems. He uses poems as a powerful weapon to spread the message about the environmental threat to nature caused by man. The poet remembers his childhood days when there were rains for six months and all the rivers were live and vibrant with water throughout the year. To quote from Dr. Dominic's paper presented at SAARC Literary Festival in Agra: "In summer almost all rivers are dry with little flow of water. Greedy land mafia appropriates government forests with the help of politicians and corrupt bureaucrats and deforests thousands of acres. Similarly, sand mafia mines sands of the rivers, digging them to die" (Dominic, "Kerala: God's Own Country").

The present study aims to explore the selected poems from K. V Dominic's two poetic collections, *Winged Reason* (2010) and *Write Son, Write* (2011), which exhibit the major environmental issues.

Prof. Dominic's first poem "Write My Son, Write" is a message to the entire humanity. Human beings have superior thought of being the finest creation of God and that they have the right to destroy animals and nature for their existence. The poet says that God loves all creatures and things in this world and man has no right to exploit both animals and nature. The poet expresses philosophical views in the last part of the poem:

> Enough, my son,
> enough;
> nothing more
> to tell your species.
> If they heed
> they will be saved;
> other beings
> will be saved;
> plants will be saved
> and the universe
> as such will be saved.
>
> (*Write Son, Write*, 37)

The endless agony of God toward man, who is created by God in His own image, is best explained in the poem "I am Just a Mango Tree". The tree stands like a 'Himalayan Umbrella' to give shelter to the students who are "waiting for the buses". The tree is very proud of itself because it is the source of fruit, bed, and shelter for all creatures. But all the happiness of the tree is thwarted when it overhears a conversation between a boy and a girl:

> "Darling, where shall we wait
> when they cut this tree?
> "Dear, why should they cut this tree,
> a cool shelter to countless?"
> "They plan to build a waiting shed here."
>
> (*Winged Reason*, 41)

The tree can't believe the words of the children so that she asks God, her creator:

> God, what do I hear? Is it true?"
> 'True, my daughter, I am helpless.'
> Can't they spare me and
> build it somewhere else?
> Don't I do them good as to all?
> Don't I have feeling and pains
> though I endure in silence?
> Haven't I the right to live?
>
> (*Winged Reason*, 41)

The heart-stricken words of the tree have really unveiled the cruel face of human beings. The tree is also the creation of God; she also has feelings; and she asks a painful question: "God, why is your man so selfish and cruel?" (*Winged Reason*, 41)

God is totally helpless because he has created man in his own image. He hadn't thought of this type of a creation in this world. Human beings are causing an endless agony to their Creator, Father. The poet here generalizes the agony of God to the agony of all fathers. But how can a father kill his sons?

The poet, like a true environmentalist, feels that nature moans only because of the brutal hands of man. Man's cruel consumption of nature will lead to his own destiny and this is clearly expressed in the poem "Nature Weeps". Man ill-treated mango tree, paddy fields, flowers, and everything around him. Tigers started searching food in villages because "the people killed their preys" (*Write Son, Write*, 71). Even the sun is angry at man because of his act of cutting trees.

*Philosophical Musings for a Meaningful Life*

The poet is very keen on expressing minute aspects of man's cruelty toward all creatures. The sky is covered with the fumes of plastic so that the sound of the cuckoo is changed. The poet could identify the minute change in the sound of the cuckoo because cuckoo is singing for the poet himself. Now cuckoo is not waking him up in the morning because he has no trees to sit on (*Write Son, Write*, 73). The poet brings out the consequences of man's treatment of snakes and improper waste management:

> Snakes appear on
> roads and lanes:
> their havens are furnaces
>
> Mice and rats multiply
> and trouble human beings:
> man litters food around
>
> (*Write Son, Write*, 73)

The poet reminds us of a major problem that is the scarcity of water, which lays the foundation of our life and "going to be more precious; than gold and diamond" (*Write Son, Write*, 91). "Water, Water, Everywhere...", a poem composed on the World Water Day, is a very big question focusing on our near future. Destruction of natural resources, increasing construction, urbanization, etc. are all the pivotal causes for the scarcity of water. Absence of rains will wipe out a number of lives. The poet expresses his anguishes:

> Lifespan dropped to thirty-five;
> thirty five looked eighty-five.
> Dehydration caused wrinkles;
> smooth skin turned
> sore and scaly;
> lovely long haired women
> appeared shaved-headed ghosts.
>
> (*Write Son, Write*, 91–92)

Water is the panacea of our life, but we get only mineral oil packed in disposable bottles, that also is hazardous for nature: "heaps of garbage everywhere" (*Write Son, Write*, 92). Flowing water will become a ration and many people will suffer from kidney failure. Extreme climate change and water scarcity will be a vital source to produce a wave of the next world war. The poet writes:

> Water stolen
> at gun point;
> armed forces guarded
> water reservoirs of nations.
>
> (*Write Son, Write*, 92)

Scarcity of water will lead to anxiety, depression, displeasure, aggression, and aversion. The climate change will bring out the danger by restricting our access to the basic needs of our life. The future is very critical in the sense that: "Sea level rose every day; / low lands disappeared / one after another (*Write Son, Write*, 92).

Enormous and unlawful consumption and treatment of natural resources of man has become the real problem behind all natural calamities and scarcity of natural resources. The poet foresees the tragic situation through the poem "God is Helpless". Even God, the sole creator of the world, is helpless when man prays for his mercy to have rain and save their land. The poet gives a clear answer to the doings of man in this poem. God, the merciful Almighty, asks mankind many unanswerable questions and the poet experiences the helplessness of God.

> "I am helpless,
> my beloved children.
> I did supply
> whatever you needed;
> The same I gave
> to all non-human beings;
> I created the earth,
> an oasis for men,
> animals and plants;"
>
> (*Write Son, Write*, 63)

We human beings have put the axe to our own branches. We are responsible for cutting all the trees, emitting toxic gases to pollute the skyn and dig our own grave. Plant and animals can't live because of the atrocities caused by man to them. The poet writes:

> All complain of;
> your cruelty and torture;
> they have no food;
> they have no water;
> they have no shelter;
> and not even air
>
> (*Write Son, Write*, 64)

All creatures are pleading to God to call man back; otherwise they could not live in this earth. God is totally helpless and it is we who are answerable to all questions. ". . . only if man learns to live in harmony with nature and His creations, he has the possibility of survival; if his exploitation of humanity and nature continues, nothing can save him" (Chambial, 178).

A number of movements came into existence to protest against the environmental hazards. Writing poems is a promising mission to make some changes in the minds of the readers. So environmental crisis can be always kept alive through poems and it can be used as a vehicle for social change. Here the poet's purpose is to convey the inner and outer connection between nature and humanity. The survival of nature and humanity are interdependent. The life of nature enables the life of human beings. Only true lovers of nature like K. V. Dominic can see the reckless exploitation of nature by man. He has opened our eyes to the environmental issues through his poems, such as "I am just a Mango Tree", "Nature Weeps", "Water, Water, Everywhere...", and "God is Helpless". These poems equally manifest pedagogy of environmental alertness. The poet reminds us of our responsibilities toward nature and environment.

## Works Cited

Chambial, D. C. "K. V. Dominic--A Humanitarian in Conception and Socio Consciousness: An Analytical Study of *Write Son, Write*. *International Journal of Multicultural Literature* 2.2 (July 2012): 177-182. Print.

Dominic, K. V. *Winged Reason*. New Delhi: Authorspress, 2010. Print.

---. *Write Son, Write*. New Delhi: GNOSIS, 2011. Print.

Dominic, Prof. Dr. K. V. "Kerala: God's Own Country Turning to Devil's Own Hell." SAARC Literary Festival at Grand Hotel, Agra on 11 Mar. 2013. Web. 11 Aug. 2013. Reading. <http://www.boloji.com/index.cfm?md=Content&sd=Articles&ArticleID=14257>.

Prem, P. C. K. "K. V. Dominic's *Winged Reason*: Poems of Man's Earthly Life and Painful Realities." *Labyrinth* 2.2 (2011): 104-110. Print.

Speek, Tijo. "Environment in Literature: Lawrence Buell's Eco-critical Perspective." 160-171. Web. 16 Aug. 2013. <http://www.eki.ee/km/place/pdf/kp1_18>.

# Chapter 23 -
# Ecological and Social Issues in K. V. Dominic's Multicultural Symphony by Dr. Arbind Kumar Choudhary

K. V. Dominic is one of the most vibrating Indian English poets of the post-independence era, who credits three poetry collections—*Winged Reason*, *Write Son, Write*, and *Multicultural Symphony* published in the year 2010, 2011 and 2014 respectively. His intense passion for the burning social and national ailments makes him a disciple of Ezekielean School of poetry in Indian-English literature. His poetic passion for natural beauty, animal world, rural landscape, and imaginative poetic approach keep him beside the Romanticists in Indian-English poetry. Though K. V. Dominic belongs to Ezekielean school of poetry, yet Aurobindonean cultural essence of his poetry can hardly be ruled out. There are a number of critical works, reviews, poems, awards, editorial board memberships of many literary Journals, and several other honorable posts in the literary field to his poetic credits that make him an out-and-out Indian-English poet in the firmament of Indian-English poetry. The most impressive poetic tool K. V. Dominic uses is the application of native words—such as matha, beedi, ma, mafia, surkhi, mahouts, jungles, karma, and many others—frequently found from alpha and omega of his poetry books in general and *Multicultural Symphony* in particular for the overall literary prosperity of Indian-English poetry up to the global level.

Though Jayanta Mahapatra and K. V. Dominic belong to Christian community, they express their firm faith in the rituals of Jagganath Puri of Odisha and Advaita philosophy of Shankaracharya situated in Kerala. K. V. Dominic's comment in his preface makes his concept of life clear:

> "Basically I am a follower of Advaita philosophy. Though I am a Christian by birth I believe in Advaita. My commonsense doesn't allow me to see God as a separate entity. I believe that there is a supreme power or energy which is controlling this universe. We call it God or the Creator. That power is the spirit or soul of the universe and its element is present in all its creations including atoms. Thus divinity is there in all bodies, both living and nonliving" (*Multicultural Symphony*, 8).

Like Jayanta Mahapatra, K. V. Dominic presents a painterly picture of Keralscape in general and ruralscape in particular that makes him out and out an Indian English poet in the popular creative milieu. His firm faith in one god and one world government exhumes his poetic fragrance in Indian-English literature. The Romantic poets were adept in using a number of birds throughout their poetic gardens. Like the Romantic poets and Assamese Romantic poet Raghunath Chaudhari, K. V. Dominic has shown his proficiency over the use of a number of birds—bats, owls, kites, eagles, pests, cuckoos, skylarks, fowls, nightingales etc.—throughout his poems that make him a poet of the birds in Indian-English poetry. Here lies one such stanza in support of his intense love for these mute birds:

> When will we begin to love
> kites, eagles, bats, owls
> as we long for parrots, cuckoos
> skylarks and nightingales?
> when will we stop the massacre
> of animals, birds and fish
> and learn to respect
> other beings and their right to live?"
>
> *(Multicultural Symphony, 51)*

Like the Romantic poets, K. V. Dominic is a great lover of nature who cherishes the animals, birds, insects, and other living beings in his poetry. Human generations try their best to establish their own kingdom at the cost of nature's annihilation for which they get themselves eternally cursed in the court of sovereignty. Though all natural objects—living and non-living things—are for the sake of the human race, they are brutally killed in the kingdom of human beings. Comparing human and animal world, K. V. Dominic, the poet, inhales the essence of the innocent world of the animals in this stanza:

> How sweet and musical
> are the sounds of animal world
> when compared to the toxic sounds
> vomited by the human species
> defiling air chaste and pure !"
>
> *(Multicultural Symphony, 59)*

As an ecologist, Dominic cites example of Charles Darwin, patron saint of animals, and razes the irrational theories of the religious fanatics because men have been found prone to vice than virtue. The animal world rarely commits crime with human world or natural world unlike humans that are ever found engaged in crimes, killings, tortures, and annihilation for their own sake of selfishness. His proverbial line "we inhale what plants exhale" is the mantra of his poetic life in Indian-English literature. Believing his firm faith in karma rather than fate, this poet prefers the role of the deeds to action of the fate in life. His proverbial dialog "Peace and happiness are fruits of karma!" seems an echo of the Bhagwad Gita in which the deeds of the human beings have been strongly supported rather than the fate in the human life. Man is the maker as well as the destroyer of his fate in this world. Ridiculing the human world that makes divisions, not only between man and woman but also between man and animal, he elicits the significance of the creator who has made only man and woman to run the human race in this world. The women are forced to lead the cursed lives from birth to death because they are humiliated everywhere. Surprisingly women, who are treated as the incarnations of the goddesses, are not even allowed to be priests in churches, mosques, or temples. Like Stephen Gill, K. V. Dominic wishes for a world government because national governments are led by selfish people at the cost of humanity, purity, and divinity. The poet sings:

> Let there be no India, Pakistan or China
> America, Africa, Europe or Australia
> But only one nation THE WORLD
> where every being lives in perfect harmony
> as one entity in multicultural world.
>
> *(Multicultural Symphony, 23)*

The political propagandists in disguise of political leaders befool the masses in the name of religion, culture, race, language, region, caste and various other divisive things that make a demarcation line between men and men in this beautiful world of God, the creator of this universe. God made the world and men made the country. His homage to Swami Vivekananda, who highlighted the cultural wisdom of India in Chicago exhumes the spiritual humanism in this monetary-minded kingdom of human beings. His other poem "Mother's Love" brings to light the selfless motherly love for the children she renders throughout her earthly life. Martyrs are nothing but the products of the political battlefield. His remembrance of his childhood life sends him to the seventh heaven for the time being because that peace and pleasure haunt him from his life now laden with a crown of thorns rather than bed of roses.

His satire on modern education, agony of the world champion, the pathetic life of the Naxalite-hit areas, homage to Sakuntala Devi, celebration on the eve of grief, childbirth, focus on land mafia, description of caste politics, child labor, global warming, and various other social ailments make him a disciple of Ezekielean school of poetry in the firmament of Indian English poetry. Here lies some proverbial lines: "This unity in diversity makes beauty of universe", "Peace and happiness are fruits of karma", "We inhale what plants exhale", "Millions are spent for senseless rituals and ceremonies", "I have a soul as vibrant as yours", "He who creates destroys as well", and several others that appeal most to poetry lovers and critics alike in the literary world. K. V. Dominic is one of the leading contemporary Indian English poets from the fertile literary soil of Kerala who has started to perfume the Indian poetic paysage with capital ideas, innovative poetic approach and literary tradition of writing for the literary prosperity of Tom, Dick and Harry in general and the poetry lovers in particular on this strife-stricken earth. I wish to inhale more and more of his poetic fragrance in the womb of time.

Literature is called the mirror of the society. K. V. Dominic paints a horrible picture of this immoral society in which the old parents and other helpless members of the family become a burden for their own children. The house in which they serve their family for the whole life is later treated like the burden of the same family in their old age. As a result, he paints a shameful picture of the existing immoral society in which ungratefulness of the people has been shown with great poetic accuracy in his poem "Musings on My Shoes":

> Same is the plight of proletarian
> They are shoes worn by the rich
> Service being complete
> they are spat out like curry leaves
> Women too are often treated like shoes.
> Mothers and wives when old and weak
> Become burden to sons and husbands.

(Multicultural Symphony, 58)

K. V. Dominic evokes the problem of the global warming for which none but the western developed countries are solely responsible via polluting air, water, and nature. They are the original culprits of the global warming rather than the third world countries. He also ridicules the western sensual attire and the *carpe diem* theory that are far away from the essence of the eastern spiritual philosophy. His tribute to Sakuntala Devi, the human computer, deserves appreciation amidst the poetry lovers in India and abroad.

K. V. Dominic who composes free verse dazzles the poetic passage with his innovative poetic approach and poetic philosophy over a number of burning issues throughout his poetic career. There are a number of social, national, global, natural, and historical issues he raises very eloquently in one poem after another. His selfless dedication to the literary world, intense passion for the moral society, and message of natural harmony reserve for him a permanent berth in the history of Indian English poetry.

## Work Cited

Dominic, K. V. *Multicultural Symphony*. New Delhi, GNOSIS, 2014. Print.

# Chapter 24 -
# Holistic Musings: K. V. Dominic as a Poet with Purpose
# by Kavitha Gopalakrishnan

"Omnia vivunt, Omnia interse conexa" -- Cicero
(Everything is alive, everything is interconnected.) (qtd. in *Business Insider* N pag.)

>Write, my son,
>Write.
>Teach your folk
>their position.
>All the other beings aware
>of their humble position;
>only your species
>ignorant of his position. (*Write Son, Write*, 33)

    These lines sum up the mission, vision, and intention of K. V. Dominic in writing poetry. In his three collections—*Winged Reason*, *Write son, Write* and *Multicultural Symphony*—he tries to push the limits of his all-encompassing vision to a more rigorous investigation of nature—both Mother Nature and Human nature. His poetry advocates Art for Life's sake and emphatically believes that a piece of art must carry a message for mankind. His poems showcase man's nocuous neglect of the pain and care of other creatures and fellow beings. He points out several corrigenda committed by man, which constantly concerns him and thus calls for immediate attention. He focuses on man's exploitation of the biosphere, the apathy shown toward fellow beings and other living creatures, and tries to wake them to their heinous indifference. His poems painfully voice his concern over man's corrigenda.

    Dr. Dominic's poetic oeuvre is driven by a holistic belief, which is characterized by the belief that the parts of something are intimately interconnected and explicable only by reference to the whole. This is what imbues his poetry with direction and purpose. Dr. Dominic—poet, critic, short story writer, editor of IJML and WEC, Secretary of GIEWEC—is one poet who seeks life in nature and exemplifies the interconnectivity between Man and Nature. He sees God in nature and all beings—animate and inanimate. The poems propagate this philosophy of his, which is mandatory to maintain the balance of our ecosystem. Thirty-nine poems of *Winged Reason*, thirty-one poems of *Write Son, Write*, and forty-seven poems of *Multicultural Symphony* bring to light the sensitive heart and analytic brain of the poet that reasons out the contemporary world in a manner that is realistic and convincing. His poems are an expression of his holistic views and philosophy. He openly states in the preface to *Multicultural Symphony* that he is a follower of Advaita philosophy. He says:

> My commonsense doesn't allow me to see God as a separate entity. I believe that there is a Supreme Power or Energy which is controlling this universe... That power is the spirit or soul of the universe and its element is present in all its creations including atoms. Thus divinity is there in all bodies, both living and non living. Based on this reason I cannot find human beings better than other beings or dearest to the creator. (*Multicultural Symphony*, 8)

The poet's "sacred wish" is to instill grace and nobility in man. He thus takes up the task of enlightening the human souls to the marvel of nature:

> My son,
> I have a mission
> in your creation,
> God spoke
> to my ears.
> . . . . . . . . . . . .
> Write, my son,
> write.
> Write till
> I say stop.
>
> (*Write Son, Write*, 21)

He voices the predicament of Lord Almighty on seeing the indifference and apathy of mankind:

> Don't you feel
> the symphony
> of the universe?
> It grieves me that
> your species seldom
> senses my rhythm.
> Plants and animals
> dance to my number.
>
> (*Write Son, Write*, 22)

Even God is pained to see the callousness of humankind. Man kills other beings for sport, for food, and for various other wants. The poet writes in Part Seven thus:

> You speak to them
> in strange tongue,
> and they reply
> in divine speech;
> unintelligible,
> you scourge and
> even kill them.
>
> (*Write Son, Write*, 26)

He then further elaborates in Part Nine as to how man treats nature and other beings with indifference and callousness.

> I breathed in him
> celestial values:
> happiness, beauty,

# Philosophical Musings for a Meaningful Life

> peace, love, mercy;
> but he fosters
> hate and violence;
> kills his kith and kin;
> shows no mercy
> to animals and plants. (*Write Son, Write*, 28)

The extremeness of man's apathy and animosity is highlighted when he pens the desperate question of God:

> Who gave you right
> to kill my creations?
> The way you torture
> fowl and cattle,
> bereft food and water,
> caged and chained,
> . . . . . . . . . . . . . . . .
> The fish you catch
> struggle for breath
> and cause your glee!
>
> (*Write Son, Write*, 29)

As a plea to mankind, he painfully asks Man in Part Eleven:

> Why don't you
> learn from Nature?
> Animals and birds
> present you models.
> Models of pure love,
> happiness, hard work,
> suffering, kindness,
> patience, sharing,
> fellowship, gratitude.
>
> (*Write Son, Write*, 30)

He, in this comprehensive manifesto to the entire humanity, also dwells on the vainglorious mankind basking in his own attempts and glory:

> Alas! Vainglorious
> he thinks
> the master
> of all wisdom;
> tries to conquer
> the universe:
> . . . . . . . . . . . . .
> He defies me,
> assumes my position,
> haughtily claims
> as the noblest
> of my creations!
> He gives me shape,

and boasts,
embodiment of God!

*(Write Son, Write,* 27–28)

Dr. Dominic asserts the fact that only when we are empathetic toward other creatures, we can realize the intertwining network between various beings and understand how every action has its own repercussions on beings who are part and parcel of this network. In "Multicultural Harmony", Part One, he painfully asks:

My dear fellow beings
when will you learn
the need for
multicultural existence?

*(Multicultural Symphony,* 15)

In the Part Four of the same poem, he speaks to us in the tone of a spiritual leader:

Dear my fellow human beings
be humble as all other beings
This planet is a home
to all objects living and non living
Kindly learn your position

*(Multicultural Symphony,* 20)

Just as he dwells on the philosophical plane, he is equally grounded on the philosophical plane. He addresses the issues plaguing our country and countrymen through his poetry, and sends the right message across. He has adopted a conversational style in poetry, which again attracts the ordinary readers. His sense of language is competent enough for him not to be obtrusively bizarre. The simple, lucid language provides little cover for the subtle dig he takes at various situations. In "Indian Democracy", he writes:

Thus democracy reigns
drinking tears of thousands!
Criminal MPs,
brought from jails
to prove majority on floor
horse-trade of billions!
. . . . . . . . . . . . . . . . .
still democracy shall prevail
or tyranny will
sit on the chair.

*(Winged Reason,* 60)

The apparent simplicity of his language, however, conceals the depth of his thought. Just as in "International Women's Day":

International Women's Day;
celebrations all over the world;
. . . . . . . . . . . . . . .
her praises sung hoarse
coarse in her life's course
mockery's rhetoric in these celebrations!

# Philosophical Musings for a Meaningful Life

(*Winged Reason*, 42)

At places, the lines become epigrammatic. As in "Lal Salaam to Labour", he writes:

> the more we give, the more we get
> Put charity in humanity
> a spiritual bliss that never dies.

(*Winged Reason*, 45)

The terse, epigrammatic, pungent style is also seen in "Human Brain":

> If heaven is happiness
> and happiness heaven,
> they are in
> and we are out.

(*Winged Reason*, 59)

In the Preface, he mentions in detail how terrorist attacks, corruption, rich-poor divide are the thorns that 'pierces' his heart every day and how seeing this "gushing blood runs through his pen to paper" (*Winged Reason*, 13). In "A Blissful Voyage", he writes:

> I wish I were a bullet
> and shoot into the chest of that terrorist
> who compels that teenage boy
> to explode and kill that innocent mob.

(*Winged Reason*, 21)

These lines bare open the poet's heart, which bleeds at sights of terrorist acts. His heart also aches when he sees corruption and the rich-poor divide that exists all around us just as he writes in "Haves and Have-nots":

> When millions die of hunger,
> thousands compete for delicacies.
> Minority always luxuriates
> at the cost of
> majorities' necessities.

(*Winged Reason*, 36)

We see the same sentiment in "Lal Salaam to Labour":

> They sow the seed;
> reap the corn;
> and we eat and sleep.
> They build houses
> where they never rest,
> and there we live and snore.

(*Winged Reason*, 44)

He openly speaks against corruption as in "Indian Democracy":

> Parliament elections:
> several billion business;
> stage of heinous means.

(*Winged Reason* 60)

In the same poem, he also brings to light how all these atrocities are performed under the guise of service to God:

> Secularism butchered;
> caste and religion
> raise their hood;
> . . . . . . . . . . . . .
> National parties play
> trump card with communalism;
>
> (*Winged Reason*, 60)

Yet another poem, "In the name of God", highlights this point:

> Corruption is promoted
> in the name of God.
> God is dethroned
> in the name of God.
>
> (*Winged Reason*, 70)

The poet thus is undoubtedly concerned with the presenting issues of the world, but this does not mean that he has severed his association with his native place and surroundings. He rather frequently resorts to native themes, traditions, sensibility, and bindings. This is clear in his poem "Onam". In it, he relates the festival Onam, recounts its legend, and brings to light the essence of the festival, the thought behind it, and finally strikes a chord when he shows how the ostensible affluence fails to impress Maveli:

> But granted him a boon
> to visit his people
> once in a year.
> Maveli visits on Onam;
> Fed up he
> he returns in tears.
>
> (*Winged Reason*, 54)

"He" is repeated twice—in the second last and last line. This sends across the feeling that probably the poet is in tears and is sobbing along with Maveli.

The poet is equally moved at the plight of animals and plants. We are moved to tears when we read "I am Just a Mango Tree." We wonder how man can act so mercilessly:

> "Dear, why should they cut this tree,
> a cool shelter to countless?"
> "They plan to build a waiting shed here."
> . . . . . . . . . . . . . . . . . . .
> Can't they spare me and
> build it somewhere else?
>
> (*Winged Reason*, 41)

We are filled with similar emotion when we read "A Sheep's Wail":

> The milk for my lamb
> you suck and drain
> and grow fat and cruel
> . . . . . . . . . . . . . . . . .

# Philosophical Musings for a Meaningful Life

> Man, you are the cruelest,
> you are the most ungrateful
> of all God's creations. (
>
> *Winged Reason*, 24–25)

He is able to read the mind of these speechless beings and pens down their heart-rending cries. He seems to be in total communion with them when he writes in the same poem:

> If a heaven is there
> we will reach there first
> and pray to God to shut you out.
>
> (*Winged Reason*, 25)

Or when the Mango tree sighs in "I am just a Mango Tree":

> God why is your Man so selfish and cruel?
> Did you create him,
> to disturb this earth's balance?
> This planet would be a paradise
> if you kindly withdraw him.
>
> (*Winged Reason*, 41)

The poet then further relates how he was blessed with an all-encompassing compassion for other beings. In "My Teenage Hobby", he writes:

> Once when I pulled a fish,
> flashed a horrible vision:
> I am pulled from the sky;
> death struggle on the line.
> Awestruck and repentant,
> I unhooked the fish
> and dropped in the water. (*Winged Reason*, 48)

And he shows how he means in letter and spirit of what he says in "How I Became a Vegetarian":

> lived non-veg life;
> believed in the teachings
> that man is the centre of universe
> . . . . . . . . . . . . . . . . .
> my eyes are opened at last
> and I have become
> a pure vegetarian.
>
> (*Winged Reason*, 76)

He conveys this all encompassing love for beings in a lighter vein in "A Spider in my Bathroom":

> A spider in my bathroom
> To smite or spare?
> Lives on mosquitoes
> Who inject me
> The creator has sent
> it along with mosquitoes
> Being a poet vowed

> To love all creations
> what shall I do?
>
> *(Multicultural Symphony,* 52)

Dr. Dominic envisions a harmonious world and thus calls for a change in outlook and mindset of mankind. Only if human beings understand the cohesion between the sapien, flora, and fauna, a change in the world can be expected. Dr. Dominic hopes and wishes to write verses that would act as a catalyst in changing the mindset of man—his thinking, outlook, and attitude toward other beings on earth. This is one merit that elevates Dr. Dominic to a position of great distinction among many skilful practitioners of the noble craft. And of his many poetic skills, the most exemplary is his tidy constructions of thought. His philosophical heritage is imbued with the human awareness of a divine order visible in Creation in which different creatures are intertwined in a Great Chain of Being.

The whole world thus is bound with mutually reinforcing or mutually destructive interdependencies. Dr. Dominic makes a sincere attempt to effectively bring to the fore the need of coexistence and the need of cultivating empathy and benevolence for a harmonious, peaceful life on the face of the earth.

## Works Cited

Dominic, K. V. *Multicultural Symphony.* New Delhi: GNOSIS, 2014. Print.

---. *Winged Reason.* New Delhi: Authorpress, 2010. Print.

---. *Write Son, Write.* New Delhi: GNOSIS, 2011. Print.

Matai, D. K. "We are all One." *Business Insider.* Web 11 Mar. 2011.

# Chapter 25 -
# Interview with Prof. K. V. Dominic
# by Prof. Elisabetta Marino

**EM:** Good morning Prof. Dominic! Your scholarly and artistic careers are equally amazing! Can you outline them?

**KVD:** I have been a faculty member of the Post Graduate and Research Department of English, Newman College, Thodupuzha, Kerala, India, for twenty-six years till my retirement from service on 31 March, 2011, at the age of fifty-five. I have been teaching both UG and PG English literature students research methodology and MLA style of documentation for their project papers. In addition, I have been the editor of the international biannual refereed journal *Indian Journal of Postcolonial Literatures*, a publication of the PG department of English. Thus I came into contact with hundreds of university/college professors, research scholars, and professional writers in India and abroad. I found much thrill in editing the issues of the journal with minimum mistakes and using the correct latest MLA style. I have been very punctual in publishing the issues in the due months themselves and sending copies to the subscribers and contributors in the respective months. This punctuality in the release of the issues created a huge impression and trust among the subscribers and contributors and the journal thus flourished.

I took the editing and publishing of the journals as a mission—a mission of serving research scholars and college teachers. Hundreds of PhD research scholars could publish their research articles—a requisite of their course, and innumerable college teachers got promotion by publishing their articles in my journal. This service rendered to them gave me much happiness and boost for further editing, and thus I started editing anthologies. Fortunately, I got a great scholarly publisher—a lover of literature who is very selfless and never profit-minded. I am talking of Mr. Sudarshan Kcherry of Authorspress, New Delhi, who is my soulmate now. Thus our teamwork resulted in the creation of several edited books. So far I have edited/authored 22 books, of which 18 have come out and four are under print.

On 23 September, 2010, nearly ten well-known professors-cum-writers from different parts of India assembled in my college for a national seminar I had organized and in that evening, we gave birth to a guild of writers entitled, Guild of Indian English Writers, Editors and Critics (GIEWEC). I was elected as the Secretary of the guild and other different office-bearers. The main objectives of the guild are: promote Indian-English Literature in general, publish an international refereed biannual journal entitled *Writers Editors Critics* (WEC) for the contributions of the members, inspire and enlighten the members in creative and critical writing, assist Ph.D. scholars in thesis writing, make the members aware of research methodology and the latest documentation style and conduct annual conferences in various states. The guild was registered as a society and the first issue of *Writers Editors Critics* came out in March 2011.

After my retirement in March 2011, I started editing and publishing another international refereed biannual journal, called *International Journal on Multicultural Literature* (IJML). The maiden issue came out in July 2011. Thus I am now busy with editing and publishing both the journals. WEC's issues come out in March and September and IJML's issues in January and July. I am very prompt in releasing the issues in the respective months. The Guild has now 164 members of which 74 are life members. IJML has 107 subscribers within this short period. Due to the high quality we are maintaining, both journals have been indexed and abstracted by Literary Reference Center Plus, EBSCO Host, USA. As fulfilment of the objectives, annual literary conferences were held in Kochi (Kerala) and Mumbai in the last two years. In addition, I have conducted several workshops on research methodology and MLA style of documentation in several parts of the country.

Now coming to my creative activity, I take poetry and short story as a weapon and reaction to the evils of the society. The function of poetry is to instruct and delight. To me, the aspect of "instruct"—impart great values and messages, seems more important than "delight". Hence I don't care much about rhythm, rhyme, or such decorations which add musicality to the lines. I write in free verse, using very simple vocabulary with minimum figural language. I have a very clear vision in my compositions: even an uneducated man—one who can just read and write—should be attracted to my poetry and thus the message should enter into his/her mind. Unlike T. S. Eliot and several other modern great poets, I write for the masses and not for just elite and educated.

**EM:** It seems to me that both branches of your career aim at uncovering channels of communication, at fostering peace. Can you please expand on that? Did you have any source of inspiration? Did your father and mother have a strong influence on that?

**KVD:** As I have explained, I have a mission and vision, which I have been scholarly fulfilling through my journals and edited books. The main objective of our life is happiness and we can attain this happiness best by serving others. That's exactly what I have been doing by editing and publishing journals and books. Since good literature imparts the message of peace and happiness, the critical studies on them underline and focus on this great message. Exhortation for peace and happiness is the main theme of my poetry and short stories. Acting as a social critic, I charge at men as well as their customs, traditions, beliefs, superstitions, pseudo-philosophies, and all such narrow thoughts which annihilate peace and happiness in societies. I am a champion of the marginalized, oppressed, and downtrodden. I have composed several poems on the problems of working class, sexism and ageism, child labor, cruelty to animals, casteism, etc.

I have been greatly influenced by my father and mother in molding my philosophies and attitude to life. They were very generous and humane not only to the people associated with them but to animals also. I have dedicated my first poetry collection to my father and the second one to my mother. The second collection *Write Son, Write* has my tribute to my mother in the poem "Elegy on My Ma". My wife Anne, who is also a postgraduate in English Literature, is my constant inspiration and the first critic of my creative works. Romantic and Victorian poets—Wordsworth, Shelley, Keats, Browning, Tennyson, Arnold—and Indian poets in English—Tagore, Nissim Ezekiel, and Jayanta Mahapatra—have exerted influence on me. Buddha, Christ, Swami Vivekananda, Gandhi, Nehru, etc. are the philosophers and statesmen who influenced me.

**EM:** Focusing more specifically on *Write Son, Write*, it seems that writing is turned into a strong and powerful tool. The title itself looks like a prompt, to act and change the world. Some of the poems, like the one dedicated to Aung San Suu Kyi, seem to confirm this idea. Can you expand on that?

**KVD:** *Write Son, Write* is my second collection of poems, published after *Winged Reason*. I do believe that whatever I have written or am going to write is inspired by poets' poet—God. A poet is a sage and God speaks to the world through his/her pen. Thus the title of the book and the title poem "Write, My Son, Write" is justified. This title poem is the longest of all my poems, 483 lines in twenty-one sections. In fact, it is my manifesto, my philosophy of life. My concept of God and creation, the triangular relation between God, human beings, and other beings, how human beings play discordant notes to the symphony and harmony of universe, how other beings, though less intelligent, are superior in feelings and emotions, how religious, political, and intellectual mafia exploit the innocent, illiterate laity, etc are dealt in detail in this poem. When religious and political leaders and intelligentsia fail to inject values into the masses, only poets, who are like prophets, can save this planet and its inhabitants from imminent devastation. Aung San Suu Kyi is such a prophet.

**EM:** The animal world seems to be characterized by a moral code, a sense of friendship and companionship and a respect for life and nature that is quite difficult to find in humans. Can you tell me more about it?

**KVD:** Man has to learn a lot from nature, especially from the animal world. It's a perverted concept that man is the centre of universe and God has created the earth for his existence. It is his intelligence which makes him think so selfishly, distort the Creator as he likes, and subject the animal world and plant world to his whims and fancies and comforts and luxuries. Man, the latest evolutionary being, has to respect his predecessors and ancestors, and allow them also to coexist with him. There are eleven poems dealing with animals and birds in my collections and most of them portray the cruelty done to animals by human beings. I believe that all creations of God are beautiful and there can be nothing ugly among his creations. As Keats says, "A thing of beauty is a joy for ever," these creations—both plant world and animal world are sources of happiness for those who observe them. Man can learn many values from animals: love, kindness, friendship, cooperation, industry, cleanliness, etc. I am of the opinion that non-human beings are dearer to God than human beings because they don't sin against Him. They move with perfect rhythm to His eternal symphony.

**EM:** What do you wish for Mother India, cherished in your writings?

**KVD:** In my poem "Victory to thee Mother India", in *Write Son, Write*, I have expressed my wish for Mother India. At present, the Mother's heart is being torn and her blood is being devoured by three mafias—religious, political, and intellectual. Tagore, Gandhi, and Nehru were her great sons who filled her heart with happiness. "No doubt, your womb / will bear more great children, / who will lift us from this trance / and tether us back to the global home, / and you will sleep on the lap, / fondled by your Mother World" (*Write son, Write*, 43). I dream of a global family where Mother India becomes an affable, sweet, and darling daughter to Mother World.

**EM:** Plans for the future?

**KVD:** I would like to continue my literary activities, both scholarly and creative, with more zeal and fervor. The only problem is lack of time. Since I don't have any assistants for the office work of the Guild—for countless email answers and phone calls—much of my time every day has to be diverted for it. As membership rises, I will be overburdened. Still fighting against time and physical ailments caused by overuse of computer, I will go on editing and publishing journals and books, and at the same time find time to involve in creative activity of composing poems and short stories.

**EM:** Thank you very much Prof. Dominic for sharing your views and philosophies with the readers in India and abroad.

**KVD:** It's my pleasure and pride dear Prof. Elisabetta to be interviewed by an Indian-loving literary celebrity like you. Thanks to all readers.

## List of Contributors

**P. C. K. Prem** (**P. C. Katoch** of Malkher Garh-Palampur, Himachal), a trilingual author of more than forty books in English and Hindi, post-graduated in English Literature from Punjab University, Chandigarh, in 1970, taught English in various colleges of Punjab and Himachal before shifting to civil services, and after retiring from IAS, served as Member, HP Public Service Commission. Katoch Prem is the only major poet, novelist, short story writer, essayist, and critic in English from Himachal Pradesh. Presently, he lives with his wife Shakun in his farmhouse at Palampur-176061, Himachal. Currently, he is working on ancient Indian Literature, particularly the portions that try to interpret various philosophic thoughts, religious anxieties, and spiritual quests of man.

**Dr. S. Kumaran** is working as an Assistant Professor at the Department of English, University College of Engineering Tindivanam, which is a constituent unit of Anna University, Chennai. He has received his doctorate from Anna University and has obtained PGCTE from English and Foreign Languages University, Hyderabad. Further, he has qualified both State Eligibility Test and UGC-National Eligibility Test. He is actively engaged in research work and his research contributions include: 30 journal publications, 3 books, 35 paper presentations, 8 papers in various anthologies, and guidance to doctoral students. Moreover, he is the Treasurer of Guild of Indian English Writers, Editors, and Critics (GIEWEC), Associate Editor of two refereed international biannual journals—*Writers Editors Critics* (WEC) and *International Journal on Multicultural Literature* (IJML)— and member of the editorial boards of various journals from India and abroad.

**Dr. Sudhir K. Arora** teaches English at Maharaja Harishchandra P. G. College, Moradabad, affiliated with M. J. P. Rohilkhand University, Bareilly. He has authored a number of books, including *Aravind Adiga's The White Tiger* and *Multicultural Consciousness in the Novels of Kamala Markandaya*. The voluminous critical work *Cultural and Philosophical Reflections in Indian Poetry in English* in five volumes is his magnum opus. He resides at B-72, Deendayal Nagar, Phase-2, Near Sai Temple, Moradabad-244001 (UP) India, and can be contacted at drsudhirkarora@gmail.com

**Dr. D. C. Chambial** Reputed English poet, critic, short story writer, and interviewer, is the Editor of international biannual journal *Poetcrit*, Maranda, Himachal Pradesh, India. His critical and creative works have been widely published in India and abroad.

**Prof. Dr. T. V. Reddy** worked as Lecturer, Reader, and U.G.C National Fellow & Visiting Professor, and retired as Principal of Govt. Degree College in Dec. 2001. He is a renowned poet, critic & novelist of international repute. His poems appeared in French journals in Paris. M.Phil and Ph.D. theses have been produced on his works. He has received innumerable national and international awards for his poetry. He has authored and published seven collections of poems, two novels, two books of criticism, and a book on grammar. He is the President of Guild of Indian English Writers, Editors & Critics (GIEWEC).

**Dr. Sugandha Agarwal** Assistant Professor in English, Moradabad Institute of Technology, Moradabad, U.P., India, is the Editor of *MIT Journal of English Language and Literature* and also the Review Editor of *Writers Editors Critics* (WEC) and *International Journal on Multicultural Literature* (IJML).

**Dr. Rob Harle** is a writer, artist, and academic reviewer from Australia. His writing includes poetry, short fiction, academic essays and reviews of scholarly books, journals, and papers. His work is published in journals, anthologies, online reviews, and books, and he has two volumes of his own poetry published—*Scratches & Deeper Wounds* (1996) and *Mechanisms of Desire* (2012). His art practice involves digital-computer art both for the web and print. His giclée images have been exhibited widely. His thesis is on Freud's notion of the subconscious and its relationship with Surrealist poetry.

**Dr. J. Pamela** Assistant Professor of English & Head, Kasthurba College for Women Villianur, Puducherry, India.

**Dr. Bhaskar Roy Barman** reputed English poet, short story writer, playwright, critic, essayist and columnist from Agartala, Tripura, India. He has numerous publications to his credit.

**Dr. S. Ayyappa Raja** Assistant Professor of English, Department of English, Annamalai University, Annamalai Nagar, Tamil Nadu, India. He has published many research papers in national and international journals.

**Dr. Arbind Kumar Choudhary** Reputed English poet &critic, is the Head of the Department of English, Rangachahi College, Majuli, Assam, India-785104. He is the editor of the research journals *Kohinoor* (ISSN 0973-6395) & *Ayush* (ISSN 0974-8075).

**Anisha Ghosh Paul** Guest Lecturer in English, Siliguri Mahila Mahavidyalaya, Siliguri, West Bengal, India.

**Joseph Palathunkal Mathew** M.A., MHR, and PGDM, is a poet, writer, and teacher based in Ahmedabad, Gujarat, India. Contact: josephpalathunkal00@gmail.com.

**Dr. Patricia Prime** reputed poet, reviewer from New Zealand, is the co-editor of *Kokako*, reviews/interviews editor of *Haibun Today*, and writes reviews for several journals including *Takahe, Gusts* and *Atlas Poetica*. She is the co-editor of *100 Tanka by One Hundred Poets*. She is also the co-editor of the forthcoming contemporary haiku anthology: *A Vast Sky*. She writes haiku, tanka, haibun, tanka prose and renga and has published her poetry worldwide. Her poetry, interviews and reviews have been published in the *World Poetry Almanac* (Mongolia) from 2009-2012. Patricia is a member of GIEWEC (India) and is on the Advisory Board of *Writers Editors Critics* (India), *International Journal on Multicultural Literature* (India) and *New Fiction Journal* (India).

**Dr. Mahboobeh Khaleghi** is an emerging critic from Iran. She has won her PhD on the topic "A Study of the Novels of Toni Morrison and Gloria Naylor from a Feminist Perspective" at University of Mysore, India. She has to her credit innumerable publications in reputed international journals and books. Dr. Mahboobeh is the Associate Editor of *International Journal on Multicultural Literature* (IJML). She is in the Advisory and Editorial Boards of several international journals. She is also the co-editor of the book *Indian Literatures in English: New Directions, Newer Possibilities*.

**Sangeeta Mahesh** Assistant Professor of English, Moradabad Institute of Technology, Moradabad, U.P. India, is an English poet and critic. Her maiden collection of poems *Ocean of Thoughts: Poems about Social Issues and Human Values* was published in 2014 by Authorspress, New Delhi.

**Dr. Radhamamani Sarma** retired Professor of English from Chennai, is a reputed English poet and critic and has authored several books.

**Dr. S. Barathi** Assistant Professor, Department of English, Srinivasa Ramanujan Centre, Sastra University, Kumbakonam, Tamil Nadu, India. She is an emerging critic from India.

**Rincy Mol Sebastian** is HSS Teacher in English, Government Higher Secondary School, Eranhimangad, Nilampur, Kerala, India. She is also a PhD Research Scholar at Calicut University, Kozhikode, Kerala.

**Kavitha Gopalakrishnan** is Assistant Professor of English, Baselius College, Kottayam, Kerala, India. She is the Review Editor of *Writers Editors Critics* (WEC) and *International Journal on Multicultural Literatures* (IJML).

**Prof. Dr. Elisabetta Marino** is tenured Assistant Professor of English Literature at the University of Rome "Tor Vergata". She published a book on Tamerlane in English and American literature (2000) and edited the volume (2002) of proceedings of the "Asia and the West Conference" organized at "Tor Vergata" by Professor Lina Unali in 2001. She co-edited the collection of essays entitled *Transnational, National, and Personal Voices: New Perspectives on Asian American and Asian Diasporic Women Writers* (2004), and in 2005, she published a volume entitled *Introduzione alla letteratura bangladese Britannica* (An introduction to British Bangladeshi literature). In 2011, she published a book entitled *Mary Shelley e l'Italia. Il viaggio, il Risorgimento, la questione femminile* (Mary Shelley and Italy). She has published extensively on travel literature, Asian-American and Asian-British literature, Italian-American literature, and on the English Romantic writers.

# Index

## A

A Blissful Voyage, 16, 17, 62, 87, 113, 135, 156, 205
A Desperate Attempt, 130
A Sheep's Wail, 19, 54, 63, 99, 129, 135, 146, 149, 187, 206
Advaita Vedanta, viii, xiii, 123, 181
Agarwal, S., 214
Agitation Through Farming, 185
Aham Brahmasmi, 61, 136
Ammini's Demise, 19, 64, 90, 129, 132, 146, 153, 157, 177
Ammini's Lament, 19, 89, 132, 146, 153
An Elegy on My Ma, 40, 66, 79, 140, 159
apathy, 203
Arora, S., 213
Asuras, 175
Attachment, 65, 91, 129, 146, 149, 188

## B

Barathi, S., 215
Barman, B., 214
Beach Beauticians, 36, 73, 185
Beena's Shattered Dreams, 73, 163
Beevi, R., 57, 102, 184
Bharat Matha, 163
Browning, R., 2, 23, 77, 87, 123, 179, 210
Buddhism, 210
Bulbul's Nest, 170

## C

caste, 6, 12, 13, 36, 50, 59, 78, 79, 111, 112, 118, 145, 146, 155, 161, 163, 199, 206
Celebration of Girl-child's Birth, 126
Chambial, D.C., vii, 39, 117, 122, 194, 195
Chambial, D.C.., 213
child labor, ix, 58, 73, 107, 109, 127, 142, 145, 167, 174, 175, 199, 210
Child Labour, 73, 78, 93, 109, 127, 163, 174
Choudhary, A., 214
Cicero, 201
Coconut Palm, 41, 57, 67, 140, 146, 148, 170
Cohabitance on the Planet, 72, 129, 162

Coleridge, S.T., 40, 80, 87, 90, 91, 93, 95, 169, 173, 179
Cry of My Child, 176
Cuckoo Singing, 88, 146, 148, 156, 188

## D

Darwin, viii, 76, 93, 104, 105, 123, 142, 198
Das, K., viii, 87, 119, 123
deforestation, 169, 170, 188, 189, 191
Dhanalakshmi, 36, 78, 109, 174
Dickinson, E., viii, 123
Dignity of Labour, 74, 78, 93, 124, 163, 168
disharmony, 14, 51, 93, 149
Drowned Dreams, 73, 163
Dryden, J., 179

## E

Ezekiel, N., viii, 123, 210

## F

For the Glory of God, 57, 102, 160, 184
Frost, R., viii, 87, 123, 190

## G

Gandhi, viii, xiii, 14, 17, 27, 35, 40, 51, 55, 68, 76, 80, 87, 102, 121, 123, 134, 140, 183, 210, 211
Gayatri, 26, 54, 63, 88, 127, 132, 139, 156
George Joson, 15, 26, 53, 61, 79, 87, 97, 131, 155
Gill, Stephen, xiii, 181, 198
global warming, 36, 58, 67, 68, 72, 104, 141, 142, 146, 160, 162, 191, 199
Global Warming's Real Culprits, 72, 104, 141
God is Helpless, 12, 91, 102, 129, 135, 146, 151, 160, 193, 194
Goldberg, M., 133
Gopalakrishnan, K., 215

## H

Harle, R., 214
Haves and Have-nots, 6, 8, 14, 17, 47, 50, 51, 54, 100, 108, 110, 125, 132, 135, 146, 147, 205
Heaney, S., 1, 77, 179

Helen and Her World, 135
Heschel, A., 137
horoscope, 33, 59, 71, 113, 146
human rights, ix, 167, 168
humanism, ix, 3, 11, 15–21, 23, 37, 45, 53, 62, 76, 87, 98, 121, 158, 188, 199
Hunger's Call, 57, 66, 103, 125, 136, 160
Hungry Mouths, 4, 74, 107, 125, 163, 176

## I

I am Just a Mango Tree, 19, 54, 88, 146, 147, 157, 169, 187, 192, 206
IAF Vayu Shakti 2010, 136, 171
illiteracy, 40, 69, 160, 174
In the Name of God, 18, 55, 111, 135, 178
Indian Democracy, 12, 16, 49, 50, 55, 100, 135, 157, 204, 205
inhumanism, 187
International Women's Day, 20, 21, 61, 63, 64, 88, 100, 103, 113, 126, 134, 135, 204
interview, 209–11

## J

Jeevatma, 61

## K

Kannappilly, V., 145, 146
Katie Sportz, 41, 135, 136
Kaumudi, 26, 55, 61, 90, 140, 183
Kaumudi Teacher is No More, 61, 90, 140, 183
Keats, viii, 27, 87, 119, 123, 177, 210, 211
Kerala, xiii, 186, 189
    dam, 185
Khaleghi, M., 214
King, M.L., 135
Krishna, 175
Kumaran, S., 213
    about, xi
    humanism, 15–21
Kurtz, P., 16, 19, 21
Kyi, A.S., 57, 65, 67, 91, 121, 135, 136, 210, 211

## L

Lal Salaam to Labour, 64, 135, 167, 205
Laxmi's Tea, 133
Leavis, F.R., 179
Leela, 131
Lines Composed from Thodupuzha River's Bridge, 58, 160, 174, 183
Lynen, J.F., 189, 190

## M

Madhya Pradesh, 111, 135, 163, 184
Mahapatra, J., viii, 1, 23, 87, 97, 123, 181, 186, 197, 210
Mahesh, S., 214
Malabar, 55, 140, 184
Mandela, N., 41, 57, 67, 91, 102, 121
Marino, E., xiv, 123, 209–11, 215
martyrdom, 171
Massacre of Cats, 40, 57, 66, 67, 79, 91, 102, 129, 146, 153, 159
Mathew, J., 214
Mother Teresa, viii, 65, 123, 134
motorcycle, 111, 163
Mukesh's Destiny, 73, 109, 127, 128
Mullaperiyar Dam, 73, 142, 185, 188, 189
Multicultural Harmony, 3, 10, 71, 77, 81, 93, 104, 112, 114, 129, 141, 146, 153, 161, 168, 204
Multicultural Kerala, 141, 162, 173, 182
Musings on My Shoes, 14, 108, 199

## N

Nature Weeps, 41, 68, 69, 79, 92, 129, 187, 192, 194
Nature's Bounties, 146, 147, 169, 188
Nayanar, E.K., 8, 16, 26, 47, 53, 61, 87, 98, 131, 132, 155, 183
non-violence, 65

## O

Odisha, 181, 197
Old Age, 9, 10, 20, 49, 61, 89, 114, 127, 132
On Conservation, 93, 110, 163, 170, 187
Onam, 9, 25, 48, 89, 184, 188, 206
ozone depletion, 191

## P

Pamela, J., 214
Paramatma, 61
Paul, A.G., 123, 181, 214
politics, 4, 6, 16, 21, 24, 27, 46, 53, 61, 124, 126, 145
poverty, viii, 4, 5, 9, 21, 46, 48, 57, 58, 61, 65, 66, 75, 86, 88, 104, 107, 108, 115, 120, 124, 125, 127, 128, 136, 139, 141, 142, 143, 145, 146, 155, 160, 163, 164, 174, 175, 184
Pragg, J., 18
Prem, PCK, 1–14, 55, 146, 165, 213
Prime, P., viii, 214
Protest against Sand Mafia, 73, 110, 142, 164

## R

Raja, S., 214

Reddy, T., vii, 213
religious fanaticism, ix, 1, 42, 58, 92, 111, 167
Rocketing Growth of India, 40, 57, 69, 92, 160

## S

sacred wish, 202
Saichen Tragedy, 188
Sarangi, 173
Sarma, R., 215
Sebastian, R., 215
sexism, 33, 88, 124, 126, 146, 210
Shankara, A., 181, 189
Shelley, viii, 87, 123, 210, 215
Siachen Tragedy, 36, 73, 93, 104, 113, 162
Singh, R.K., 117, 122
Sister Mercy, 69, 135, 184
social criticism, vii, ix, 2, 23, 53, 77, 86, 97, 123, 155, 167, 179, 184, 187
supreme being, 15, 70, 104, 158, 178, 197, 202, 208

## T

Tears of a World Champion, 73, 130
Tennyson, A., 87, 98, 123, 210
The Rose, 169, 179
Thodupuzha Municipal Park, 36, 94, 142, 164, 174, 183, 189
To My Colleague, 42, 58, 92, 111, 135, 136, 184
toxins, 191
Train Blast, 42, 58, 92, 160, 175
Tsunami Camps, 8, 9, 17, 47, 48, 54, 63, 88, 132, 175, 176

## U

unemployment, 58, 65, 120, 139, 143, 145, 174
universal rhythm, 177
urbanization, 170, 193

## V

Valueless Education, 74, 94, 185

## W

Wagamon, 41, 42, 182
Water, Water, Everywhere, 42, 68, 93, 103, 129, 160, 172, 189, 193, 194
Where Shall I Flee from this Fretful Land, 142, 184
Whitman, W., 68, 70
Who Am I, 105, 124
Wolfgang, 41, 146, 152, 189
Women's Cricket World Cup 2013, 36, 71, 112, 126
Wordsworth, viii, 58, 87, 92, 123, 181, 182, 183, 186, 210
Work is Worship, 11, 58, 94, 146, 148, 160
World Water Day, 103, 160, 172, 193
Write, My Son, Write, 39, 55, 65, 66, 81, 90, 101, 111, 135, 145, 146, 150, 151, 158, 188, 210

## Z

Zimbabwe, 103, 125, 160

Ruskin Bond has won the hearts of millions of readers with his countless charming short stories and introspective novels. From biographical tales about acting as a grandfather to children, to tales of unrequited love, the cross-cultural dimensions of Indian society, and the power and beauty of nature, Bond's more than forty novels and short story collections have made him an internationally acclaimed author.

In *Ruskin Bond's World*, Indian scholar Gulnaz Fatma, Ph.D. sheds light on one of her country's greatest and most beloved storytellers, tracing the influences in his stories from a childhood in colonial India through his time spent in Britain and his life today among India's hills and mountains. She explores the biographical as well as the imaginary elements of his fiction and explores in detail the themes of nature, children, love, and animals in his novels and short stories. Throughout these pages is revealed Bond's love for humanity in all its variety, from honorable rogues to proud beggars, heartbroken lovers, and wise old men and women.

"Gulnaz has successfully traced major themes in Bond's prolific work under the lenses of her careful examination, proving he is the product of his environment...a sincere study of Ruskin Bond."

--Stephen Gill, Ph.D., author and poet laureate of Ansted University

"I welcome this long overdue study of one of India's literary shining lights. Ruskin Bond's World opens the door to a deeper understanding of one author's imagination and deepest wisdom."
--Tyler R. Tichelaar, Ph.D. and award-winning author of The Gothic Wanderer

**Ruskin Bond's World: Thematic Influences of Nature, Children, and Love in his Major Works**

From the World Voices Series

Literary Criticism: Asian - Indic

ISBN-13: 978-1-61599-199-0

Modern History Press

www.ModernHistoryPress.com

In India, the life of women has never been easy by any stretch of the imagination. *Swati's Marriage and Other Tales of India* brings their eternal struggles to a new audience by engaging the subject head-on through the eyes of young women in the 21st century. Western audiences may have assumed that such considerations as dowries, arranged marriage, and abuse of spouses, servants, and the elderly would be tempered in the age of social media.

Instead, Ankita Sharma's characters confront these issues as they persevere in their quest for love, independence, and fulfillment in the face of centuries of social mores, traditions, and institutionalized repression. Sometimes, all they can do is put on a smile for their armor and retreat to fight another day, their only comfort being hope that their children will have it better than they did.

Here is the human condition expressed on every page—the desperate longing for meaning, for acceptance, for love and understanding that we all seek, that we all despair we may not find, that brings us together into a shared experience at the very same moment that it separates us.

"Fans of Masterpiece's *Indian Summer* and the stories of Ruskin Bond will welcome this female perspective on modern-day Indian life. These short stories are full of epiphanies and restrictions that remind one of James Joyce and Katherine Mansfield's work and show how little the human experience changes, despite cultural differences."

— Tyler R. Tichelaar, Ph.D. and award-winning author of *Narrow Lives* and *The Best Place*.

**Swati's Marriage and Other Tales of India by Ankita Sharma**

From the World Voices Series

LITERARY COLLECTIONS / Asian / Indic

ISBN-13: 978-1-61599-287-4

Modern History Press

**www.ModernHistoryPress.com**

# Introducing the World Voices Series

This series highlights the best English-language autobiography, fiction, and poetry of diverse voices from Africa, Asia, the Caribbean, and South America.

*The Blue Fairy and other tales of transcendence*
By Ernest Dempsey

*Iraq Through a Bullet Hole: A Civilian Wikileaks*
by Issam Jameel

*The Road-Shaped Heart*
by Nick Purdon

*Beyond the Scent of Sorrow*
By Sweta Srivastava Vikram

*No Ocean Here*
by Sweta Srivastava Vikram

*A Short History of the Short Story*
By Gulnaz Fatma

*Ruskin Bond's World: Thematic Influences of Nature, Children, and Love in His Major Works*
By Gulnaz Fatma

from Modern History Press
http://www.modernhistorypress.com/world-voices/

www.ingramcontent.com/pod-product-compliance
Lightning Source LLC
Chambersburg PA
CBHW082116230426
43671CB00015B/2716